When Pixies Come Out to Play

When Pixies Come Out to Play

A Play Therapy Primer

Lois Carey

When Pixies Come Out to Play

First Edition
ISBN 978-1-926975-11-5 Paperback
ISBN 978-1-926975-10-8 eBook

Published simultaneously in Canada, the United Kingdom, and the United States of America by Genoa House. For information on obtaining permission for use of material from this work, submit a written request to:

books@genoahouse.com
www.genoahouse.com

Many thanks to all who have directly or indirectly provided permission to quote their works. Every effort has been made to trace all copyright holders; however, if any have been overlooked, the author will be pleased to make the necessary arrangements at the first opportunity. See pages 253-261 for a complete list of references.

CONTENTS

FOREWORD

Being a child therapist is fraught with challenges and rewards, both for the beginner as well as the experienced play therapist and sandplay therapist.

Learning at the start of our professional careers, as therapists or counselors, how to create a safe, psychological space, or container, for our clients to be able to create and grow is an essential but not always an easy task, especially for beginners. Being able to lead without judgment and often without verbal communication and interpretation is essential in allowing children to lead in their play. The therapist needs to join with the child at the child's experience level and be able to stay within the therapeutic metaphor the child may be using. Children are naturally drawn to sandplay and play, which are natural forms of expression, just as birds fly, and fish swim, so children play as naturally as breathing. Sandplay, in particular, has the unique allure of allowing freedom in non-verbal creativity without constraint and much less self-criticism (than, say, drawing or creating something might elicit). Mastery of difficult feelings and conflicted thoughts are facilitated and healed through the therapeutic distance from traumatic events and images, many of which may be horrific.

It is difficult for many therapists to be a witness to their client's pain and resulting creative process. It requires a willingness to maintain focused attention, while you might not really know exactly what will emerge, especially with the use of sandplay. This state of not knowing allows the child the freedom to move with their creative energies and gives them space to build their worlds. In many cases, witnessing visual images is more powerful than verbal therapy because, just like the children, we, the therapists, find our own symbolic thinking processes activated. Consequently, a child's sandplay can be deeply moving for the therapist. And in the hands of a properly prepared therapist, sandplay is a powerful, invaluable modality. The children learn how to be in tune with their physical, emotional, mental, and spiritual experiences. They learn how to recapture their enthusiasm for living, and what it means to be human and gain a larger perspective.

As the therapist joins with the child at an experience level, counter-transference issues inevitably arise to the potent images and stories. We witness the children's stories of the unspeakable brutalities of humanity—violent crime, childhood physical and sexual abuse, extreme loss, family and community violence, and terrorism, among them. We may be seeing children and teens who exhibit symptoms from lack of trust in family members, distrust of adults, in general, feeling worthless, depressed, withdrawn, isolated, anxious, angry, defiant, and hyper-vigilant. They suffer from lack of sleep, nightmares, refusing to go to bed, along with low self-esteem, low frustration tolerance, learning problems, developmental delays, poor social skills, and difficulty self-regulating affect. Some of our clients rage against the world through antisocial and sexualized behaviors, while others withdraw into silence or dissociation. We cannot help but be touched at a deep level by these experiences and sharing. Being human and caring individuals, we react and may feel anger at or repulsion from what we are exposed to.

We enter into this profession out of a genuine and intense desire to help others in a meaningful way. But at times we may find our basic training and skills tested and strained, stretched to the limits, and often found wanting. Counter-transference issues that arise can make it difficult for the therapist to hold the therapeutic space, remaining an unbiased witness, so that the child can continue to deepen the experience that needs to be played out. Such reactions need to be addressed in competent supervision to keep us centered.

As we develop further along in our careers working with a wide array of presenting problems, from sexual abuse to being caught in the middle of a difficult parental divorce, requires from us a variety of skills. And we find that over time wisdom begins to emerge from all of these experiences that have tempered and molded us.

Lois Carey's voice throughout *When Pixies Come Out to Play* epitomizes that of the wise mentor who has lived through a multitude of experiences and of having been witness to difficult, heart-wrenching treatment cases, many of which pull at your heart and others that create deep satisfaction in a job well done.

When Pixies Come Out to Play is a compendium of chapters seen through the eyes of a seasoned clinician who shares her professional life and wisdom through a personal, moving voice. We learn through the poignant wisdom of her cases and experiences about sandplay therapy and the nuances and intricacies involved in implementing sandplay from a Jungian perspective. Lois Carey takes us on a personal journey from her initial training experiences in Switzerland to the intricacies of cases involving violence and trauma, attachment and loss, sexual abuse, and acting out.

The book is divided nicely into first an *Overview/Methodology* section, which offers a general overview about play therapy and sandplay therapy, along with chapters covering methodology and supervision. The second section, *Trauma and Other Disorders*, focuses on a variety of cases dealing with trauma, sexual abuse, and attachment disorders. The third section, F*amily/Cultural/Spirituality* is unique for its coverage of cases dealing with these topics, but also for the author's personal experience with a poignant case of the suicide of a client. The final section, *A Brief Introduction to Symbols and Archetypes*, gives us further insight into these critical Jungian concepts as seen through the author's treatment cases and sandplay pictures. Within each of these sections, the author shares her personalized view of her rich journey as a therapist and supervisor. We get a unique insider's view of her musings and the lessons learned along the way.

It is rare to read a book that offers up such a personalized view of a renowned sandplay therapist's professional work in such an intimate and inviting way. At the end, you come away with a true appreciation of and deeper knowing of Lois Carey and her legacy of work. *When Pixies Come Out to Play* is well worth reading for all its gems!

Athena A. Drewes, PsyD, RPT-S
Licensed Psychologist, Registered Play Therapist Supervisor
Director of Clinical Training and APA-Accredited Doctoral Internship
Astor Services for Children and Families
Rhinebeck, N.Y.

ACKNOWLEDGEMENTS

This book has been assembled from some of the numerous presentations that I have given over the past 35 or 40 years. They have been delivered in my home office, at various sites throughout the United States, Canada, Switzerland, England, Ireland, and South Africa. Some chapters are articles that I have written for the *East Coast Sandplay Journal*, the *New York Association for Play Therapy Newsletter*, or chapters that appear in books of other practitioners.

The people I need to thank are numerous for the constant love and support that I have received over these many years. If I omit anyone, please accept my apologies, but I am grateful to all. First, the Jungian analysts who have taught me so much: Dr. Ronald Grant, Dr. Edith Wallace (deceased), Dr. Gregg Furth (deceased), Dr. Edith Sullwold (deceased), Dr. John Allan, Dr. Genevieve Geer, Frau Dora Kalff (deceased), Dr. Martin Kalff, the list could go on and on. Second, my colleagues who have given so much in support: Dr. Charles Schaefer, Dr. Garry Landreth, Dr. Athena A. Drewes, Dr. Nancy Boyd Webb, and Dr. David Crenshaw. Third, my spiritual support lies with the Reverend Dr. James A. Forbes Jr., Dr. Evelyn Davis, Mrs. Emogene Stamper, Dr. Fred Dennard, and Betty Davis, among others.

A special note of thanks goes to all of my family members and friends and to Randy Hogan and Patricia Jarden for their invaluable editorial help; to Dr. Athena A. Drewes, who graciously agreed to write the Foreword; to Brad Hess for photographing my painting on the cover; and to Laura Kallen from Nyack Computer Service for her technical assistance with the images.

These acknowledgements would not be complete without heartfelt thanks for the permissions granted of reprints from various parts of chapters of my articles, as well as from chapters that I have authored in other books. Lastly, but certainly not least, a thank you to all of the adult clients and the parents of children that have given permission to have the sandplay photos and synopses of cases included in this book. Case examples are the best teaching methods that I have known.

INTRODUCTION

SANDPLAY IN SWITZERLAND—2007

I had the good fortune to attend a Sandplay workshop at Boldern, Switzerland, in July 2007. I have attended numerous such workshops since 1980, most of them in Switzerland, so when I saw this one advertised, I felt it could be the last one that I might attend and so I signed up.

The site was magnificent, high on a mountain (not quite an Alp), above a little town called Mannedorf that is on Lake Zurich, about halfway between Zurich and Rapperswill. On a clear day, we could see the snow-covered Alps across the lake.

Boldern is a conference center, so several groups were meeting at the same time. Our group had its own dining room and, I must confess, all the food (and desserts) were outstanding. I don't know how they managed to run everything so efficiently, but efficient (and tasty) it was. One time they presented us with fresh cherries that we all raved about, so on subsequent days the staff saw to it that we had all the cherries we could consume.

We were entranced with the tame rabbits that showed up at every meal outside the window of our dining room. One of them was white with black spots and black ears, the other one was similarly marked, but in brown rather than black. Those rabbits were the most photographed objects by the whole crowd—you would think that we had never seen a rabbit before, and we hadn't, at least none with those markings.

The workshop was in two sections, the first weekend was "Intensive Body Work" with Judy Zappacosta, a Sandplay therapist from California. Nine of us attended that weekend and, at the close, we didn't know how we would ever accommodate to the larger group because we had shared so much in the weekend. However, it did all work out. There were a total of only 22 in the entire group, which made for much more intimate communication of ideas.

The main part of the workshop, "Sandplay in Switzerland," was completely educational and personally enriching. Some of the participants were encouraged to present their work, which was supervised by either Judy or Martin Kalff. The audience was included in the discussions and questions that followed. Most of the presentations were of high caliber, however, a few were not because the presenters were really novices with the technique. One outstanding presentation was given by Lorraine Freedle from Santa Fe who had done a research paper for her doctorate on "Sandplay for Traumatic Brain Injury." Her work was published in an issue of the Sandplay Journal and it can be accessed on the Web with all the Sandplay pictures that were made. It was quite rewarding to see research being done with Sandplay. There are other researches being done, but this was one of the best I have witnessed.

We were privileged to have an opportunity to do three personal sand trays during the conference and I was fortunate to have mine with Martin. I have seen him (and his mother, of course), in the past, so it was a refreshing experience for me. I don't often have the chance to make my own trays, so this was definitely a plus. Martin has taken over his mother's contribution to this technique since her death and he is quite intuitive and adept.

Another important part of the workshop was taking part in six Art Therapy sessions with Sabine Kalff, Martin's wife. I have had similar sessions with her in the past, but her way of working brings out deep feelings in Art Therapy. She is quiet, non-intrusive, and offers the best of "client-centered" work. The cover of my "memoir" book, *A Salty Lake of Tears*, was painted in one of her previous workshops. Another is on my most recent endeavor, *A Little Book of Poems*. Another one is featured on the cover of this book.

During the second week, Adrienne Navone, Sandplay practitioner from Italy, who was one of Dora's early trainees, joined us. The major problem for the sections that she led was her lack of command of the English language. I know that she is far more adept at her understanding of the process than she was able to convey. During several of the sessions, Lorraine Freedle's son attended the program. He had just returned from six weeks in Italy and served as translator for Adrienne. This was definitely an asset!

We were treated to several trips as another part of the learning experience that helped the participants become acquainted with some of the many splendors of this Alpine country. One day our lectures were held at the Kalff household and that brought a flood of memories for me. I sat in the lecture hall and reflected how very much of my Sandplay training had taken place in that very room.

Martin had arranged a number of miniatures that we were free to purchase and asked that we give a donation for them. I managed to obtain quite a few, one of which had played a significant role in the first tray I ever did with Dora. I had asked her if she had a log cabin as I needed one for that particular tray. She thought for a moment and then went off to another room and came back holding one that fit the bill. I really feel so fortunate to have been able to purchase such an important personal (to me) piece.

We each brought a box lunch that day and ate in the garden together. Sabine showed us her meditation center after lunch. She is a Zen Buddhist and runs retreats for women. I doubt that I have the words to fully describe that site, however, it conveyed the utmost sense of calm and reverence that one might imagine.

The ending of that day was a pilgrimage to hear Vespers at the Einsiedeln Monastery that ends with the Salve Regina sung to the Black Madonna. I have written in other venues about my experiences there and this was yet another that causes this White Anglo-Saxon Protestant (WASP) woman to ponder once again what the spiritual connection with this Catholic figure can hold for me.

Another day trip took us by train, ferry, cable car, etc., to the Rigi, one of the Alps not too far from Zurich. We went to the Rigi by way of Lake Lucerne. That is another city that is a Swiss treasure with a famous covered bridge and numerous wonderful shops and restaurants.

I should mention that there were four of us who became fast friends and are in communication with each other, although as time goes on these communications are less and less frequent. I have found that to be the norm, unfortunately. One finds someone or several who seem to "click" with you, but eventually the magic wears off. One of the women was the aforementioned Lorraine Freedle, who at 42, appointed herself as my guardian to ensure that I didn't fall or that I got first spot in the taxi, etc. The others were Adelina Wong from Hong Kong and Weineke Goenee from the Netherlands.

While visiting the Rigi we had the pleasure of hearing four men play their Alpenhorns, and in harmony, no less! This was a treat for the ears. The Alpenhorn is an extremely difficult instrument to play and for these men to be able to harmonize so beautifully was outstanding. That same afternoon, I sat quietly alone and gazed across the vast expanse of the Alps and, once again, I was touched by the unbelievable beauty of the place and, at the same time, I experienced some sadness as I am not sure I will ever have that opportunity again. This was a physically challenging trip for me—most of my colleagues were much younger and I must admit to feeling less capable than I had ever felt before. I simply did not have the stamina that I had 20 years ago, but overall, I still managed to do almost everything, and for that I am thankful. I feel blessed to have been able to attend this conference and to continue to expand my learning of Sandplay, as that has been my passion for all these years.

Since the inception of this book, I have struggled to find an appropriate title. Shortly before it was to go to press, I had a dream that provided me with a bit of inspiration. The dream: I was returning on a train from a conference that my daughter had also attended. The train was quite crowded, but I eventually got a seat next to another woman about age 70. When her stop came, she leaned over a said to me, "The pixies will soon be coming out to play." Hence, the title. There is more, of course, because the dream also took me back to my childhood when my mother told me numerous Irish legends about fairies dancing around a certain tree, along with elves, leprechauns, etc. I don't remember much more, but they fed my imagination for years and, I am sure, led to my future profession as a play therapist.

I was in Ireland in the year 2000 and took a side trip with a driver to see some interesting sights. At one point, the road curved around a tree in the middle of the road. The driver said it was a "fairy tree" and that it was bad luck to cut it down, so they had to build the road around it.

"About one thing it is necessary to be clear from the first. The method is very difficult and calls for very prolonged training."

—Esther Harding

PART I

OVERVIEW/METHODOLOGY

CHAPTER 1

OVERVIEW OF PLAY THERAPY

WHY DO CHILDREN PLAY?

Play is the way that children have always expressed themselves. Children play before they walk or talk. Mothers and babies have always communicated through play—tickling toes, playing peek-a-boo, clapping hands—these are just a few of the ways that the process of bonding begins that is so essential for a child's healthy development. As children develop, play becomes their way to master the environment. For example, through dollhouse play, the young child replicates his/her relationship to his/her environment. When a young child sets up a dollhouse it may result in a chaotic scene or it may show a carefully constructed house with everything in its normal place. The scene that is created is largely determined by the age of the child, because some younger children (under the age of three) are not adept at arranging furniture.

WHAT IS PLAY THERAPY?

In the 1980s, professionals began to realize that play was being used by many persons as a tool for the treatment of child patients, but many had no formal training to do this type of work. Charles Schaefer, Ph.D., at Fairleigh Dickinson University in New Jersey, and one of his students, Kevin O'Conner, Ph.D., in Fresno, California, founded the Association for Play Therapy (APT) in 1981. The first APT conference was held in Queens, N.Y., in 1983. Seventy-five people attended to hear Dr. Louise Guerney and Dr. Margarita Sjolund present their methods.

Dr. Guerney is well known for her Filial Therapy technique that trains parents to do therapy with their children while being carefully monitored and coached by professionals.

Dr. Sjolund is equally well-known for her work with sand. Her method is called the Erika method and was developed in Sweden for diagnostic purposes. It differs in approach from the Kalff and Lowenfeld methods, which are used more in the United States. These are discussed in Chapter 5.

Since the time of that first conference in 1983, there has been a steady growth in attendance at conferences held in various parts of the country that attract a large number of attendees.

The original focus of APT was to formalize theoretical guidelines for professionals who work therapeutically with children and to insure that these professionals were cognizant of and trained in child development. Once these guidelines were established, comprehensive training sites were organized. The first play therapy trainings were provided in California, Texas, New Jersey,and Pennsylvania. Today, many other sites have been established and can be found on the APT website.

APT has state branches throughout the country and abroad, with each branch offering training hours through conferences and workshops. Supervision of new members is also a requirement and can be obtained through those who are Registered Play Therapist Supervisors. The requirements are quite strict and can be accessed on www.a4pt.org for up-to-date information. It is necessary to fulfill training hours and supervision requirements, with the goal being to attain Registered Play Therapist status. It has long been recognized that therapists need to develop special skills to treat children, so the establishment of play therapy has been formalized through APT and other similar organizations in other countries. For example, the therapist needs to learn how children play normally in order to differentiate what might be abnormal. After a thorough assessment, an appropriate treatment plan can then be developed.

Children's problems are treated therapeutically by several equally effective methods: puppetry, games, art, video, dollhouse play, sandplay, toy soldiers, building blocks, cars and trucks, Tinker Toys, Legos, costumes, etc. No matter which technique or toy is employed, the child and therapist use metaphoric language to communicate. They relate to each other through the characters or roles chosen, be it through a discussion with puppets, miniatures in the sand, a story told about the action in the dollhouse, or the description of an art production.

Children do not often respond to direct questions, so when play is the method of choice it is far less threatening to them than trying to get a verbal response. Instead of "Tell me what happened," children can illustrate "what happened" through play methods (dolls, puppets, art, etc.). The issues are discussed in a metaphoric form that is easier for the child to accept than through direct verbalization.

HISTORY OF PLAY THERAPY

Play Therapy has been around for many years, as far back as the early 20th century when H. G. Wells wrote *Floor Games.*[1] In that book he described how he and his sons played for hours to set up scenes with toys that spread throughout the house. The scenes often depicted problems that the children were experiencing in their daily lives. As part of the play, Wells found that toys of that period were too large for young children to handle, so he encouraged toy manufacturers to make toys that were smaller, easier for a child to handle and more "child-friendly."

In the 1920s, Margaret Lowenfeld,[2] a child psychiatrist in London, began to use play in her clinic for her child patients. Her clinic was equipped with all kinds of play materials: dolls, baby beds, bottles, housekeeping supplies, motorized vehicles, blocks to build with, a sand and water table, etc. Dr. Lowenfeld observed that the children often set up scenes with the toys in the sand tray that directly suggested their problems and concerns. She recorded her observations and followed the child's lead in treatment in order to assess and quantify her findings.

For example, one girl of 19 made a world that provided diagnostic information to Dr. Lowenfeld that led to her understanding the need for treatment.[3]

1 Wells, H.G.

2 See Bowyer, L.

3 See Urwin, C. and J. Hood-Williams, pp. 281-282

Figure 1.1 - A man threatening a giraffe

"She was brought by her mother for advice on the choice of a career, as the mother had been troubled by her daughter's frivolity and lack of concentration. From the history and behavior of the girl there was nothing to suggest the presence of any neurosis. While I (Dr. L.) was talking with the mother, the girl was asked to make a World—Figure 1.1 is the one that resulted.

"Here you see a man brandishing a stick and threatening a giraffe who is looking over the hillock at him. The other animals were on their way down to the pond in the centre to have a drink, but when the giraffe caused this disturbance, they all turned to watch. The only person not watching is the man in the top right-hand corner that is walking away and cannot see because of the bundle he is carrying."

It is clear that underneath the girl's apparent adaptation lay ideas of a paranoiac quality. The girl herself felt the World scene was absolutely normal and usual, and could see nothing in it that was peculiar in any way.

The existence of this World, however, made it possible to convince both her and her mother of the necessity for treatment.

In the first half of the 20th century, Anna Freud[4] and Melanie Klein[5] began their work with children and each developed her own theory and technique. One issue that was of importance to both of these pioneers was the role of the parent in the child's therapy. Freud occasionally met with parents, while Klein omitted them completely. Klein's rationale was that parental influence could have a negative impact on the child's treatment. In Klein's method, the child was dropped off at the door and picked up following the session; the parent(s) had no contact with the therapist at all. Today this method is rarely used because most child therapists realize that the family system is integral to the child's problems. In fact, parents are sometimes included when family play therapy is indicated; but certainly parents need to have a good working relationship with the therapist through monthly parent counseling sessions.

Following A. Freud and M. Klein, Virginia Axline,[6] a student of Carl Rogers, also began to treat children. She adapted Rogers's *Client-Centered Therapy*[7] to children and called it "Child-Centered Therapy." One of her books, *Dibs*,[8] is a classic in the play therapy field.

Space does not permit me to go further into the history of play therapy but, suffice it to say, it was and continues to be a new and exciting way to help disturbed children and their families. These techniques, through later research, have proven how very effective these methods are.

"SCHOOLS" OF PLAY THERAPY

Play therapy falls into various categories or "schools" of thought that usually reflect the therapist's primary affiliation. This is similar to individual and family therapy theories that have various "schools." Play therapists have evolved from several such backgrounds—analytic, psychodynamic, cognitive/behavioral, Eriksonian, Freudian, Jungian, Rogerian,

4 Freud, A.
5 Klein, M.
6 Axline, V., 1947
7 Rogers, C.
8 Axline, V., 1971

etc. Some forms of play therapy are designated as "child-centered" and are non-directive, based on the Rogers/Axline approach. Other forms of play therapy are behavioral, such as cognitive/behavioral, and another type, which is known as "Theraplay,"[9] was developed by Ann Jernberg. When one uses a directive form of play therapy, play therapists provide the child with toys that are directly related to his/her problem. One example that comes to mind is recounted in a videotape of Nancy Boyd Webb's,[10] in which she is treating a child who was about to enter school and who shows a great deal of anxiety about this event. Dr. Webb provided the child with a toy school bus and some toy students. She then had the child place the toy students into the school bus and transport them to school. After several sessions, this activity relieved the child (and the mother) of the child's upcoming entrance to school.

These examples illustrate that some play therapy is verbal, (metaphorical, storytelling, directive, cognitive/behavioral, etc.), while others combine non-verbal and verbal techniques, (sandplay and art therapy). The form that is used depends on the therapist's training and overall orientation.

SANDPLAY THERAPY

The history and differences inherent in Sandplay Therapy are discussed in Chapter 3 depending on which theoretical basis is used. However, Sandplay is on the cutting edge when one treats children or families, especially in cases of trauma. Corroboration of this can be found in this author's recent book, *Expressive and Creative Arts Methods for Trauma Survivors.*[11] In Chapter 1 of that book, "Neuroscience and Trauma Treatment: Implications for Creative Arts Therapists," is discussed by David Crenshaw.[12] He describes how the brain functions: our verbal abilities are located in the left hemisphere of the brain, the thinking portion, and traumatic injury is stored in the right, or non-verbal hemisphere.

9 Jernberg, A., 1989

10 Webb, N.B., 1994

11 Carey, L., ed., 2006

12 Crenshaw, D., pp. 21-38

Crenshaw sites Siegel[13] and van Der Kolk[14] in explaining this process. This suggests that non-verbal material (some of which is pre-verbal) is much more readily accessed by creative methods of therapy, such as art, music, and Sandplay.

The non-verbal aspect of Sandplay provides yet another valuable tool for this form of therapy. Once the trauma material has been accessed by a non-verbal approach, it can then be connected with the verbal, so that there is then some intellectual understanding of the trauma. An example would be that the placement of the toys in the sand (as well as the toys chosen and shapes formed in the sand, etc.) can assist the therapist in an appropriate intervention that brings the traumatic material to the forefront. After this knowledge (of the trauma) has been achieved through non-verbal means and then integrated with the verbal, the healing process can begin.

SETTING UP A PLAY ROOM

Therapists who treat children use various play materials that are designed to put a child at ease so that he/she will trust the therapist and that a therapeutic relationship will develop. It is helpful if one has a separate area from the main consulting office that is furnished with child-sized objects—tables, chairs, etc. Following are some suggested items that are important to have, others can also be used.

Necessary Items:

- Dolls of varying skin tones.
- Doll bed, blanket.
- Dollhouse and furniture.
- Baby bottle.
- Dollhouse-sized family dolls (also in varying ages and skin tones).
- Puppets, various types—cuddly, soft, aggressive, frightening.

---

13 Siegel, D.

14 Van Der Kolk, B.A., pp. 34-50

- Art materials—crayons, markers, tempera paints, pencils, various sizes of paper (an easel if space permits), clay, Play Doh.

Additional Items

- Sandplay equipment consisting of two sand boxes and an assortment of miniatures.
- Children's books that depict childhood problems.
- Therapeutic games.
- Miscellaneous other equipment such as cars or trucks, that can be ridden by the children.

CHAPTER 2

JUNGIAN THEORY

In order to assist the reader with this book, a few illustrations are included that will explain parts of the theory that are particularly relevant to an understanding of these various articles. The author believes that this will be helpful here, rather than repeating this in every chapter.

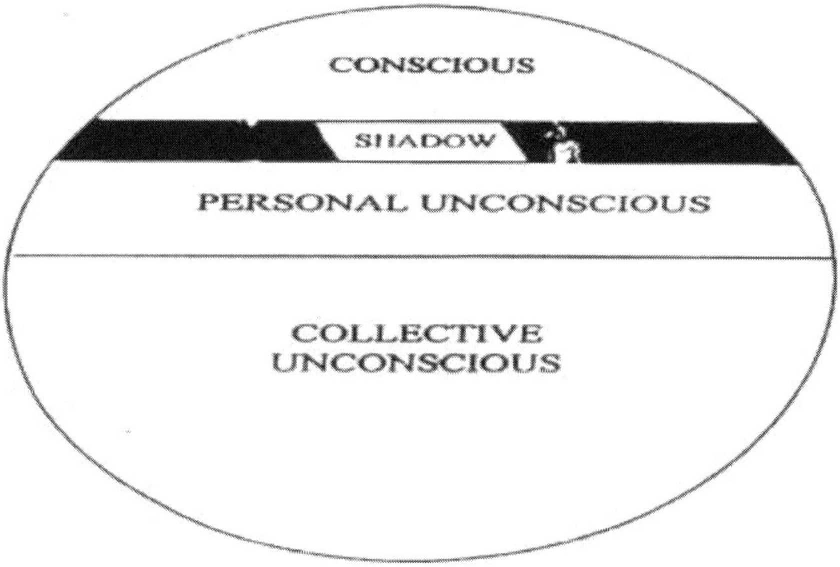

Figure 2.1 - PSYCHE

This sketch represents this author's idea of Jung's model of the psyche.

1. Note that the conscious (at the top) is only a small part of the overall psyche.

2. The shadow represents the rejected part of one's psyche that is projected onto other people. An example of what the shadow portrays is that there is possibly something about a person you have just met that is disturbing to you. This often means that something you dislike about yourself, such as a negative attitude, is unconsciously projected onto this stranger. When one begins to examine one's personal reaction, it is often possible to detect what has been projected, and thus make it available to consciousness.
3. The personal unconscious is that area of the psyche that has repressed personal issues from past experiences, such as in childhood, but that can be accessed at times through flashbacks, dreams, etc.
4 The collective unconscious is the major portion of the psyche and is the major area that caused the rift between Jung and Freud. Jung believed that each person is born with countless "archetypes" and, as one matures, only a few or several are favored.

The word psyche in contemporary analytical psychology has taken on at least two meanings. On the one hand, it refers to the faculty of the human being that is capable of experiencing the imaginary world as well as the physical world or it may refer to the entire realm of experience, both conscious and unconscious. In the first case, psyche is identified with soul in the traditional sense; in the second, psyche is the world of the soul.

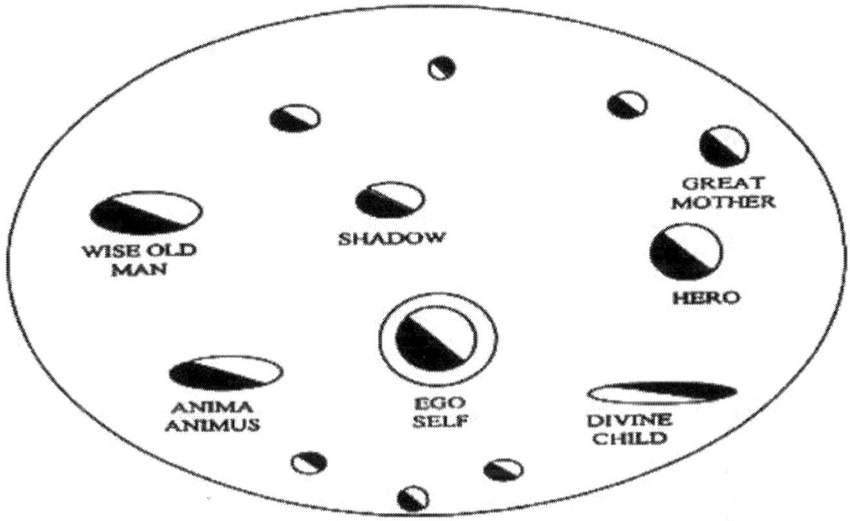

Figure 2.2 - COLLECTIVE UNCONSCIOUS

This is a sketch of the collective unconscious. Each archetype has a dark and a light side as indicated on the sketch. For example, consider the Great Mother[15] archetype. This does not refer to one's personal mother, but is considered to be the extreme of the extremes; the positive side is the nurturing, loving, cherishing part of the mother figure, similar to mother images from ancient Greece. Mary, the mother of Jesus, is considered to be an example of the Great Mother as well. The negative aspect of this archetype can best be described as the Terrible Mother[16] – she of the many rages, the Medusa – she who can kill with one glance, etc. The aim of therapy is to find a way to balance each archetype that is encountered. Again, to use the Great Mother as an example, if the positive side is dominant, one does everything to excess, to the point where there is nothing more to give. This is often the major archetype of the therapist. On the negative side, we may use the example of a man, so under the sway of the mother, that he is totally unable to relate to the real women in his life. The task becomes that of helping the client

15 Neumann, 1955, p. 18
16 Neumann, 1955, p. 21

to find a balance between the two poles. Jung believed that the ego/Self was an archetype as well.

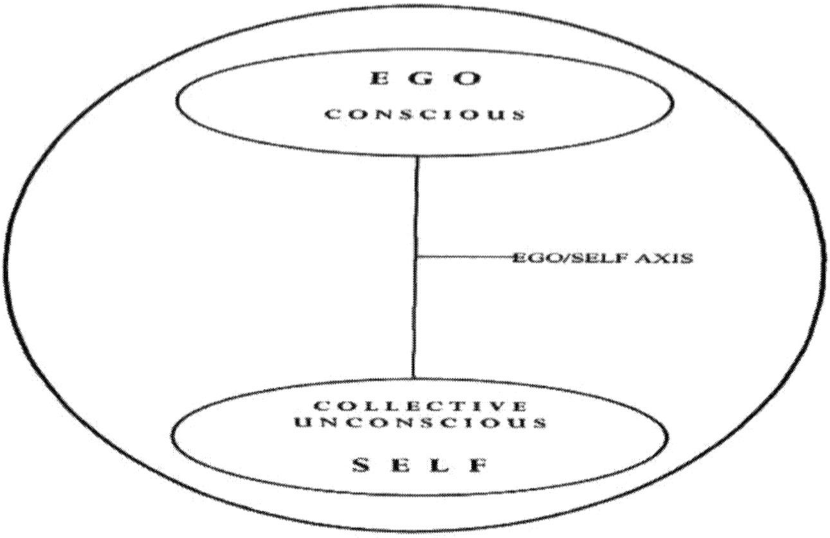

Figure 2.3

This is the ego/Self archetype. Jung believed that the ego was in the conscious part of the psyche and that the Self, the inner spiritual dimension, was buried in the collective unconscious. Jung believed that the ego and the Self were connected by an invisible thread that he called the ego/Self axis. During childhood, any assault to that invisible thread causes a split to occur. The job of therapy is to re-unite that split for true healing to occur. Any trauma, such as separation from the mothering figure, or a death in the family, or divorce, not to mention sexual or physical abuse, could cause such a rift. It is possible, in Sandplay, to actually visualize when the healing occurs in sand pictures. Later in this series, a few pictures will be shown to help illustrate this. There will be more on archetypes in a later chapter in this book.

CHAPTER 3

JUNGIAN SANDPLAY THERAPY[17]

Jungian Play Therapy (JPT) as defined by Eric Green[18] "offers an alternative to traditional talk therapy. JPT is a particular form of play therapy that facilitates healing through the expression of one's subconscious images, metaphors, and symbols based on analytical psychology."

The title of this chapter is a loosely defined term because Carl Jung himself was a psychiatrist who theorized that analysis of one's personality could only be undertaken in the "second half of life." He put that at 35 years of age. However, since Jung's time, many therapists have applied some of his theories to work with children, especially Dora Maria Kalff. Today, her method is often called "Kallfian" Sandplay.

Some Jungian principles will be presented that apply to therapy with children and also to be discussed are some other child-related theories that have been used and incorporated into Jungian work.

Jung did some very interesting writing on "The Psychology of the Child Archetype"[19] and, in his autobiography, *Memories, Dreams and Reflections,*[20] Jung discussed how he had resorted to "play" after his break with Freud. As Jung described it in "Memories," he built a miniature village out of rocks, stones, and twigs along the shoreline of his summer home in Bollingen, Switzerland. He found that this activity released a stream of fantasies that he later wrote down. This vignette is usually credited as the beginnings of Sandplay. He later moved from building this miniature village to painting his fantasies and then to stone cutting. From these endeavors, Jung gave birth to the technique of Active Imagination in which one dialogues with a dream figure (or a sandplay

---

17 Presented at various APT and NYAPT Conferences

18 Green, E., 2009

19 Jung, C.G., 1959

20 Jung, C.G., 1965

figure) and sees where it leads. This can be done in written form as well as orally.

Jung did his work during the first half of the last century and had numerous followers, some of whom stayed as his devotees, others who later moved on. One of his students, Frances Wickes, was among the first to consider how to apply Jungian theory to children. Her book, *The Inner World of Childhood,*[21] is a classic; although the thinking of that time was that all of a child's problems were directly related to the psychological problems of the parents. She demonstrated that in some cases this was true, but that the child could also have his/her own personal issues as well. At that time, Jung (and others) believed that analysis of the mother was the way to heal problems in the child.

In the 1920s and 30s, interest was growing in the field of child therapy. That was the time of Anna Freud, Melanie Klein, and Margaret Lowenfeld, all of whom were Freudian-influenced and all were working in London, as was Michael Fordham. Fordham, however, was a Jungian analyst but was also subject to the ideas of others. D.W. Winnicott was another early influence but he, too, was Freudian-trained. From what has been observed, the London group of child therapists, Freudian or Jungian, relied heavily on the analysis of everything that a child did or said and usually related it to either the sexual act or the transference relationship. Winnicott's book, *The Piggle,*[22] is a prime example. This is a case description of a four-year-old child who was suffering from the birth of a younger sibling. The book is a description of her entire analysis and every act and statement of hers is related to the birth theme. Her fantasy during part of her therapy was that she was the child of Winnicott.

One needs to differentiate the work done as counselors and therapists from that of analysts, because it is not the same thing. A child may be seen three to five times a week in an analytic setting, while play therapists are fortunate if they are authorized a total of ten weekly sessions from managed care. However, it is from these early analysts that our work has developed and therapists need to know how this has evolved.

---

21 Wickes, F., 1927

22 Winnicott, D.W., 1977

Michael Fordham[23] in London was one of the chief followers of Jung, although, as mentioned earlier, he was heavily influenced by Klein[24] and Anna Freud.[25] His work with children was very creative and he was one of the pioneers of Jungian child psychotherapy. Jungians (pre-Fordham) believed that childhood neurosis was a consequence of parental psychopathology. Fordham agreed with this view at first (parental paychopathology) and then, as he delved further into Jungian theory, he extended Jung's ideas about archetypes, the Self and individuation and applied these concepts to childhood.

In the beginning stages of child therapy, it was thought that the analysis of children and adults were similar because both approaches aimed to make the unconscious conscious. Fordham was able to demonstrate how Jung's concept of the archetype was also related to Melanie Klein's concept of unconscious fantasy.

Melanie Klein was a trainer of many early child analysts and, as part of her curriculum, she insisted that trainees have an experience with infant observation as part of their education because she believed that the training would bring up each one's personal early experiences. In this way, Klein believed that the trainees' personal analyses could be enhanced.

Each trainee was assigned a "nursing couple" – mother and baby. Many times the observation began during the pregnancy. Klein believed that careful study of the interaction between mother and baby made for better child analysts. Fordham agreed fully with this.

Klein's method was that the "couple" be observed, usually monthly, during the first two years of the child's life. The trainees were asked to visit at feeding, bathing, and bed times. Careful notes were taken and then group discussions with other trainees were held. From her studies and directly related to the Fordham/Jung view, the concept of deintegration/reintegration evolved. This means that a calm, sleeping baby is in a state of peace or reintegration. When he begins to fuss because he is uncomfortable, wet, or hungry, he is said to be in a state of deintegration. For example, a baby wakes up, looks around, and

---

23 Fordham, M.

24 Klein, M., 1959

25 Freud, A., 1946

vocalizes, thus drawing mother's attention. The mother follows up and gives a breast feed. The infant takes the nipple, sucks, looks into mother's face which leads to a glow of satisfaction and sleep returns; the child has "reintegrated." This is a continuous process until the child has longer and longer periods of reintegration. This process really continues throughout life, but here we are really considering the first two years.

Davidson,[26] another early theorist, said that the area of "play" helps the imagination grow and is the potential space between mother and baby where play can take place. This is like a sandbox, the "temenos," or intermediate healing space. If the mother's ability to manage is not firmly established, symbolic transformation cannot occur. In other words, if there is early emotional deprivation between mother and baby, this severely impairs the child's capacity to form personal relationships. This is called "attachment disorder" today.

The followers of Fordham give words to what the child is doing or saying, the object being to make the actions conscious. This is like "tracking" or "mirroring" in therapy. This helps the child to master his/her anxiety and can thus transform the child. Fordham was one of the first to show that archetypal images could be observed in children and he related these images to ego development. A primary identity exists between mother/child out of which a child evolves his/her own separate identity (deintegration/reintegration). Some examples are looking, sucking, touching, etc.

The London trainees in child analysis also have to analyze a mother under supervision in order to help them understand the difficulties that mothers have in bringing up their children. The London group also believed it was important for analysts to have some relationship to the parents. It doesn't seem to matter that a child may be the symptom-bearer in a family. It is, however, necessary to assess what in the child, him/herself, has made him/her occupy that role.

As mentioned earlier in this chapter, Jung's focus throughout his work was "the second half of life," after the age of 35. His belief was that this was the time when analysis could best be accomplished. He believed that the child was primarily an unconscious being with small islands of ego (conscious) development.

26 Davidson, M.W., 2012

In 1935, Melanie Klein was an influential force on the child therapy scene. There was very little training at that time for child psychiatrists and very limited child psychoanalysis. The children who were treated were primarily schizophrenic or autistic. Child psychotherapy was not even considered When Michael Fordham, a child psychiatrist, came on the scene, he felt that his hands were pretty much tied. Social workers worked with parents, but not analytically and so he decided to make some observations which follow:

1. Children recover from disorders no matter what was done. If they were left on a waiting list, they improved, even very severe cases. There were also no changes made in parents.
2. Archetypal material abounded and had no negative effect, as had been feared.
3. Symbolic material was found that related to the Self and ego development, comparable to individuation in later life.

These findings mirrored the views of Klein and children began to be considered as more sophisticated and complex than had been previously thought. Children had individual characteristics and could deal with intrapsychic conflicts, irrespective of the parents.

Klein's and Fordham's observations were that unconscious fantasies revealed extreme parent imagos: good and bad objects, good and bad parent images. It was also found that children developed a transference to the therapist (as good object), which is an inborn archetypal potential, directly in line with Jungian theory. Fordham demonstrated that it is in the transference that a child behaves as he does in his family; however, in cases of autism the behavior was extreme.

"The Frame" is another important concept of Fordham's that he described that related to the function of the analyst – the room, frequency of sessions, analytic attitude/style, etc. He said that psychotic children would attempt to destroy the frame, ruin equipment, attack the analyst, leave early, etc.

Fordham differed somewhat in the understanding of the Self, not as an innate part of the mother, but as a separate entity contained within the child. The idea that the Self was primary, meant that *particpation mystique* would have to be a learned response that required activity on the part of the infant. This meant that the Self had to go through deintegration/reintegration numerous times and that the deintegrates would first have archetypal characteristics. In this respect, Fordham differed from Erich Neumann because Neumann placed emphasis on mythology rather than on a real child.

One of Fordham's colleagues had analyzed a 13-month-old child, from which Fordham deduced that non-verbal communication played a much larger part with children than adults. He said that, "a child's actions in play can be taken as direct communication," but that the analyst must ALWAYS maintain the "analytic attitude." The "analytic attitude" means that the analyst holds a detached, non-judgmental, impartial attitude that allows for interpretations to be made and is, he believed, the main instrument of the analyst. The analytic attitude involved "not knowing beforehand" when assessing a child and having no previous inkling of his history, problems, etc. One needs to ALWAYS begin from nothing and see where the child leads.

One of this author's first supervisors in Social Work directed his students to interview the child without reading any history, in order that our own first impressions were formed rather than being influenced by the child's history. This was incredibly challenging and also quite helpful.

Mara Sidoli,[27] a more recent Jungian child therapist, continued with the deintegration/reintegration theory that focused on the first two weeks of a child's life. She also observed the nursing couple and viewed the baby as the protagonist. Her trainees made weekly observations for the first two years and focused on the stability of the family – the emotional tone and reliability. She observed the interactions with all relatives that appeared during visits with the family. Her techniques grew out of the Kleinian and Fordham training. Her observations were:

1. For a positive experience a child needed a good breast, a good loving mother, and a good loving baby. This constitutes the positive aspect of the mother archetype (Good Breast).

27 Personal notes, 1987

2. On the negative side, a child experiences discomfort, hate, despair, rage, violence, fear, panic – leads to the negative aspect of the mother archetype (Bad Breast).

Both of these states are absolutes for the infant who is completely involved in either experience. The good experiences need to outnumber the bad for peaceful, integrated states to predominate. This depends on "good enough" mothering to be available to provide the baby with a containing function. The real flesh-and-blood mother mediates the relationship between the baby and the innate archetypal drives.

Erik Erikson's[28] stages are also important in the overall theory, especially his first stage of Trust vs. Mistrust (see Addenda B). Erikson, Fordham, and Jung all arrived at the same conclusion: "the idea of an original wholeness is potentially there in the new-born baby."

There also needs to be consideration given to the idea of "space" as being important to child development. There needs to be enough (space), but not too much as this is the area where play and creativity can develop: "it (play) is the natural form of expression" (for the child). Playing helps a child attain more consciousness. Losing and finding are themes of many games: Bo-Peep, Hide and Seek, Hide the Thimble, etc. This is certainly something often seen in Sandplay. One author, Feldman,[29] believed that the sand tray was often not suitable for psychotic children, as they tended to throw sand around the room or at the therapist. He believed they were unable to experience the containing aspects of the tray. However, he found that these children responded well to having their own separate box of toys, a practice developed by Klein.

Several years ago this author attended a presentation that was given by a student who had worked with autistic children in the sand. It was astounding to see that these children went through the same stages as the more "normal" children who were being treated. This seems to contradict Feldman's view.

If language is not available, such as in a one-year-old or an autistic child, something like play must replace it. How the child deals with

28 Eriksen, E. 1963
29 Feldman, R. 2011

toys and the analytic space can be observed and interpreted verbally, which leads into the earliest preverbal way of communicating. For example, when a child crashes a toy car into another one, it can be done enthusiastically or aggressively, and can reveal some of the underlying dynamics.

This author's understanding of Jungian Play Therapy has come out of her own training and experience. She attended numerous summer programs in Switzerland in the 1980s and studied with people such as Dora Kalff, John Allan, and Edith Sullwold. Dora was from Switzerland, John from Western Canada, Edith from California. These programs were sponsored by the University of California Extension (Santa Cruz) that was and continues to be heavily Jungian-based. It brought together numerous Jungian analysts from those areas mentioned above, as well as many from Zurich and other countries such as Italy, Germany, and England.

In addition to Jungians, lectures were given by Alice Miller, Joseph Chilton Pearce, and others. Joseph Chilton Pearce could qualify as a child-centered therapist even though his expertise was teaching, not therapy. He believed that children did not need to be taught to read; if left untutored in the subject, they would be reading naturally by third grade. He would not be too popular with educators, but in many private schools his ideas still predominate.

One of John Allan's teachings about the multiple things that occur during every therapy session is shown in the diagram on Figure 3.1 of the following page. This example demonstrates that there are many conscious and unconscious communications that are all going on at the same time: client's to therapist's conscious; therapist's to client's conscious; therapist's to client's unconscious and vice versa; client's to therapist's unconscious and vice versa; client's unconscious to therapist's unconscious and vice versa; client's conscious to client's unconscious and vice versa; therapist's conscious to therapist's unconscious and vice versa. All of this is related to transference and counter/transference issues and demonstrates why the therapist needs to be especially conscious of all of these elements. When he/she is not conscious, good supervision is essential.

Relevant theories and practices, in addition to those of Jung, (i.e. archetypes, typology, and active imagination), such as child personality development, issues in family therapy, trauma, art therapy, puppetry, etc. are all important in the practice of play therapy, as well as others not mentioned.

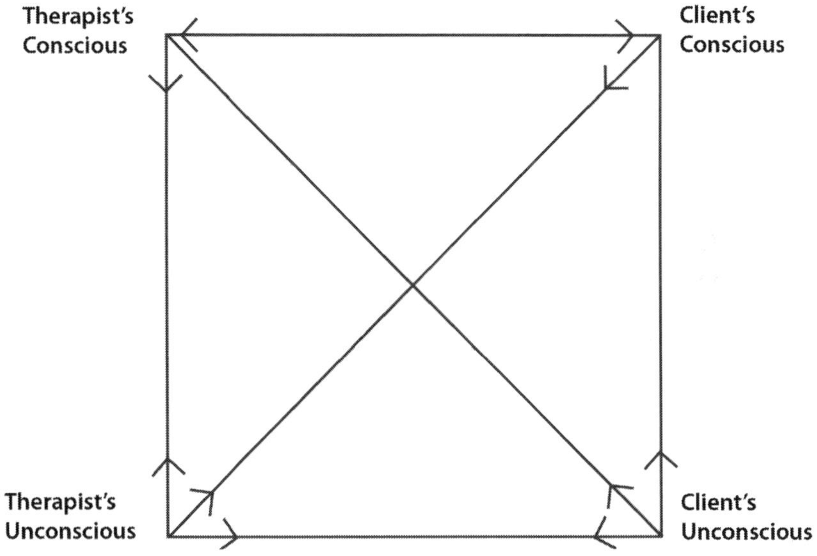

Figure 3.1

CHAPTER 4

ART AS THERAPY

Artistic expression is something that most therapists use from time to time and that Jungians use a great deal because of their interest in symbolic representation. Gregg Furth[30] and John Allen,[31] Jungian analysts, and Eliana Gil,[32] Registered Play Therapist Supervisor, must be given credit for some of these ideas.

The following twelve points come primarily from Gregg Furth.

1. What kind of feeling does the picture convey?
2. What seems odd or out of place in the picture? Always go from the known to the unknown.
3. What is actually there and what is missing?
4. If there is edging, why is it there? Perhaps as an ego support.
5. Are compartmentalization and/or segmentation apparent? These can show that the person feels split into various parts. One might also suggest that the person becomes a part of the drawing, or several parts.
6. Is transparency indicated? This can reveal impaired reality, possibly a "splitting out."
7. What season is portrayed, present season or a different one and why? Winter can reveal depression.
8. What colors are used, which ones are not used; are colors out of place, what is the intensity of the color? Notice the colors used during a series of drawings.

30 Personal communication

31 Personal notes

32 Personal notes

9. What are the sizes of the figures in relationship to the rest of the drawing?
10. Is there cross-hatching? (may reveal anxiety)
11. Are barriers in evidence? (for ego protection or for isolation)
12. What is the perspective, bird's eye, worm's eye, normal?

There has been a lot of interpretation about drawings of trees. If one looks at the drawing of a tree as representing the same age as the person who drew it and there is a hole in the trunk, it is possible to estimate that there was some sort of major wounding at half the age of the child. For example, if a child is 12 and draws a knot half-way down the trunk, one should explore what happened to him/her around the age of five or six. Other things to notice on the tree are whether or not the branches seem open. If the branches appear closed, this can indicate possible withholding of feelings or else (if the branches appear open) that the feelings are beginning to come out. An angry state can be surmised if there are spike-like branches. If the branches are scribbled over, anxiety is present. The size of the trunk and the root system are important as well. Are they seen or not? There are many things you can learn about a person from a tree drawing in addition to those listed here.

The kind of media selected needs to be observed as well. Does the person use pencil, pen, crayons, markers, finger paints, or plasticene. Each media can suggest different things. One has more control when using a pencil rather than a pen. Crayons and markers take one to a younger age; selection of colors can also indicate certain things. For example:

- Black and/or gray suggests sadness or depression.
- Red, anger or passion.
- Blue and green, calm.
- Orange, excitement, happiness.
- Purple, frightened.

Also important is how the client approaches the task, what is the process that can be noted: hesitancy, anxiety, verbal comments, etc.

A great amount of material and information can be gathered about a client, such as:

1. What developmental level is depicted in a figure?
2. Does it have most of the body parts?
3. How is space used - are there baselines, folding-over, x-ray, elevation?
4. Is the present season depicted? (Spring, summer, fall, winter)
5. If rain, snow, or wind is shown, one can assume that there is sadness; if the wind is blowing, it sometimes can indicate pre-psychosis.
6. Overall schema - is it appropriate, flexible, stereotyped, advanced, conceptual, or perceptual?
7. Color - is it appropriately related to the object, or is it used as fantasy?
8. Encapsulation – are figures separated by being "boxed-in," which often suggests serious issues, such as physical, sexual, or emotional abuse?
9. Aggressivity – seen in things like piercing eyes, reinforced fingers, large fingers, hands, arms, legs thrust wide apart, hair reinforced.
10. Insecurity, inferiority - small size of figure relative to page.
11. Inability to complete picture, few details can indicate depression.
12. Placement on the page:
    a. Upper part of page - need security OR can be aloof, unapproachable.
    b. Farther to the right - more able to delay gratification, can be introverted.
    c. Farther to the left - impulsive, extraverted, living in the past.
    d. Lower part of page - insecure, inadequate, can be depressed.
    e. Edge of paper - need for support.
    f. Upper-left quadrant - normal in young children (can be regressed in an adult).

13. Pressure used:
    a. Very heavy - tense, can be organic or psychotic.
    b. Light - depressed, inadequate, fearful.
14. Strokes:
    a. Straight line - assertive.
    b. Circular - dependent.
    c. Broken, reinforced - anxiety, tension, stress.
15. Erasures:
    a. uncertainty, self-dissatisfaction.
16. Detailing:
    a. Lack of - withdrawal, emptiness, depression.
    b. Excessive - obsessive/compulsive; incipient schizophrenic process.
    c. Excessive detailing - stiffly drawn trees or animals; relatively weak ego, striving to hold on.
17. Person rigidly at attention - body and head erect, legs closed together, arms straight, close to body - self is closed off against the world, cannot relate spontaneously to others.
18. Symmetry:
    a. Lack of - inadequate feelings.
    b. Too much - obsessive/compulsive.
19. Homosexuality - if male draws female figure with high heels and/or eyelashes on the figure. (MOST people draw their own sex first)
20. GENERIC RED FLAGS:
    a. Lack of facial features - disorganization or disintegration.
    b. Distressing written messages.
    c. Sometimes compartmentalization.

Red flags usually signal the need for further assessment.

21. The drawings of abused children may include some of the following features:

a. Wide-open mouths.
b. Startled eyes or covered-up eyes.
c. Containment around the body.
d. Developmentally regressed drawings.
e. Presence of exaggerated, prominent genitals.
f. Written messages asking for assistance (sometimes these are drawn in the sand).

However, no single feature in art is conclusive of child abuse. The therapist must make sure he/she listens to what the child has to say about his or her drawing and note the affect associated with the drawing. The same feature may mean different things at different times.

Art can be the child's preferred treatment of choice, in which case verbal therapy may or may not be valued or desired. It can be useful to have therapeutic dialogue about the art (or sandplay) work, but it is not always necessary since much art and sandplay engages unconscious processing.

This chapter summarizes in brief form some of the aspects related to how therapists without formal art therapy training can begin to understand what is being portrayed. It offers some hints that are useful to know when one is evaluating a client's drawing. When a therapist is concerned about a drawing, or a series of drawings, it is advisable to seek a competent supervisor.

CHAPTER 5

THREE METHODS OF SANDPLAY THERAPY[33]

Erica, Lowenfeld, Kalff

This chapter will acquaint the reader with the various methods and history of sand tray/sandplay therapy. There are other methods that have sprung from these three as well but these are the ones most prevalent in the United States and Europe.

1. The Erica Method

This method is not too well known in this country – its major practitioners are in Sweden. It was developed at the Erica Institute in Sweden by Gudrun Seitz,[34] who had been influenced by Margaret Lowenfeld, Melanie Klein and Anna Freud. It was originally designed as a diagnostic assessment tool and was an attempt to organize unstructured approaches into a standardized form.

The equipment consists of 360 miniatures that are scaled to size and kept in a 12-compartment cabinet. Figure 5.1 is a diagram of how the cabinet is to be arranged.

The Erica Method begins with three observation sessions that illustrate normal or pathological issues with particular attention paid to sequence, form, and composition. The therapist makes note of indifferent placement, sorting, configuration, simple categorization, juxtaposition, conventional, and whether or not the construction provided a meaningful whole or was chaotic, bizarre, and/or closed.

33 Presented to the Children's Play Therapy Center, Ireland, 2010, and to the New York Association for Play Therapy Conference, Poughkeepsie, NY, 2011

34 Sjolund, M. 1981

Organization of Toy Cabinet
Erica Method

	Aggressive	Peaceful	Peaceful	Aggressive
Moving Objects (Vehicles)	Airplanes	Trains	Cars	Boats
Active Objects (People and animals)	Soldiers Cowboys Indians	People	Farm animals	Wild Animals
Static Objects	Fire Cannons	Houses Churches Trees	Furniture	Fences Traffic Signs

Figure 5.1

There are two lines of development in the Erica Method:

1. Toys are placed without paying attention to what they represent. The child cannot combine the toys in any meaningful way. This is probably most often seen in children under age four. The levels of composition are:
   a. Indifferent placement.
   b. Sorting.
   c. Configuration.

or

2. Toys are placed meaningfully together, most often seen after a child is five or six:
   a. Simple categorization.
   b. Conventional grouping.
   c Meaningful scene.
   d. Juxtaposition.
   e. Chaotic grouping.
   f. Bizarre groupings.

g. Closed world.

Needless to say, the child who is most in need of treatment is in the last three categories: chaotic, bizarre or closed.

The Erica Method began as a diagnostic tool but eventually moved on to become a well-respected therapeutic method.

II. Margaret Lowenfeld[35]

Margaret Lowenfeld was born in Poland and later moved to England. She was a sickly child and spent much time in bed where she would read and play with her toys in an imaginative way. During this time she read *Floor Games* in which H. G. Wells described play with his two young sons. This had a later influence on her when she used toys in her child therapy treatment. Margaret later added psychiatry to her pediatric practice and opened a clinic in London called The Institute for Nervous Children. In this clinic, she had all the usual areas set up – housekeeping, kitchen, dolls, cars, trucks, etc.

In one corner she had a sand and water table with some miniature figures nearby. She noted that the children put the figures in the sand and, when she analyzed what was presented, she realized that the children were telling her what their problems were. Lowenfeld gave credit to the children for developing the technique.

Lowenfeld[36] eventually called her method The World Technique that she introduced in two parts. In the early phase of treatment she would tell the children that this was a "Bridge" and suggested that a child's life and adults' lives are on opposite sides of a river and this method helped them connect with each other.

She referred to this method as "Picture Thinking" because she believed that the infant perceived his/her world in pictures, rather than in language, and she told the young child that some things cannot be expressed in words and to try to do it through a picture (art or sand).

35 Bowyer, L., 1970
36 Lowenfeld, M., 1979

Lowenfeld believed that "Play" serves four purposes:

a. It is a child's means of making contact with his environment.
b. It makes a bridge between a child's consciousness and his/her emotional experience.
c. It represents to the child the externalized expression of his emotional life.
d. It serves as relaxation and amusement, as enjoyment and rest.

Lowenfeld believed that the objective data seen in these pictures could be gathered and analyzed in a scientific manner. Several of her followers did research in her methods: Charlotte Buhler, Liselotte Fisher and Hedda Bolgar, among others.

Lowenfeld minimized psychoanalytic theory, including the transference, and in order to limit this she would change a child's therapist from time to time because she believed that the transference should be to the tray and not to the therapist. Needless to say, this caused a great many problems (including some comments that were voiced by Winnicott, Melanie Klein and Susan Isaacs) and she later changed this practice.

There were other criticisms directed at Lowenfeld for her lack of attention to the developmental level of the child, which seemed appropriate as related to sand pictures. In the beginning, it was believed that her methods were only for diagnostic purposes, but she firmly believed that they served a therapeutic purpose as well.

There are a number of books available by and about Lowenfeld that describe her history and childhood and that are included in the bibliography. In addition to her work with children in the sand, she also developed several other testing methods, known as mosaics, poliediblocs, and kaliediblocs that are beyond the scope of this book.

An interesting fact that emerged while preparing this chapter was that in 1940 a cousin of Lowenfeld's was killed in Auschwitz. This fact so dramatically affected her that she experienced a near breakdown and entered Jungian analysis and the influence of symbols and archetypes is clear in her postwar work.

A Lowenfeld quote that this author particularly likes is:

> "Play in childhood is a function of childhood. Toys to children are like culinary implements to the kitchen; every kitchen has them and has also the elements of food. It is what the cook does with these implements and elements that determines the dish."[37]

III. Dora Kalff[38]

Frau Kalff was a Swiss housewife with two young sons who lived in a village near the Jungs. Her children used to play with Jung's grandchildren and it was Jung who noticed her ease with children. He asked her what she did with them (the children). because when they came home they were in a very happy frame of mind. Jung urged her to enroll in the Jungian Institute in Zurich and she entered personal analysis with Emma Jung, Carl's wife. As part of her training, she heard Dr. Lowenfeld lecture about her work with children in London. She spoke to Jung about it and he persuaded her to go to London to study with Dr. Lowenfeld.

Frau Kalff spent a year (1950) in London with Lowenfeld in order to learn all that she could about the World Technique. She returned to Switzerland where she added her Jungian background that included knowledge of archetypes and symbols to her other major interest, Zen Buddhism.

Frau Kalff searched for a theory that could help her understand what she observed in the sand pictures that the children made. She was fortunate to hear a lecture by Erich Neumann, a German analyst, who was exploring his ideas of child personality development. She was able to see that the stages that the children went through in a sandplay process were closely related to the theories of Neumann. They had spoken together and had agreed to do some research; however, that did not occur. Neumann's stages are chaos, animal-vegetative, fighting, ego-Self, and adaptation to the collective. Kalff was able to discern another facet that she called "the Manifestation of the Self" in which she saw that the ego and the Self were now in harmony.

---

37 Urwin, C. & J. Hood-Williams, 1988

38 Personal notes

Dora Kalff became well-respected for her work with children because Jungians were primarily adult-oriented at that time. In the 1950's the San Francisco Jung group brought her to this country where she lectured many times and gained numerous adherents to her method. Her fame spread far and wide and, in Japan, Sandplay is the number one form of therapy. This was confirmed to this author by one of the participants in a workshop. This attendee was from Japan and had worked for a psychologist there before beginning her studies of play therapy.

Today, Sandplay is practiced in many countries in the world and, while still relatively unknown, is the preferred method of therapy with many child therapists. In 1980, no one in New York had heard of it except Estelle Weinrib[39], Jungian adult analyst. This author, however, experienced how powerful and effective it was with the children she treated and began to train other child therapists in the method.

"DON'T FORGET TO TRUST THE PROCESS!!!" was Frau Kalff's favorite supervisory advice given to her trainees.

Recommended Equipment:

1. Two sand boxes, one half-filled with wet sand, the other with dry. The reason for two boxes is that the choice of sand can be diagnostically important. Most children (and adults) prefer the damp sand; however, some diagnostic categories prefer the dry, such as schizophrenics and sometimes those who have been sexually abused. The size of each box is 19 ½ x 28 ½ x 4 inches deep with the bottoms and sides painted blue so that when the sand is pushed aside it represents water or sky.
2. Miniatures in use usually represent the interests of the therapist; however, certain categories are included:
    a. Animals (domestic, wild, prehistoric).
    b. Birds (many varieties including storks, peacocks, penguins).
    c. Buildings (houses, barns, churches, etc.).
    d. People (various occupations, men, women, children, babies, black, white, Asian, Indian).
    e. Spiritual/religious /fantasy figures (fairy tales, superheroes).

39 Weinrib, E., 1983

f. Natural items (trees, shells, stones, rocks, feathers).
g. Transportation vehicles (cars, trucks, planes, boats).
h. Miscellaneous items (fences, bridges, caskets, headstones).

The collection of miniatures can be as broad as space and money permit; however, it is suggested that one's collection hold only those items of which the therapist has some mythological or archetypal understanding. "On the shelves of every sandplay therapist, their unconscious lies open for all to see."[40]

40 Bradway, K., 1981

CHAPTER 6

SUPERVISION FOR SANDPLAY THERAPISTS[41]

There has been a large body of work written about supervision for traditional "talk therapy" in books and journals such as Social Work, Marriage and Family Therapy, Counseling, Trauma, etc. but only recently has attention been paid to expressive and/or creative arts types of therapy. These types are of a different milieu and require a wide range of experience and knowledge in order for one to be an effective supervisor. First and foremost, much of this work requires comfort with a non-verbal approach to therapy that differs markedly from the more common verbal skills needed for traditional supervision. In addition to having sufficient clinical experience with a wide range of cases before one takes on the job of supervision, one also needs to have supervisory training and be well-versed and knowledgeable about symbolism and archetypes that one encounters in many of the non-verbal methods.

Supervision has been an essential part of training in all of the mental health disciplines and has gone through many evolutions since it began. When this author was a student, she was required to keep extensive clinical notes for weekly appointments with her supervisor. At that time, it was also the practice to audiotape sessions that could then be played to the supervisor for his/her comments. This was in the early 70s. Her first supervisor, during her field placement told her, "It takes ten years to make a good therapist." Her response was, "I don't have ten years!" She was about 45 at the time. After ten years, she knew exactly what he meant!

Many supervisory books cover frameworks and models for supervision, supervision in clinical practice, and issues within integrative supervision. Topics include different models of the supervision practice: anti-oppressive practice, spirituality and supervision, counseling supervision

41 Published in the East Coast Sandplay Journal, 2010

in health care, supervision of organizations, self-protection for supervisors from complaints and litigation. For example, if a supervisee is sued for malpractice, the supervisor is also liable and can also be sued. These supervisory practices are wide in scope but rich in detail, and are essential reading for psychotherapists, counselors, consultants, and students involved in the supervision process. In addition, all supervisors, both verbal and non-verbal, need to include cultural and ethical issues in supervision. The bibliography contains supervision material that is pertinent to what verbal and non-verbal practitioners do; needless to say, there has been much more written about supervision but very little on supervising the creative process.

Videotapes of sessions have recently been used for supervision and currently it is possible to have telephone conferences or online supervision. The possibilities are much more manageable today, but some form of supervision is a must, especially for the novice practitioner.

The Association for Play Therapy (APT) is now in its 21st or 22nd year and has diligently sought to accredit those clinicians who are members of the organization by setting up standards for Registered Play Therapist (RPT) status, as well as for supervision status (RPT-S). There are branches of this organization throughout the United States as well as some abroad. In New York, the NYAPT, provides workshops and an annual conference where play therapy is the focus. Information about this organization and its many branches is available at www.a4pt.org.

Supervision and clinical work with sand and art are interconnected and those who supervise play therapists using sand and/or any type of play therapy or creative arts methods need specialized training in order to appropriately explore these processes. The purpose of such supervision is to provide clinicians with the opportunity to understand the unique problems that may arise when using sand trays and/or other play therapy methods. Some of the areas to be considered when supervising play therapists include those that refer to decoding non-verbal messages, keeping boundaries, an understanding of symbolism and archetypes, cultural issues, ethical standards, and case conceptualization. Private consultation is especially useful (and part of the requirements of APT) for colleagues who are working towards attaining Registered Play

Therapy (RPT) status and/or the Supervisor (RPT-S) credential in play therapy. Please see the APT[42] website for further information.

Practitioners who use sand in clinical work are enriched through participating in their own process in sandplay and are strongly encouraged to do so by those who offer training in this method. Process work enables the clinician to understand how very powerful this medium can be. This is a requirement for anyone who wishes to become a certified Sandplay Practitioner through the Sandplay Therapy Association of America (STA). However, many practitioners choose not to join that organization because of geographical and/or financial constraints. If a Sandplay therapist and/or a supervisor are not available, it is sometimes possible to witness and observe one's own work in the sand, but it is more advantageous to do so with a non-judging, compassionate, informed colleague. Neither of these types of supervision (alone or with a colleague) is the method of choice, but they are sometimes the only available possibility. Sandplay is not usually done alone because of the power that is inherent in the work. Each practitioner needs a witness to add another "lens" to the process. Today, with modern technology some practitioners are using Skype for supervision purposes and even for witnessing someone making his/her own tray.

This author made a sand picture alone one time because of inordinate stress that she had experienced at that time. She had been asked to teach a 5-week course on Sandplay at the Jung Institute in New York City. After the first meeting, she received a message that she had not included "archetypes" in her lecture. This seemed to be incredible because all the sand pictures were full of archetypes, she simply had not named them as such because she assumed that the group would understand. She was wrong and this was quite a lesson for her. One afternoon before the second class, she took out all the books in her library that dealt with archetypes hoping to explain "archetypes" more effectively to the class. She was fully engaged in putting together some sort of logical explanation when suddenly the thought occurred to her, "I am NOT a head (thinking type) person, I work from the "gut" (feeling type)." She immediately threw the books down on the floor and went into the sand

42 www.a4pt.org

room. The sand was quite wet from a previous session, but Figure 6.1 is an image of what appeared.

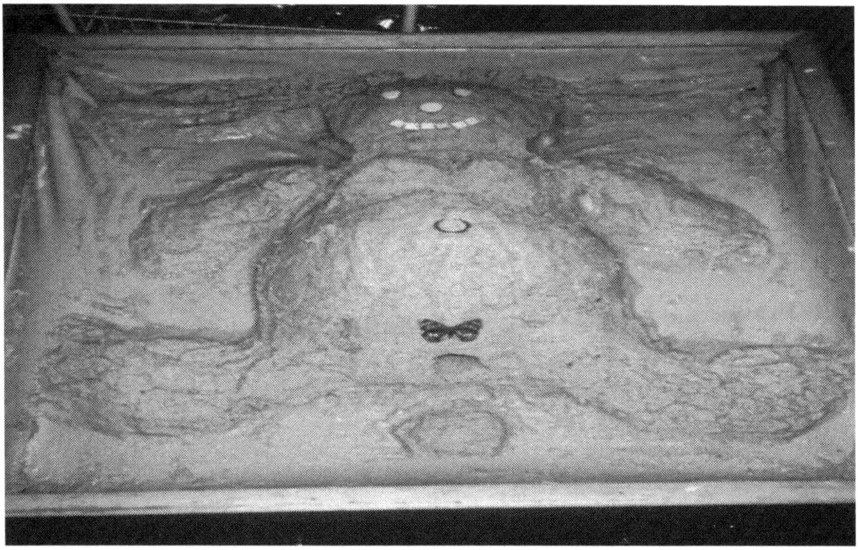

Figure 6.1

In examining the photo, it is truly an image of the Self. She placed her hands on that pregnant belly and could feel the transfer of energies. She had no further problems with that class when she could listen to her inner guide.

Supervision at times can be problematic, particularly if it is a poor fit between supervisor and supervisee. We often speak about "counter transference" and that usually suggests a negative experience; however, Kay Bradway, one of the founders of the Sandplay Therapy Association, speaks of it as "co-transference," meaning that it is a collegial pursuit. In other words, the supervisor/supervisee relationship also includes the case being discussed at that time. This author asked one of her supervisees to describe her impression of what "good supervision" entails. This led her to discuss a very negative supervisory experience that had affected her ability to accept supervision for quite some time. The quote follows:

"As a new social work intern, I was paired with a supervisor in a school-based mental health clinic in an extremely at-risk elementary school.

My supervisor had suffered some personal losses recently, and within two weeks of the start of my internship, she changed jobs to another part of the agency. She informed me it would be my responsibility to make provisions to travel nearly an hour to attend supervision now (on my own time where the clinical hours would not be counted), and that I was expected to find ways to get my process recordings to her, and that she would be 'checking in' on me through the other members of the staff. She was almost never available, was extremely critical when we met and made me scared of the entire supervision process. No one ever bothered to explain to me that supervision was not a conflictual experience that was fraught with feelings of fear and powerlessness.

It came to a head one day when I refused to drive the hour to meet for supervision. I'd had a particularly bad day with a very difficult client, and asked if we could meet the next day. She told me I had to come, and I finally stood my ground and said no. A week later, she called and said that she couldn't recommend me to move forward in the program because of my "anger issues" and "defensiveness." I was devastated. I finally called my wonderful and supportive field instructor, who listened to me cry and took action in my defense. This supervisor had let her stuff get in the way, and, because I didn't know any better, I took it personally.

This experience, although now ten years ago, left its mark. To this day, sometimes, supervision makes me anxious and I have had to work hard to take constructive criticism as constructive and as an opportunity to learn. Even sharing how I feel about supervision makes me a little anxious that there will be some sort of retaliation. Fortunately, I've had enough therapy now to know that that won't happen and I'm a lot more open to the process and what can be learned.

I find supervision most helpful when it offers an alternative perspective in how to approach a case. I like concrete suggestions of different things to try, and resources in the forms of reading, websites, or other people to whom I can speak. It is also helpful when my supervisor treats me like a colleague as opposed to emphasizing the power differential in the relationship. As a busy working mom and student, the flexibility of phone sessions and the ability to email pictures of art work and sand trays is incredibly helpful in being able to keep up with regular supervision despite the many demands on my time."

To return to the subject of Supervision, we need to be able to identify "red flags" in sand that may signal the need to be alert to deeper issues that may be emerging. I have seen numerous examples of children's work in sand that can divulge the deeper meanings of their experience.

One pictorial example was similar to many that this boy had done over the past couple of years. In this picture, he is feeding one animal to another that can suggest how he feels "swallowed up" by many parental battles that he witnessed. The parents live at some distance from each other, so this child has spent innumerable hours "in transit."

Another area that is critical for us as sand therapists is our role in dealing with parents. This is something that this author focuses on with her supervisees. Following are just a couple of important areas to cover with those whom you supervise; I am sure there are others.

1. Do you have a difficult time dealing with parents of clients?
2. How do you explain sandplay to parents?
3. Do you wonder how to talk about your work as a play therapist?
4. Can you establish credibility and legitimacy with parents, professionals, and work sites?

This author knows from experience that professional play therapists often have difficulty advocating for play therapy interventions with parents, as well as with other members of the mental health and educational community. Several therapists whom she has supervised have resisted working with the parents at all, and frequently the father is the most difficult for them to reach. In these cases, one might suspect that the supervisee has unresolved parental issues and needs to refer them for personal therapy.

The website of APT now has a very well-done video that explains play therapy to parents and is something that can be shown to parents as it is only about seven or eight minutes long. These are all issues that an experienced supervisor can help the less experienced clinician with.

Supervisors (of any method) need to *constantly* be aware that supervision is not personal therapy, that strict boundaries are essential. This can become problematic in non-verbal methods such as sand tray because of the unconscious issues that are often inadvertently exposed.

In order to correct for this, a photograph of the sand picture can be taken and printed so that the supervisee can take it to his or her therapist for discussion.

Following is an example from a group supervision process that was an experiment with a more directive type of supervision. Credit for this method must be given to Rie Rogers Mitchell[43] for "Mentoring supervisors: a process model" in *Supervision of Sandplay Therapy* (2008, USA and Canada: Routledge). The supervisor asked those present to think of their most difficult client and to build a scene. One of the clinicians had presented a difficult case of a young woman. After the scene was completed, the supervisor observed and then commented, "That (pointing to the cleared spaces) almost looks like kidneys."

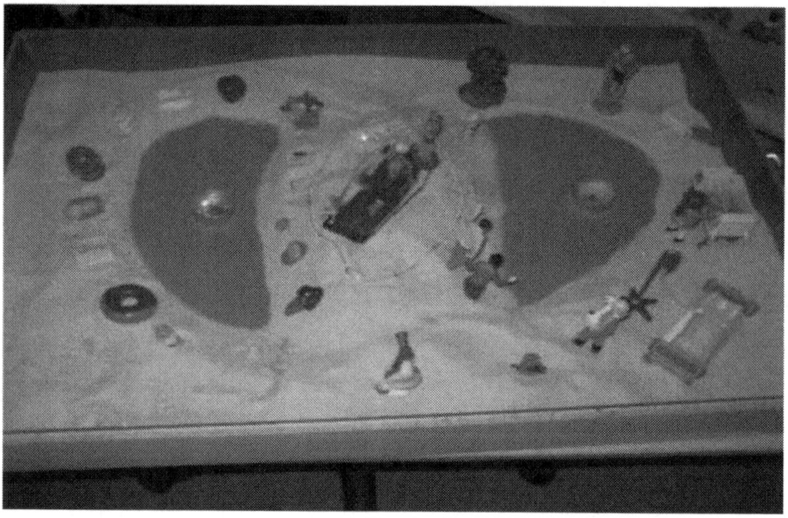

Figure 6.2

The following week, the therapist reported that the young woman had been hospitalized during the week with kidney failure. There was certainly no indication that this was about to happen, but somehow the supervisor's intuitive process was activated by the supervisee's sand picture and this comment was the result.

43 Friedman, H. and R. Mitchell, 2008, Chapter 14

One additional observation needs to be reported about this construction. You will note that there is one candle in each of the cleared spaces. When the supervisee tried to light the candles, one kept going out and attempts to make it burn were fruitless. Finally, she gave up and said something like, "Oh well, just let it be."

Jungian clinicians need to examine sand pictures that have been produced using three of our four functions: feeling, sensation, and intuition. We do have a fourth function, thinking, but since this modality (sand) reaches us on the non-verbal level, thinking needs to be eliminated, at least in the beginning.

1. Ask your supervisee what *feeling* is evoked in him/her by the scene.
2. Then, ask him/her what is notable about the scene – any colors or numbers of items grouped together or placed strategically that might suggest anything? This is the *sensation* function.
3. Then, focus on any hints or *intuitions* the supervisee might have that are suggested by the scene.
4. Try to avoid providing answers, but help the supervisee to begin to understand the scene using his/her own resources.
5. Ask the supervisee to make associations to the symbols, particularly of any figures that are repeated from session to session, etc. It may be helpful to refer him/her to a symbol dictionary or else to look it up on the web.

Another approach might be for one to think of his/her most difficult client and build a scene. It is truly amazing what often is illustrated like the example given above.

In conclusion, the supervision of sandplay therapists who work non-verbally entails much more study and research than that in verbal supervision. It is also important to help guide the supervisee to adapt his/her thinking to a symbolic approach. This is no easy task, but when we "put our heads together" the work is broadened considerably.

CHAPTER 7

SANDPLAY, ART, AND PLAY THERAPY TO PROMOTE ANXIETY REDUCTION[44]

INTRODUCTION

Traumatic stress is an overwhelming response to violent acts such as those described by Dr. Nancy Boyd Webb[45] in Chapter 1 of her book. The terrorist events at the World Trade Center, the Pentagon, and the downing of the plane in Pennsylvania that occurred on 9/11/01 are prime examples. This chapter discusses creative techniques that are helpful in resolving disturbing responses to many situations of trauma.

I am a social worker in private practice in a suburban area of New York City. My office is approximately 25 miles from what is now known as "Ground Zero" and, as such, is somewhat removed from the epicenter of that particular tragedy. However, many families who live in this area are employed in the city and, unfortunately, a number of their members were victims. In addition, many of our local police officers and firemen are employed in the city and were on volunteer duty for the weeks and months following 9/ll. I will be presenting a case in this chapter of a child whose father was involved in the rescue efforts.

In addition to being a play therapist, I am also a family therapist and have incorporated into my work some creative forms of therapy along with more traditional verbal therapy in both individual and family treatments. My primary specialty is Sandplay Therapy, with Art Therapy as my secondary interest.

Many cases throughout my years in practice have involved children traumatized by sexual abuse, loss and bereavement, adoption, and

---

44 Excerpts reprinted from N. B. Webb, 2004

45 45 Webb, 2004

neurological impairment. These cases cover many of the standard diagnostic categories such as anxiety, depression, ADHD, oppositional disorder, developmental delay, and Tourette's syndrome. In this chapter, I will present the case of an anxious child whose symptoms were exacerbated by the events of 9/11.

SANDPLAY, ART, AND PLAY THERAPY

Why does one choose Play Therapy, Sandplay, or Art Therapy? Primarily because children readily accept and understand these techniques which help to immediately lower any resistance to being "in therapy." Play Therapy has become the accepted method for most child therapy, because play is the way that children traditionally handle their problems. Garry Landreth[46] tells us,

> "For children to 'play out' their experiences and feelings is the most natural dynamic and self-healing process in which children can engage. Play is a medium of exchange and restricting children to verbal expression automatically places a barrier to a therapeutic relationship by imposing limitations that in effect say to children 'You must come up to my level of communication and communicate with words.'"

One can readily see, therefore, that any form of therapy that is essentially creative and that can be non-verbal as well as verbal, holds a definite advantage for a child who has been traumatized, no matter what the cause. My preference, because of my training, is to utilize Sandplay Therapy, Art Therapy, and Play Therapy, all of which were used in the case that will be discussed.

Sandplay Therapy is directly related to Art Therapy and Play Therapy (See Chapters 1 - 4).

The physical arrangement of my office allows for a separate space for both verbal and non-verbal sessions - the Sandplay/Art room is separate from the interviewing office. This affords the child an initial choice between the two when he/she comes for therapy, having seen both areas

46 Landreth, G. 1991

during the intake appointment. There are times when both areas are used within a given session and at other times the child chooses one or the other site. Because the work I do is child-centered, I follow the child's lead.

The Sandplay Therapy process begins by inviting the child to touch the sand in both boxes to see which one might "feel better." He/she is then directed to look at all the miniatures that are arranged in shelves around the room. The child then selects as many or as few toys as needed in order to construct a sand scene. I tell the child that a photograph of the scene will be taken when he/she states that it is complete. I take two pictures: a Polaroid that the child can keep at the conclusion of therapy, and a slide that I explain is for teaching or writing purposes. The parent signs permission for this, and the child gives his/her permission as well, depending on the age and understanding of the child.

When the child has completed his/her first (and subsequent) sand scenes, I invite him/her to either say something about it, to name it, or to tell a story about it. However, if they do not want to say anything, that is fine as well. The most important part of Sandplay is that any verbalization is kept within the metaphor of whatever has been depicted in the tray. For example, if there is a threatening scene with a tiger about to devour a kitten, one might say something like, "I see you have a tiger and a kitten , I wonder what the tiger and/or the kitten might be feeling." In this way, the therapist acknowledges the feeling tone in the scene without interpreting it as a real-life situation or assigning roles to the figures. This is similar to some forms of Play Therapy interactions: one takes great care in moving slowly towards the deeper, somewhat more obvious (to us), connections. Our belief is that the child will eventually make connections when he/she is ready to do so and that if we move too quickly, the child can become defensive and unavailable to the therapeutic process.

The healing process in Sandplay appears to come about through the *process* of creation, rather than through the *content* of any single picture. Sandplay moves through developmental stages, in accordance with a child's chronological and psychological age. The role of the therapist here is vitally important. The sand tray is the healing vessel, sometimes called the "temenos" (place of healing), and the therapist's function is to witness and "hold" the unconscious of the child's psyche while a transformative process takes place. My belief is that it is the person of the therapist, combined with the medium of the sand equipment that determines success or failure with this technique. Anyone can own a sand box and toys, but the training, care and compassion of the sandplay therapist will determine just how healing this form of play therapy will be.

CASE EXAMPLE

The following case example involves an "indirect victim" of the World Trade Center tragedy. This was a young boy who was brought to me by his mother in October 2001. I will call this boy Alexander. He suffered from severe migraine headaches that had become much more frequent after the World Trade Center attacks.

During the intake I explored all of the relevant facts about Alexander and his family and used the Tripartite Crisis Assessment developed by Dr. Nancy Boyd Webb.[47] This assessment describes three different sets of interacting variables that should be considered for each unique crisis event:

1. The nature of the crisis.
2. The idiosyncratic characteristics of the individual.
3. The strengths and weaknesses of the individual's support system.

THE NATURE OF THE CRISIS SITUATION

The nature of this particular crisis was unlike any that had ever been experienced in this country prior to September 11, 2001. The World Trade Center in New York City was one of the targets of terrorists who had highjacked four planes and deliberately crashed two of them into the twin towers. Our entire way of life was immediately changed and threatened, this country had never before experienced such a horrific act. Indeed, we had never heretofore had a major attack on our homeland. The impact of this tragedy was felt by people throughout the country,

47 Webb, N.B, 1999

but most especially in the New York City and Washington, D. C., areas. All four of these planes had been deployed to those two cities, but only three succeeded in their mission. The fourth one, meant for Washington, was brought down in Pennsylvania due to the incredible courage of passengers on that flight.

Other parts of the country were affected as well. However, the closer one was to any of these crisis areas, the more intense the effects were felt.[48]/[49] Therapists, too, in these geographical areas were deeply shaken, having had very little, if any, prior experience with such an overwhelming event. Although there had been some earlier terrorist attacks, such as the 1993 World Trade Center bombing, as well as the Oklahoma City bombing, none were of the magnitude of this atrocity. All of us in the helping professions were aware that our services would be vitally needed for quite some time because of this tragedy. We struggled to maintain our own balance in order to be of assistance to those who might need our help and expertise.

THE IDIOSYNCRATIC CHARACTERISTICS OF THE INDIVIDUAL

A complete psychosocial history is integral to the assessment process. Alexander, a latency-aged boy, had suffered with migraines since the age of five. Some were preceded by an aura. This appeared to stem from an anxiety disorder. The headaches had been controlled with medication. Prior to 9/11, he experienced approximately one headache per month. After that date, he had about ten per month. His anxiety appeared to acerbate his symptoms. Many of his headaches necessitated full-day absences from school; with others he was able to attend only part of the day.

Alexander was a nice-looking, well-groomed boy who attended school in his community. He was an honors student and took his schoolwork seriously. In addition, he was active in sports, in which he was one of the star players. He was a very serious-minded boy who was polite and respectful, almost to excess. For example, when I would reach for a toy

48 Pynoos and Nader, 1989
49 Nader, Pynoos, Fairbanks, & Frederick, 1990

or art materials for him, he would always say "thank you." Sometimes there might be ten or twelve "thank you's" within five minutes. I assured him that he did not need to thank me so profusely. Everything he did, from his schoolwork performance to his sports activities to parties that he attended, was accomplished with the utmost intensity and enthusiasm. His history, according to his parents, was that he had always been a tense child and appeared to internalize things deeply. He never had to be reminded to attend to his responsibilities and diligently did whatever was required of him.

THE STRENGTHS AND WEAKNESSES OF THE INDIVIDUAL'S SUPPORT SYSTEM

When one assesses a young child it is important that the family dynamics be explored, as well. This intact family, which I will call "Hopkins," consisted of:

Client: Alexander, age ten, 5th grade, history of migraine headaches.

Mother: Jeannette, age 39, part-time sports coach.

Father: Anthony, age 40, New York Ciy fireman.

There was a very large, close-knit, extended family that celebrated numerous family events.

On 9/11, Mr. Hopkins, along with almost all the firemen and policemen in the New York City area, was assigned to the World Trade Center site and spent two to three months there as part of the search and rescue team. Numerous other rescue volunteers came to assist from across the nation and from foreign countries as well in the frantic search for survivors and/or remains.

A significant number of Mr. and Mrs. Hopkins's friends and colleagues unfortunately died during the rescue operations. These deaths required attendance by both parents at numerous funeral services. The children also attended one or two of the services because they were friends of the children whose parents had died. The mood in the Hopkins household was one of devastation and utter depression as one funeral followed another.

Alexander, the child of this couple, was the one that internalized most of the family pressures. He had a history of tension and anxiety as evidenced by migraine headaches. His tension was further revealed by the fact that he was a nail-biter and his nails were bitten quite far down. He had been taken to many specialists for his migraines, for which he was medicated. Up until 9/ll, the medication was effective, at least most of the time. After that, it did not appear to help.

Alexander's family-support system included both his nuclear family and a close-knit, extended family. He performed well in school, in sports, and had good peer relationships. He was well thought of by teachers and peers. He had many ego strengths, but his coping mechanisms did not always serve him well. His major complaint was the migraine condition that was traced to those times when he became too anxious and intense over a test or a sport activity or even, at times, playing too hard at family parties.

This is the information I acquired during the assessment process. During that time, I also explained my method of treatment to Alexander and his parents. I requested that Mrs. Hopkins keep a log in order to see what precipitated his headaches.

TREATMENT

Alexander had numerous headaches during the first month to six weeks of treatment and there were several reports of his being "nervous" prior to sessions, but he always wanted to attend. Most of the reported headaches occurred in relation to excessive over-exertion, to being over-tired, to being over-excited. A record was kept of the numbers of headaches he had during the first six or seven months of therapy: ten in October, eight in November, seven in January, none in February, two in March, two in April, and two in May.

As part of my evaluation of a child, I frequently use The House Tree Person[50] test because it is a good indicator of some of a child's personality features and/or can provide the trained therapist with clues to the child's needs. I asked Alexander to complete these drawings during our first individual session.

50 Jolles, Isaac, 1983

Figure 7.1

The instructions are to draw a house on one page, a tree on another page, and a person on a third page. In order to save space, I have placed all of the drawings on one sheet. They are reproduced here in their actual size, but each was drawn on a separate page measuring 8 1/2 x 11 inches.

Each drawing was executed quickly, suggesting that this was an anxiety-ridden task. Several things are notable about these drawings. First is the very small size of each image. This usually indicates how small and helpless the child sees himself. I assumed, therefore, that Alexander needed some self-esteem and ego-boosting measures, as well as a significant amount of anxiety reduction. The house has windows on the lower floor that almost look like teeth that suggest some oral rage. This might indicate that he has internalized much of his anger, which could be a contributing factor to his numerous migraine headaches. It is a two-dimensional house, which is unusual for a child of this age, and there is no ground line, suggesting that he does not feel that he has a solid base. In other words, his feelings of security have been badly undermined.

Like the house, Alexander's tree has no ground line, and there is a hole halfway up. When one looks at a tree with a hole in it, one considers that the height of the tree represents the age of the child and the relative placement of the hole indicates the age of a past wound or trauma. If we consider that Alexander is now age ten and the hole is halfway up, this might suggest that the trauma occurred around age five, the age when his migraines began. There were no significant family events that anyone could recall during his fifth year.

The person that Alexander drew is of a nondescript nature, with the arms raised, almost like a baby reaching up for his mother. This drawing is typical of a much younger child. Also of note is, once again, the lack of a ground line and the fact that the feet point backward. The placement of the feet suggests that he felt safer in the past than at present.

Alexander did his first sand picture during that session and it revealed some amount of inner chaos – many figures were used, with no logical theme. In order to conserve space, this scene is not replicated. Chaos is typical of many first pictures, especially for children with an anxiety disorder.

As discussed earlier, Sandplay Therapy reveals developmental stages. Chaos can often be the first stage, followed by the animal/vegetative stage, the fighting stage (with the theme of good/evil), and next, an indication that a state of positive ego development has been reached and there is movement towards an increased ability to deal with problems. Dora Kalff found, in some cases, that a spiritual connection was revealed and this she termed "The Constellation of the Self." She believed that it signaled a turning point in therapy, and it was a positive indication to her that the ego and the Self, formerly separated by trauma, had been reconnected.

Space does not permit the illustration of all of these elements. However, I would like to focus on a few examples. Figure 7.2 is a typical fighting stage with teams facing off against each other.

Figure 7.2

This was made about three weeks after the first picture. Note the large dragon (upper left) with a soldier on his head, gun pointed down (his migraines?)

Figure 7.3

Figure 7.3 was made about six weeks into therapy and is Alexander's version of the rescue scene at the Twin Towers. He asked me what I might have that could represent the towers and I showed him two miniature oil wells in my collection. He added an airplane soaring nearby. Then he placed numerous firemen and rescue vehicles in attendance. Alexander and I both felt a sense of loss and devastation as we looked at this scene.

Three or four months after therapy began, Alexander asked if he could draw rather than use sand, and he produced Figure 7.4.

Figure 7.4

This is a picture of the firemen attempting to rescue those falling from the two buildings. One building is red and signifies the fire. This same type of drawing was made by numerous children after 9/11 that I saw during crisis work in New York City.

Figure 7.5 was made about five months after Alexander began therapy and was his depiction of people visiting the Statue of Liberty. They appear to be paying homage to what she (the statue) represents.

Figure 7.5

I commented to him that it looked as if the people (who formed a cross) were placing their hope for the future with God. He was quite moved by my observation and agreed. I intuitively believed that his innate spirituality was being revealed unconsciously in this picture. This is an example of the spiritual component in a sand picture.

The resolution, or turning point, of Sandplay Therapy is often illustrated by a sand picture, sometimes in a mandala form, such as that seen in Figure 7.6 and which Dora Kalff would refer to as the "Constellation of the Self." This scene shows Superman in the center of a circle of wild animals, which in turn are surrounded by a circle of trees.

Figure 7.6

Alexander has progressed from the very tiny self-portrait illustrated in Figure 7.1 to Superman (possibly his new self-figure) taking on the wild animals. One can only hope that Superman (Alexander) will be the victor!

This series of sandplay pictures and artwork illustrates the power that can exist in a non-verbal milieu. A child is able to verbalize his or her deep concerns in a way that is non-threatening, non-verbal, and non-confrontative.

The art and sand pictures, however, do not cover all that transpired during Alexander's therapy. Several sessions were held with one or both parents, some without Alexander and some when he was present. Mrs. Hopkins, particularly, carried a tremendous burden. She was concerned not only about Alexander, but also about her husband and the many losses they all had suffered.

Alexander began to exhibit a major separation anxiety condition when his mother had to go on sports-coaching assignments. This disorder developed shortly after the World Trade Center incident. Many of her travel dates were directly associated as a contributing factor to his headaches. He was able to verbalize that he was terrified that she would have an auto accident and thus be taken from him. Needless to say, he was quite anxious on those occasions.

Alexander became somewhat resistant to therapy after about six months that coincided with an appointment to see his neurologist for a medication review. At that time, Mrs. Hopkins brought up Alexander's resistance to therapy. The doctor suggested that therapy should definitely be continued, but thought perhaps play therapy was "too babyish" for Alexander, who was eleven by now. My own opinion was different. I believed that Alexander was stuck in the separation/individuation phase that is usually mastered by children by the age of two or three. In addition, his nail-biting and overall tension continued and I sincerely believed that play therapy was the treatment of choice. However, given this family's cultural background where "doctor knows best," there was nothing I could do but switch to a more verbal form of therapy.

The picture where Superman was Alexander's apparent self-image (Figure 7.6) was constructed during that time. This indicates a more age-appropriate stance with regard to the separation issue – Superman did not need a dependent relationship – and, it was hoped, Alexander no longer needed to cling to it either.

The neurologist encouraged Alexander to take control of his own condition, rather than Mrs. Hopkins being the monitor; that is, he would ask his mother when he felt the need for medication. The neurologist asked to see him again in six months and it was hoped that eventually Alexander may not need much medication.

During the re-evaluation session with Alexander, we agreed that treatment should be continued for the following several months on a bi-monthly basis and that we would focus on more expressive, non-verbal activities. This decision was based on my knowledge of Alexander, particularly his underlying anxiety state combined with his resistance to verbalizing any of his concerns. It appeared to me that a non-verbal modality was a far better approach to reducing his continuing anxieties than a verbal one. Alexander was due to begin school again and that would undoubtedly contribute to an increase in his stress level. I explained to the parents and the child my difference of opinion from the neurologist's by saying that I truly felt the way to best treat him was to focus on his underlying anxiety rather than on the number of migraines that he experienced. This new treatment plan was based on his stated wish to overcome some of the separation anxiety that continued to persist when his mother needed to travel. I explained the positive sign that showed Superman in Figure 7.6, but that Superman needed now to meet and confront some of those other things that continued to keep him from achieving true ease and comfort with his situation.

SUMMARY

This chapter has focused on one anxious child's reaction to the events at the World Trade Center on 9/11/01. He was at risk because of several factors: (1) his history of migraine headaches, (2) his father's role in search and rescue operations, (3) the exacerbation of a separation-anxiety disorder.

Art Therapy, Sandplay Therapy, and Family Therapy were all employed in this child's treatment. Improvement was noted after the first few months, signified by the lessened frequency of his migraines and confirmed by what was revealed in the sand pictures. Alexander's resistance to attending therapy was ameliorated by decreasing the frequency of the sessions and by his recognition that his symptoms, though not fully resolved, were abating.

Several pictorial examples of Alexander's journey towards healing have been included. These demonstrate how, through the use of these creative milieus, he did indeed accomplish some resolution of his fears. In so doing, he was able to reduce some of his symptoms. Alexander agreed to continue therapy with the objective being to help him with his remaining anxieties.

I would add that while the case example described is one of an existing condition that was exacerbated by a national crisis, the techniques used are applicable to other children who suffer from anxiety, depression, family issues, or overall limited emotional and/or developmental functioning. Sandplay Therapy and Art Therapy are valuable avenues to explore when children have limited verbal skills or lack the maturity necessary to help them express their innermost fears.

The immediate post-9/11 time was one of major significance for all of us in the helping professions. We struggled to keep our own equilibrium and not to allow our personal issues to infect the work that we were doing, in order to serve the children and families that came to us. Numerous personal and professional stresses were plaguing me at the time and I considered retiring. However, with the help of colleagues, friends, and church, I continued to perform what I believe to be the prime mission in my professional life – to serve children and families to the best of my ability, using my knowledge, my creativity, and my past experience in this career that I have chosen.

CHAPTER 8

AGES AND STAGES OF CHILD DEVELOPMENT

Therapists who treat children need to be fully cognizant of normal child development; otherwise, there would be no framework for what is abnormal. This chapter is a quick overview of the normal stages of development.

I. Pre-school and entering school – Age 3 – 6.

- a. Careful assessment is needed - what problems are best treated with which approach - individual, family, group, all of which can use art, puppets, story, sand, dollhouse.
- b. Part of assessment – House-Tree-Person Drawing.
- c. Typical problems – developmental delays, anxiety, depression, rule out sexual abuse, parenting issues (separation/divorce), toilet training, selective mutism can begin here or in next stage.

II. Elementary School - Age: 6 – 11 (two phases, 6 – 9, 9 – 11 (pre-adolescent)).

Problems that surface and are often picked up in school:

Phase 1.

- a. Learning problems, stealing, cheating, self-esteem issues, family break-up, depression, anxiety.
- b. Helpful therapeutic techniques - games, mastery, team playing, sportsmanship (use of metaphor) role play, role reversal with individual, group, or family using puppetry, art, sand, storytelling.

c. Typical problems – family break-up, learning disabilities with anxiety, depression, shy child; bully (either recipient or aggressor), socialization.

Phase 2.

a. Pre-adolescent issues – emphasis on sex education (including body image), peer and family relationships.

III. LATENCY DEVELOPMENT - Ages 6 – 11, 12 (approximately)

Latency really comes in two periods:

1. Early latency is from roughly 5 ½ to 8. Oedipal urgings begin along with repression of same. The superego is harsh, there are issues of guilt and problems can surface at school. Anal and oral themes emerge in Sandplay.
2. Late latency is approximately from 8 to 11. The ego is stronger, superego is firmly established, sexual excitement is under control.

This is Erikson's[51] stage of Industry vs. Inferiority; the superego becomes consolidated during this stage so that children are very much aware of good and evil. It is the fighting stage in Sandplay therapy.

The tasks of latency are to resolve Oedipal strivings and to consolidate the superego through identifications with both parents. By early latency, children have their gender identities firmly established. Between 5 and 10 children keep gender identity strictly enforced – girls identify with feminine clothing, boys identify with stereotypical masculine values. These identifications arc visual in their Sandplay productions as well.

Pre-oedipal factors play a major role in organizing and resolving the oedipal struggle. During latency the changes are more gradual, there is more balance and equilibrium which leads to positive ego development and a well-functioning superego by 7 or 8. The child is now able to use cognition and social relations in a satisfying and esteem-promoting way.

51 Erikson, E., 1963

Girls usually mature earlier than boys, sometimes as early as 9 or 10. Children begin to realize that parents are not omnipotent. Between 9 and 11, there is further ego consolidation and pre-adolescence begins.

Rules, right and wrong, winning and losing are all major issues. Sometimes children strictly adhere to rules, others "bend the rules" and try to cheat to win.

School and peers become the focal points during the latency stage. By 8, children are ready for organized sports that help with their physical as well as emotional development.

In the latency stage, girls, particularly, struggle with body-image issues and there can be incipient anorexia that develops during this period.

Children's personality styles are also formed during this period. Some girls develop "pleasing behavior," while others become "tomboys."

Some of the major problems can be related to over-programming by two working parents; there can be idealization of a missing parent in separated or divorced households; school problems, including learning disabilities, can surface during this time; self-confidence may be weak; boys begin to fear their own aggression. Fantasy plays a major role During this time, which is why sandplay is such an effective modality.

This is the period during which most children who are in need of therapy are identified, which is why therapists need to understand normal development as well as abnormal.

When family crises accompany the normal developmental stages in children, the children are often affected in some way. A crisis can be anything from separation or divorce, illness in parent or child (grandparent or other relative), death of a significant family member, a geographical move that necessitates changing school, neighborhood, etc. The child, in the midst of such a crisis, becomes the symptom bearer and either needs to have therapy for her or himself or else the whole family needs to be treated. Each case needs to be evaluated on its own terms, there are no hard-and-fast rules. This is why a careful assessment must be made before one decides who the identified patient is – child or family.

Adolescence – 12 – 18 (two phases – 11 - 14; 15 – 18).

The early adolescent phase is puberty – that time when physical changes occur – especially for girls. The onset of menses is one of the most critical times for girls. It is an easy transition at times but can be extremely painful. Sometimes, the pain related to menses continues and can include migraine headaches as well. As the girl moves into full adolescence, the symptoms usually subside; however, for far too many girls, they continue until after the birth of the first child.

For boys, puberty is often accompanied by "wet dreams" – a condition that is embarrassing for the boy as he feels ashamed that he cannot control this nighttime emission. He needs to be told that this is not a disgrace, but merely a stage and that it means he will be able to father a child in the future.

Peer relationships are the most significant factor in adolescence, as well as these tasks:

1. Beginning of separation from family – leads to stress within the family.
2. Effects of older or younger siblings.
3. Typical problems that can emerge—drug, alcohol, or sex experimentation, school relationships, depression, anxiety.

For those who work with adolescents, two good books on the development and the need for ritual for the adolescent are found in the bibliography. One is by Kaspar Kiepenheuer[52] and the other one is edited by Louise Mahdi[53], et al. I especially refer you to the chapters in the Mahdi book by John Allan (Chapter 2, p. 23) and Edith Sullwold (Chapter 7, p.111).

This chapter is of particular importance and this author has found that many supervisees need a review of this subject in order to be as effective as possible.

52 Kiepenheuer, K., 1980
53 Mahdi, L. et al (eds.), 1987

CHAPTER 9

THE MIND/BODY CONNECTION IN SANDPLAY[54]

The mind/body connection in Sandplay has been a topic that has been a challenge to formulate and to articulate, but one that has important implications for both play therapy and sandplay therapy.

When one discusses "mind," immediately the brain is thought of. The brain is an organ that has numerous regulatory functions. "Mind" as a concept implies thinking, memory, recollection, opinions, the seat of consciousness, the intellect, etc. "Body," on the other hand, denotes the entire physical structure and substance of a person. Many times "brain" and "mind" are used interchangeably. The mind/body connection is intended to convey how the body and the mind/brain interact in subtle, inexplicable ways and how the medium of sand can provide a positive link.

All therapists are aware that one's emotional life (mind/brain) can affect bodily functions.

For example, when someone is traumatized in any way, one's blood pressure often spikes and the heart rate increases. One can become short of breath or totally unable to breathe; some people faint under these circumstances. Similarly, when one is excessively worried about something, the stomach will often tie itself into knots and sometimes an ulcer will form. In other situations people develop irritable-bowel symdrome. There are numerous possible psychogenic illnesses, too numerous to mention here.

Please refer to the diagram in Chapter 2, (Figure 2.3 p. 26, Ego/Self) and, if one substitutes "Mind" for Ego and "Body" for Self, this same diagram might be useful in describing the Mind/Body connection. According to Jung, the problem that exists for clients is that the ego

54 Workshop at Center for Sandplay Studies, 1996,2008

has become separated from the Self. The task of treatment is to heal the split that has occurred and that is recognized by the symptoms and distress that leads the client into therapy in the first place. Jung believed that the ego and the Self, (which he termed the "spiritual center of the psyche,") were originally contained within the psyche of the Mother. Gradually, as the child developed, he/she achieved full psychological separation from the mother and became able to develop his/her own ego and Self. Jung proposed an imaginary line that connected the ego and the Self which he termed the "ego/Self axis." (See diagram) Jung said that the therapeutic task was to reconnect the ego and the Self in order for the client to achieve optimum functioning. Jung's reasoning was that the birth trauma was the original insult to that connection and any subsequent traumas made the connection weaker.

Many of today's researchers have demonstrated how certain prenatal influences can shape a child's destiny. "Ghosts from the Nursery[55]" that has been mentioned in other chapters of this book is one that is quite impressive. "Ghosts" discusses prenatal influences that contribute to a child's propensity for violence, which these authors believe is the number one problem facing society today. Much of what these authors say is intended to alert the reader to the issues of prenatal conditions of the mother, particularly the use of drugs and/or alcohol, and the effects on the brain of the developing fetus. However, the body is also affected, i.e. low birth weight of the baby is one example. It is most interesting to note that the father's substance abuse also plays a part because of changes in his semen.

Rene Spitz's[56] and John Bowlby's[57] studies in the 1940s and 1950s are of special interest when the role of the "mind/body" split is considered in a child's early developmental experiences. Bowlby studied institutionalized children who had been separated from their mothers. He was able to illustrate the effects of the lack of touch or other bodily stimulation on the psyche/mind of the infant. He demonstrated that babies as young as two months of age developed signs of depression that

55 Karr-Morse & Wiley, 1997
56 Spitz, R., 1945
57 Bowlby, J. 1969

he termed "anaclitic depression." His research, however, did not include an examination of prenatal issues.

The role of touch is a requirement in normal child development and is an area that has been discussed in the past and continues today. Harlow's[58] research in the early 1900s examined the importance of touch on the later socialization of monkeys. The experiments involved monkeys that were fed by one of two kinds of "wire mothers" – a robot-like construction with nothing soft about it, or one that had a soft cloth draped over it. The monkeys that were fed by the cloth-draped "mothers" related much better to other monkeys as they matured that confirmed Harlow's hypothesis.

In the early part of the last century, in Western society, child rearing was far different from what it is today. At that time, no matter how much or how hard a baby cried, he/she was not fed more often than every four hours, and it was on the dot of four hours – not five minutes before nor five minutes after the specified time. This practice seems to be antithetical to positive child development from today's viewpoint. John Bowlby was concerned about the effects on the babies he treated. He believed that such a rigid feeding schedule was not in every child's best interest. He proved his assumptions through his studies of institutionalized babies and examined all aspects of their care – from feeding practices to the importance of eye contact and to the role of touch.

In Bowlby's sample, many babies were housed in a large room, each baby in his/her own crib. The sides of each crib were draped with sheets or blankets so that the babies could not see beyond their own crib. The nurse/caretaker did not provide any sort of nurturing touch or affection. The babies' diapers were changed with as little interaction as possible, and their bottles were propped up on pillows. When a baby was first placed in that environment, he/she would cry long and hard for attention; however, as time went on and there was no response from the environment, the cries eventually became whimpers and finally ceased altogether. Anaclitic depression or "hospitalism" (Spitz's term) was the result. The observers noted that the babies developed depressed affects and vacant stares, almost like some of the pictures of concentration-camp victims.

---

58 Harlow, H., 1963

Sandplay, as practiced today, links one to the non-verbal realm and, as an earth element, inherently calls up Great Mother issues from the depths of pre-history. These ideas will be returned to in Chapter 29. Some knowledge of the early pioneers of play therapy will be presented here.

Bowlby's[59] studies began in England and brought attention to the need to change how institutionalized children were treated. One of the first things to disappear was the sheets that were draped over the sides of the cribs. Then, the walls were painted with pleasing colors and pictures were hung. The nurses or aides were instructed to hold the babies when feeding them and to hold and cuddle the infants like a birth mother might do. The babies began to respond to this new system of being held and smiled at and they learned to smile in return. This seems like "old hat" today, but it was revolutionary thinking in the 1940s.

Considered to be the father of psychoanalysis, Sigmund Freud[60] was the forerunner of the psychoanalytic method and many theorists followed from his pioneering efforts. In Freud's method, he placed himself on a chair and sat behind the analysand, who lay on a couch and "free-associated." Touch was totally forbidden; not even a handshake was proffered on entering or leaving the office. The early pioneers treated adults only until, little by little, the field began to recognize that if problems could be addressed earlier rather than later, much suffering could be alleviated. Anna Freud,[61] following in her father's footsteps, was one of the first therapists to do analytic work with children.

The people who have contributed to this process are many and their methods may differ significantly. Some things are common to all approaches, however. Primary, of course, is that all methods agree on the importance of the first few years of life, including the prenatal experience.

---

59 Bowlby, J., 1969, 1973, 1980

60 Freud, S., 1922

61 Freud, A., 1946

Many therapists departed from a strict Freudian method and explored other theorists such as Carl Rogers,[62] B.F. Skinner,[63] Milton Erikson,[64] Alfred Adler,[65] and Carl Jung,[66] all of whom abandoned the couch in favor of sitting fact to face with patients and interacting with them.

Virginia Axline[67], an important pioneer of child therapy, was a student of Carl Rogers. She adapted his "client-centered" philosophy to her work with children. This later became known as "child-centered" play therapy. It is interesting to note that she kept a supply of sand in her play room. Other major contributors to play therapy were Karen Horney[68], Clark Moustakis[69], David Winnicott[70] and Margaret Lowenfeld[71]. Many, many more have followed and this brings the reader to Dora Kalff[72] and sandplay therapists.

Sandplay Therapy is one medium that is quite effective in linking the break between mind and body. This is primarily due to its connection to the non-verbal aspect and the tactile dimensions of the medium. Many other chapters in this book are devoted to the positive aspects of Sandplay Therapy so they will not be repeated here.

---

62 Rogers, C., 1955
63 Skinner, B. F,. 1953
64 Erikson, M., 1954
65 Adler, A., 1927
66 Jung. C. G., 1959
67 Axline. V., 1947
68 Horney, K., 1950
69 Moustakis, C., 1997
70 Winnicott, D., 1977
71 Loewenfeld, M., 1979
72 Kalff, D., 1980

PART II

TRAUMA AND OTHER DISORDERS

CHAPTER 10

SANDPLAY THERAPY WITH A TROUBLED CHILD[73]

HISTORY OF SANDPLAY

Sandplay therapy was developed about 30 years ago in Switzerland by a Jungian psychologist, Frau Dora Kalff. Her therapeutic work grew out of her studies in London with Dr. Margaret Lowenfeld who had first used sand and miniatures with her patients in what was termed the World Technique.[74] Frau Kalff refined and adapted this technique with her own Jungian orientation and called it *Sandplay*[75] (1971, 1980).

Jung himself had used a similar method during a particularly difficult period of his life that he described in *Memories, Dreams and Reflections.*[76] He had felt completely blocked in his creative process. When he suddenly remembered how he had played as a child, he decided that he had to return to a childhood frame of mind to recapture and free his creative imagination. Each afternoon he went to the shore of the lake in Bollingen to build a miniature village out of rocks and stones. He became almost obsessed with the project. He found that this activity freed his psyche in a way that enabled him to proceed with many of his creative ideas. This experience led him, somewhat later, to encourage Kalff in her work with children. Jung had heard Lowenfeld lecture in England about her work with the World Technique, which used sand and miniatures as a projective test. Jung was struck by the similarities to his own miniature village, and likened the sandtray to an alchemical vessel because of its transformative potential that is an integral aspect

73 Carey, L., 1990

74 Lowenfeld, M. 1979

75 Kalff, D. 1971

76 Jung, C. 1965

of sandplay. Kalff has drawn on Neumann's[77] theories and she outlines three broad stages wherein a child's sandplay work parallels Neumann's stages of development:

a. The animal-vegetative stage.
b. The fighting stage.
c. Adaptation to the collective.

The stages overlap and recur numerous times in any given therapeutic process as the psyche works and reworks the conflicts. Further, a particular critical period occurs during treatment that Kalff has termed the "Constellation of the Self." This is the point when the ego and the self, or spiritual center of the psyche, are in harmony and that Kalff sees as the turning point in sandplay therapy. Images at this period can be intuitively recognized as transformative, when all the elements for psychological healing are made visible to the therapist. It is the turning point. Further integration is usually needed to insure the psyche's stabilization.

To interpret any sandplay picture one needs to have a fairly solid understanding of Jung's work with imagery and the archetypes of the collective unconscious, a background in normal and abnormal child developmental theories, and a working knowledge of play therapy, drama therapy, and art therapy. Sandplay therapy reveals the unconscious contents of the psyche through the miniatures selected, the way the sand is shaped or molded, the overall cohesiveness of the picture, and, most important, the interactions with the therapist. The sandbox itself can provide a *temenos* or place of healing. The analysand's stories that accompany each picture provide an opportunity to express the inner conflict in a safe and protected way. At times, the sandplay therapist is an active participant with full discussion of the material; at other times, the process is non-verbal, yet one that holds both the conscious and unconscious of therapist and child as they meet in the intermediate space with the sandbox as the unifying, transformative medium. The process of sandplay therapy allows the child to discover and elucidate his or her own individual myth, with the help that a clinician can offer

77 Neumann, E. 1959

through support, education, interpretation, integration, ventilation, and an intuitive understanding of the possibilities as they emerge.

EQUIPMENT

A sandplay room can be elaborate or simple. The basic necessities, however, include two sandboxes (approximately 23" X 28" X 4") that can be mounted on legs or set on a table. This size limitation is so the entire contents can be observed in a single glance. Kalff has termed the environment of the sandbox "a free and protected space." Two boxes are needed so that one can contain wet sand and the other dry, because very different things emerge when sand of differing consistencies is used. The bottom and sides of the boxes should be painted blue so that, when the sand is pushed aside, water or sky can be illustrated. The boxes should also be waterproof, as water is often added, especially by children. This author has lined her wooden boxes with heavy blue vinyl such as is used to line swimming pools. Some sandplay therapists have used metal or plastic boxes. Necessary also is a collection of miniatures to be placed in the sand. Here each therapist's creative selection occurs. Some basic requirements include houses, people (of all types and occupations), cars, trucks, boats, planes, animals (prehistoric, wild, domestic), trees and shrubbery, fences, bridges, fantasy figures, cowboys and Indians. These miniatures can be displayed on shelves around the walls or kept in boxes or drawers readily accessible. Lastly, a source of water is required.

THERAPEUTIC RATIONALE

Sandplay has been effectively used with a diverse range of diagnostic categories (Bradway[78]) such as the affective disorders, eating disorders, adjustment disorders, enuresis, encopresis, and others. It has also been effective with more serious conditions such as schizophrenia and autism. Sandplay effectively combines certain aspects of play therapy, art therapy, and drama therapy, and also adds its own tactile dimension. The unconscious conflicts of the client are quickly illustrated by the emerging sand picture. Sand offers an opportunity for both symbolic

78 Bradway, K. 1981

and realistic grounding to occur. It is an earth element and serves as the link to the prima materia, the Great Mother, the preverbal uroboric level of the psyche (Weinrib[79]). During treatment it is especially important to sense when verbal interpretations need to be made as well as when nonverbal acceptance of the process might be more effective and possibly less intrusive. Additionally, it is extremely important for the therapist to bring to the work a sense of play, along with clinical expertise, for this process to be most effective.

Sandplay therapy, as will be illustrated by the following case, derives its unique quality from the particular way in which certain factors are combined. Among these factors are:

- Sand is tactile, yet provides a total kinesthetic involvement. This leads to a concentrated focus or meditative space that allows the inner, protected self to emerge.
- Limits are set on the action by the size of the sand tray, which ultimately assists the client in his or her own limit-setting capacity.
- Sandplay allows the child (or adult) to be in total control of the action and, consequently, to experience a sense of his or her own power.
- Sandplay can encourage verbalization in those cases where poor verbal skills exist and can also be used nonverbally for those who use excessive verbalization as a defense.
- Transference issues can sometimes be lessened by the use of sandplay and in other cases they can be intensified. The box itself often can become the transference vessel rather than the therapist. This sometimes serves to neutralize negative transference issues when they arise.
- It may be that a deeper level of the psyche can be reached more quickly than is possible with other treatment modalities, due to the very concrete nature of the grounding that occurs through the use of sand. (Carey[80])

---

79 Weinrib, E. 1983

80 Carey, L. 1990

CASE EXAMPLE

Jack C. was a nine-year-old boy referred to me by his school psychologist who suggested that Jack could benefit from an independent evaluation and play therapy. The psychologist's concerns were that the child was demonstrating enuresis, encopresis, and pica, among other symptoms. A comprehensive physical examination proved negative. Jack was in a class for neurologically impaired children and had a history of speech and language disorders. His IQ was in the low normal range. His father had died suddenly about a year earlier and his mother had just taken a full-time job. There was some depression in evidence.

Further, the school psychologist had inferred from her projective testing that this child was either being sexually molested or sexually overstimulated in some way. She believed that this was occurring within the family, which was of prime concern to Jack's mother as it directly implicated one of her other children. This allegation was resolved satisfactorily very early in my assessment when Mrs. C. confronted her older son with the school's conclusion and was convinced that no overt sexual molestation had occurred. This was corroborated in my assessment of Jack's sandplay work, discussed below.

Although Jack was not being sexually molested, he was sexually overstimulated. He was the youngest of four boys; the others (aged 16, 14, 12) were immersed in their own adolescent struggles and had also lost their father and experienced the mother's return to work. It was while Mrs. C. was at work that the older sons had discovered X-rated movies, which they all, including Jack, watched. These movies turned out to be the source of Jack's sexual knowledge and, hence, overstimulation.

Further history presented by Mrs. C. revealed that Jack had always been an accident-prone child. He had had numerous hospitalizations for falls, concussions, stitches, broken bones. He had also taken an overdose of his grandmother's blood pressure medication at the age of four for which he required hospitalization.

About two weeks after his father's death, Jack choked on a gum ball and again was hospitalized. Two months later, he developed a severe allergic reaction and was hospitalized for several days. Six months later, he broke an ankle and had to have surgery, which necessitated another two and a half weeks in the hospital. All of these hospitalizations were extremely traumatic for Jack, contributing further to his feelings of separation and loss. He was much less competent in overall functioning than any of his family members and with a very weak ego structure and correspondingly low self-esteem.

At the age of two and a half, Jack was tested for slow language development and was diagnosed as speech and language disordered. He received treatment for this condition and his speech was much improved when he entered kindergarten; however, he was placed in a learning-disabled classroom so that he could continue to receive individualized attention. The original diagnosis was changed to "neurologically impaired" when his speech improved, but his need for individualized instruction remained. Mrs. C. reported that Jack still had problems in speech, with retrieval of information and, as she described it, "major processing in the brain." Jack also had difficulty in the area of peer relationships. He had no friends, nor did he seek any. His pursuits at home were either solitary or fraught with competition with his three older brothers.

Jack's history reveals a child with severe developmental problems who was making adaptive progress within his special-class placement until his father's sudden death and his mother's return to work, two profoundly significant events in his life. It undoubtedly felt like double abandonment to him. Both happenings caused severe repercussions. Jack was struggling in his adaptation to these parental losses, and in this struggle mimicked his brothers as his role models. Their normal adolescent sexual curiosity was observed by and intensified in Jack, who was not developmentally ready for this stimulation. It was the underlying cause of his distress. However, it is to be noted that this family had functioned quite well until the sudden loss of Mr. C., and that Jack's special needs appeared to have been met at each step along the way.

TREATMENT

Jack came into the sandplay room that first day, his blue eyes open wide with wonder. His mother had told him there would be a sandbox here, but he was unprepared for the vast display of miniatures arranged on shelves that extend from floor to ceiling. He examined every miniature in the room, one at a time. He surreptitiously glanced at me. I stood nearby, but not too close, as I did not want my presence to be too intrusive on that first visit. I told him he could use any of the figures to make a sand picture and suggested he look everything over so that he would know what was available. He took down the things he could reach: the cars, trucks, houses, shells, farm animals, people, cowboys and Indians, dinosaurs, snakes, sea creatures and much more. Then he glanced at the higher shelves. I suggested that we move a chair so that he could climb up and examine those items that were out of his reach. His eyes lit up and he gave me a broad grin, which I felt was the beginning connection with this child, a sign perhaps that a positive transference relationship would be possible. He took a large, two-headed dragon and examined it in minute detail. This particular dragon was to play a large part in the course of Jack's therapy.

After thoroughly checking the contents of the room, Jack glanced around at me as if to ask, "Now what?" I showed him that there were two sandboxes. I explained that one contained wet sand, the other dry and that he could use whichever one he wanted. I told him that he might want to touch both of them to see which felt best to him. The wet sand and dry sand are available for two reasons: (a) to provide the child with an initial choice of the medium to use, and (b) to provide the therapist with diagnostically useful information. Jack's initial selection of dry sand is typical of children with learning disabilities as well as of those with enuresis and encopresis (personal notes from Kalff lectures). Wet sand often is too regressive and threatening in the beginning stages of therapy for such children.

As Jack placed the figures he had chosen, we talked a little about his understanding of why he was here. He answered in a drawling monotone, "because my brother bothers me." I asked what he meant. "N. touches my private parts and I want him to stop it." In response to my questions, he went on to say it was only when they wrestled; he was never naked and he never touched his brother's private parts, nor was he ever asked to. He said that I should explain this to his Mom. He had already told her this but seemed to need me to tell her as well. I believe he wanted me to do this so he could not be accused of tattling on his brother. It was at this time that Jack told me that he and his older brothers were watching X-rated movies while their mother was at work. I encouraged Jack to tell his mother about the movies in my presence, and she put an immediate stop to both the wrestling and the movies. She seemed able to enforce this even when she was not at home.

Jack's manner of speech was often difficult to understand. He spoke in a monotone with minimal affect. I often asked him to repeat a word or phrase, which would make him impatient and angry with me and demonstrated the beginning of some negative transference. I interpreted to him that it must make him angry when others, such as his family or teachers, fail to understand what he means. It was apparently helpful to him to know that I, at least, could accept and understand his angry feelings.

Figure 10.1

In Jack's first sand picture he placed the two-headed dragon in the upper left corner, a castle on a hill with two knights nearby (one on horseback, one with upraised arm), a magician, a princess, and Santa Claus (this was a week or two before Christmas). As I searched this first sand picture for clues as to what else might be troubling Jack, I noted first the two-headed dragon that had initially caught his eye. The upper left comer, in which the dragon was placed is the area in the sandbox often associated with the mother, sometimes with a negative connotation (Kalff lectures).

Cirlot[81] wrote about the dragon:

> But, broadly speaking, present-day psychology defines the dragon symbol as 'something terrible to be overcome.' Jung goes on to say that the dragon is a mother-image (that is, a mirror of the maternal principle or of the unconscious) and that it expresses the individual's repugnance towards incest and the fear of committing it, although he also suggests that it quite simply represents evil.

The dragon, in this instance, can possibly be extended to include not only Jack's personal mother but my presence as well, as it was a two-headed dragon and could be viewed as combining two aspects of the feminine in one symbol. It suggests a multitude of possibilities - his personal mother, my presence as transference figure, the archetypal Mother with positive and negative qualities, terror of the unknown, and the hero's quest to slay the dragon.

When I asked Jack what he thought of the dragon, he immediately associated it to his mother, saying that "sometimes she roars like a dragon." He gave a loud roar to illustrate what he meant. I asked if perhaps he saw me as a dragon as well, in as much as I was a woman something like his mother. Jack was quick to answer that he didn't see me as a dragon, but that he was afraid his brothers would think he was crazy if he had to see me. I followed his lead and asked Jack if he thought he was crazy. He said that he did and that he also knew he was stupid. I assured him that he was not crazy but his feelings sometimes made him think he was. I also asked him what he thought stupid meant. He said it meant you had to go to the "stupid class." I explained that being in that class made him feel different but that did not mean he was stupid

81 Cirlot, 1971

or could not learn, but that he and his classmates each learned things in their own way and in their own time.

The struggle toward autonomy is applicable to all children, but becomes crucial to a child with Jack's history. The knight on horseback is mounted and, facing the dragon, ready to do battle. The castle is another important element in this first sand picture. The castle, again according to Cirlot[82], symbolizes "an embattled spiritual power, ever on the watch." For Jack, it may have depicted his struggle to find his own inner strength. The question for him became not only to find his inner strength, but to help him internalize it so that he could draw on it to cope with the many traumas he had experienced in his short life. This castle, positioned on top of a hill, could possibly reveal his beginning awareness of his own place for inner sanctuary. Of course, the castle (or any symbol) can have numerous interpretations.

With most children it is helpful, indeed essential, to get their own interpretation before one offers any amplification; otherwise, the sand picture becomes merely the therapist's projection and, as such, is not particularly useful. Sandplay, like all therapies, is interactional and requires at least two points of view (i.e., those of the child and those of the therapist).

Jack had placed a magician in a black cape beside the castle. It could be hypothesized that this figure combined Jack's depressive feelings (black) with his "magical thinking" (magician), his belief that he had in some way caused his father's death, and that he could undo it as well.

As I searched Jack's first sand picture, I looked for clues to possible sexual abuse that did not seem to be apparent. With children who have been sexually abused, it is often observed that the figures are buried in the sand from the waist down. This was not the case in Jack's picture. I did note, however, that Jack had placed a fairy princess (lower left), so that he had provided a balance to the dragon, as a negative mother figure, in this more positive aspect of the feminine in his psyche.

Santa Claus was another figure in the picture and can also represent various psychological aspects. Jack attributed its presence to the fact that Christmas was only a week or two away. I accepted his interpretation, but felt on a deeper level that it could also have represented his unconscious

82 Cirlot, 1977

hope that I (as Santa Claus) could bring his father back to him, could help him in his feelings of stupidity, could help his feelings of being crazy.

I prognosticated that this was a good beginning. Jack had his task outlined (battle with the dragon), a safe haven (the castle), a sensitivity (the princess), and the means to accomplish this struggle (the mounted knight), and there did not seem to be any suggestion of sexual abuse.

One of the things we talked about during those early weeks was Jack's fantasy that "if you go to the bathroom (e.g., eliminate feces) you will have a heart attack." I asked Jack to explain this to me. He told me that, on the night his father died, his Dad had gone to the bathroom and that was why he had died. I asked Jack if he, too, thought that somehow he might die, especially if he went to the bathroom. He nodded a vigorous assent. He then began to cry and said that if he wasn't so stupid his father would not have died. I spent most of this session explaining to Jack that when people are having a heart attack, they sometimes feel sick and need to go to the bathroom, but that going to the bathroom did not cause the heart attack. I explained how the heart and the digestivesystems work in terms that I hoped he could understand. The confusion related to heart attacks and elimination turned out to be the cause of this child's encopretic episodes, which stopped almost immediately after that session. I stressed that Jack had not caused his father's death, nor had his brothers, nor his mother. I interpreted to him that by trying to hold in his feces he was trying to hold in his feelings about his father's death.

Jack's second picture, the following week, further explicated his situation.

Here we see a topsy-turvy world: cars and trucks upside down and a wounded soldier ready for the ambulance. The topsy-turvy world showed how his world felt upside down to Jack and the presence of the ambulance indicated to me that he unconsciously expected the therapy (i.e., ambulance) to be a place to heal his wounded feelings. It was through this image that I believe Jack was showing me his deep woundedness and asking me to help set things right for him. This message was a nonverbal one, but I interpreted this to him nevertheless and he nodded in agreement. In the upper left corner he added a gasoline pump. Although the overall look of the scene was quite hopeless, energy, represented by the gasoline pump, was available to him.

Figure 10.2

Four or five weeks went by as Jack continually buried and unburied many objects. Sometimes he buried dinosaurs, sometimes outer-space figures, occasionally the wounded soldier. In this activity, Jack seemed to be processing some of his Oedipal/sex/aggression themes and, most especially, the death and resurrection themes surrounding the loss of his father. During these sessions, Jack talked to me about his activities at school and about some new friends he had made. He also became curious about my life, which indicated to me his positive transference feelings. He asked me if I had kids and whether my husband had had a heart attack. I answered his questions honestly and said that I guessed that he wished in some ways that he could live with me, where things appeared to be more normal. (My office is in my home and he occasionally caught sight of my husband.) He nodded his silent agreement.

Around this time, Jack had also asked his mother if she would get him a new daddy.

The route to my office took Jack past the cemetery where his father was buried, which was, perhaps, part of the impetus to the burying and unburying motif.

For a while, traveling this route contributed to some resistance because the feelings he experienced, as he confronted death and loss, became extremely painful for him. It was also a reminder that going to therapy meant to him that he was crazy. He was trying to integrate all the conflictual feelings that were being aroused.

Symbolically, the act of burying can indicate at least two things: (a) rage that is being buried, and/or (b) attempts to hide and protect a fragile ego. In Jack's case there was the additional association of his father's burial. (This form of complete burying is not to be confused with the previously mentioned half-buried figures of sexually abused children.) In Jack's case, the burying seemed to be indicative of both his rage and his efforts at ego protection, along with some integration of his feelings about his father's death. It is possible that other feelings of loss related to his mother's return to work were also being addressed by the burying activity. His choice of objects to bury was significant. The dinosaurs could well have represented his primitive, instinctual urges that were beginning to surface and to need containment; the cars and trucks, his attempts at mobilization; the outer-space figures, his feelings of being "crazy, spaced-out." The wounded soldier in every instance seemed to indicate Jack's own wounded feelings.

Some three to four months after starting therapy, Jack became interested in using fire in his sand pictures. Fire can symbolize several widely divergent ideas such as positive masculine potency, castration anxiety, and inner rage as well as feelings that are out of control. There is a ritualistic element around the use of fire extant in all cultures throughout recorded history.

Jack produced the next picture showing the depth of his primitive, instinctual energy, which is represented here by prehistoric figures - yet in a very ordered, very organized way. To me, this picture seemed to be what Kalff might term the "Constellation of the Self." There is a feeling of reverence associated with the light in the center, which seemed to hold primitive forces at bay. It was as though he had found his own inner light. We both admired this picture and I gave him a great deal of verbal support. These primitive energies were now available to him in an entirely new, cohesive manner. He had placed a candle center stage, as if to highlight the importance of this picture. The candle was shaped like a pyramid and seemed to serve the same function the castle had in an earlier picture - a safe, protected space. Not visible in the photograph, a dinosaur was devouring a crocodile. This could represent the depth of Jack's rage and his fears of being swallowed up by his feelings of inadequacy when he compared himself to his brothers who were all older, stronger, and better adapted than he. In almost every session, Jack referred to himself as the "stupid one." I continually interpreted this to him in ways that might modify his poor self-image. Jack had used wet sand for the first time in executing Figure 10.3.

Figure 10.3

Use of the wet sand was a positive signal to me that Jack had been able to move to a deeper psychological level than previously. He felt safe enough in this environment to reveal his deepest conflicts. His use of the dinosaurs further corroborated this observation. Not long after Jack produced this picture, Mrs. C. reported that he was becoming quite outspoken at home and was "showing his temper." I felt that for Jack this was positive growth in that he was beginning to assert himself.

On the positive side, his mother also reported that Jack's bad dreams had apparently stopped; he no longer requested a night light, and his enuresis had not recurred. The pica had not continued past the first or second session.

In Figure 10.4. Jack had the castle with candles in the turrets, the dragon with candles in each of its two mouths, and the pyramid-candle surrounded by outerspace figures.

Figure 10.4

The dragon and the outer-space figures may serve, for Jack, to link the very distant past and the future. He appears to be attempting to find his place in the continuum. Under the pyramid (Figure 10.5), a man lay buried, which seemed to be another reworking of his earlier burial themes. Here Jack had made a funeral service that illustrated some of his feelings about his father's death. In that session, we talked again of how very difficult it was for him to attend his father's funeral with all the feelings he carried of being lost and alone. In the same session, he manipulated the dragon so that he burned the genital area, which seemed to signify (again) his initial sex/aggression theme as well as to affirm his own phallic potency. This ritual, however, could also indicate his unconscious rage at his mother for his fantasy that she might have been responsible for his father's death, another aspect that I had discussed with him. Still another possibility to be considered was that I, too, was part of his dragon symbolism. The burning could have represented his unconscious rage at me for not having restored his father to him and an unconscious linking of some of his rage toward his mother, which extended to me as another maternal figure. Further, by confronting me in this symbolic way, he may have been trying to control his fears by not verbalizing them. Facing these very deep feelings is always painful and, with Jack, was compounded by all the previously discussed material.

Figure 10.5

In the fifth month of Jack's therapy, he wanted to use both sandboxes during a single session. This is somewhat unusual. However, I have observed this in some children who have lost a parent through divorce or death. In this normal stage of Oedipal development (Freud[83]), the boy unconsciously wishes for the death of the father so that he can have the mother all to himself. In Jack's case, his unconscious wish was granted, which led to an overwhelming guilt reaction on his part. He

83 Freud, S., 1922

also experienced the conflictual need for his mother's comfort, as part of the grief resolution, along with the fear of total engulfment and the need to push away from her toward his own autonomy. It seemed that he very much needed to use two boxes in order to express all these issues.

Jack used all the available tools of the sandplay environment to illustrate and integrate his numerous conflicts. As can be seen, Jack connected the two boxes with a bridge, which was in itself quite significant. This bridging seemed to indicate that he had a way to get back and forth, from inner to outer, from conscious to unconscious, from masculine to feminine.

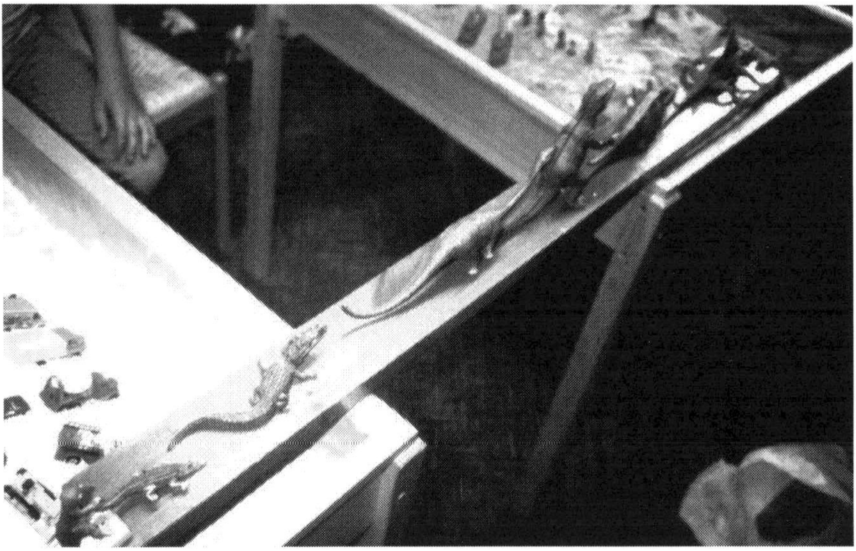

Figure 10.6

Jack was more or less nonverbal during the times when he used both boxes. He appeared to be totally engrossed in the sand pictures and gave a deep sigh when they were completed. Then he would glance up at me and grin as if to say, "How's that?" It seemed to me that not much verbalization was required at that time and, so, when he was finished I joined empathically with him as we admired his work. I did attempt to engage him in a discussion of what the experience evoked in him and his comment, "I've already told you everything," seemed to say it all.

Jack repeated this configuration in the following two or three sessions. It is, of course, possible that part of Jack's impetus for using both boxes may have been an unconscious need to accomplish as much as possible in the few weeks remaining before the planned summer break; however, it appeared more directly related to a healthier adaptation.

School reports indicated that Jack had much more concentration on his school work; there were no more episodes of enuresis, encopresis or pica, and his peer relationships had improved. Jack began to feel more comfortable at home, and reports from his mother indicated that family interactions were within a more normal range. His position of family scapegoat was lessened as his brothers began to treat him as one of them, rather than as the stupid one.

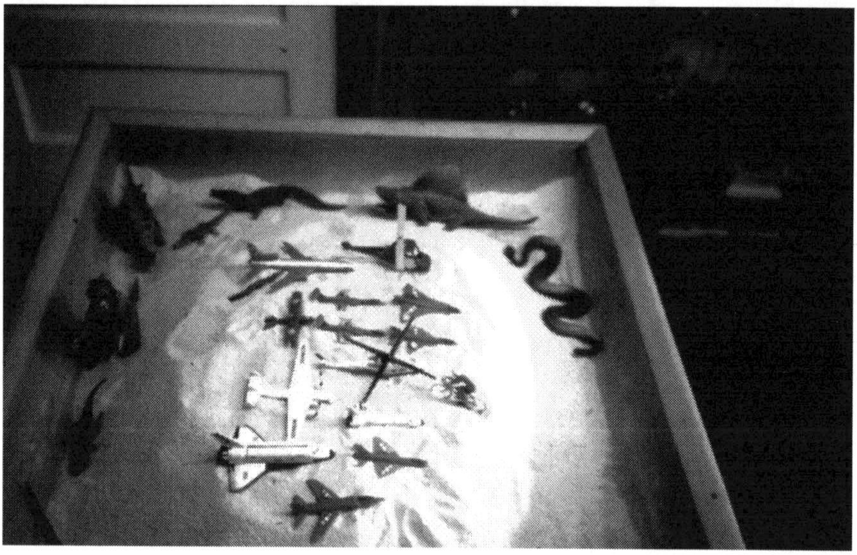

Figure 10.7

Jack placed every airplane I had in the office on top of the hill (Fig. 10.7). They were all pointed toward the other box. He next placed alligators, snakes, octopus, lobster, and fish around all the airplanes. He set a gold Volkswagen near the center. This VW was another important symbol for Jack. The car, in dreams, is at times a symbol of the self. In Jack's case, his oldest brother drove a VW; therefore this appeared to be another way that he could identify with an older male role model. In addition, gold often symbolizes a very special aspect of the self, the inner treasure, and is associated with the sun and masculine creative energy. The placement of this car, near the center of the box, again seemed to confirm that the car, as Jack's self, was in a centered, more grounded spot. Also in this picture, Jack placed a large plank to serve as a bridge between the two boxes and made a procession of dinosaurs marching across the bridge. He shoved a human baby down the throat of one dinosaur, which repeated an earlier theme, that of being devoured. Perhaps it was his still-fragile self going into the belly of that huge instinctual force. I made an interpretive comment about the baby's terror of this huge monster. Jack said that was a silly idea because the monster was going to throw it up anyway. He seemed to be more in control of his inner rage (the dinosaurs) and more able to determine the fate of the baby. Then a fascinating thing occurred. Jack arranged a second procession on the bridge that came from the opposite direction. It was made up of an Indian brave, a black warrior, and an Indian chief smoking a peace pipe! This Indian procession met the dinosaurs face to face, peaceably. Jack had clearly illustrated his key to making peace with the monsters. He proudly announced, "That Indian isn't afraid of anything!" We both broke into laughter about that one.

A look into the wet sandbox revealed similarities to the dry one. Jack had carefully piled and patted all the sand into the center of the box, forming an island surrounded by water. He positioned a number of boats on the island, which included one boat being carried in a truck and one being pulled on a trailer. Perhaps placing the boats this way showed some lingering discomfort at this stage with using wet sand. So, in one box, things of the air are all set to take off and, in the other, things of the sea. He was able to sort and categorize by this time and I mentioned to him that it seemed the boats were on dry land instead of in the water. He said he didn't know why, just that that was how he wanted it. On the bridge between the two were all the powerful forces of his unconscious and yet they were met by positive, healing, masculine figures. I was quite impressed with his choice of figures and commented how brave those figures seemed to be on their way to meet the dragons. Jack shrugged and grinned as he left the session,

This same theme (with slight variations) was portrayed over the following two weeks. At one of the sessions, Jack added some farm and domestic animals in the wet sand, which seemed to be movement toward a more domesticated level of the psyche. There was still some confusion for him, however, as some of the animals were in the water and some on the island, although the boats remained high and dry. The theme of things needing protection (like the boats on the island) was repeated in various ways throughout his treatment and spoke of his own underlying need for continued protection,

In the last of this series, the cars were alone on their hill while underneath the bridge, hidden from sight, was a car that he said had gone in for repair, I asked what had happened to the car. Jack replied that it had had a bad accident and that it wasn't fixed yet. This indicated to me Jack's concern that he, too, was not yet "all fixed." I did not make a verbal response to this but merely held my observation as the summer break was at hand and it did not seem appropriate to comment. The dinosaurs marched across the bridge as before, but without gobbling anything up. He placed some soldiers and other fighting figures in the wet sand, which told me nonverbally that the inner battle still continued, but perhaps in a more accessible, open way. In the center he had positioned the wounded soldier (himself), which had appeared for the first time in his second picture some months before. When he finished and we stood admiring his work, I asked him which figure was in the most danger. He pointed to the wounded soldier in the center, then picked it up and put it into the ambulance in the dry sand. He had found an appropriate caring container for his woundedness by the miniatures chosen and the way he used them.

This picture of the soldier seemed to represent another very complex theme for Jack, because it spoke of all his wounded aspects: his numerous handicaps, the loss of his father, his ordinal place in his family, and his Oedipal concerns. By being able to insert and remove the soldier in the ambulance, he was able to begin to take control of his feelings. Another positive aspect of this figure was related to the fact that Jack's oldest brother was a volunteer with a local ambulance crew. The use of this miniature had given him the opportunity to identify in a very real way with an older male figure much as the gold Volkswagen had done.

The ambulance is very often symbolic of the therapeutic relationship, linked as it is with a place of emergency treatment and healing. Jack's insertion and removal of the solider seemed to represent several motifs for him. As mentioned, it enabled him to identify with a male role model (his brother). In addition, because of the transference that had been established (and which was illustrated by the ambulance) the insertion and removal of the soldier seemed to indicate that this was a healing experience for him. He, Jack, was now in charge of the wounded soldier.

Through sandplay therapy, Jack's losses were integrated, his family and peer relationships had improved. In addition, his self-esteem had increased and his ego boundaries were stronger. He had experienced positive and negative transference feelings and had found the safety to express these feelings both in the sandbox and verbally.

Jack's case was terminated at this point although continued treatment was recommended in order to stabilize and further integrate the healing process. However, there are many factors to be considered by a child therapist, a major one being parental support and understanding. In Jack's situation, it was Mrs. C.'s decision not to continue therapy in the Fall as we had planned. Mrs. C. was pleased with Jack's progress and could see no reason to continue even though Jack (and I) had requested it. Her rationale was similar to that of many parents (i.e., the shame that they associate with having a child in therapy, the concept that they are bad parents if they can't take care of their child's needs, and a general fear and misunderstanding of the psychotherapeutic process). These factors applied to this woman who was rearing four sons under very difficult circumstances.

SUMMARY

This case has demonstrated the use of sandplay therapy with a child who had multiple problems. A selected progression of sand tray pictures has been examined and the therapeutic interaction has been discussed. Jack's sandplay process moved from a chaotic beginning into a much deeper uncovering of his feelings, and revealed his subsequent integration of these feelings through his transference reactions. He was able both to illustrate and to talk about his low self-esteem and his frustrations over his own limitations. He succeeded in resolving a large part of his grief reaction and guilt around his father's sudden death through the repetitive burying and unburying of objects as well as the one funeral scene, which was described and illustrated. The feelings of abandonment and rage occasioned by his mother's return to work were partly illustrated by the burying as well as by the burning of the dragon. The final series demonstrated how the archetypal forces in his psyche were being organized, assimilated, and tamed. He had, on the bridge, used the healing symbol of the peace pipe to make peace with the primitive rage seen by the dinosaurs. In this way, Jack began to come to peaceful terms with the uncontrollable, archaic energy that resided within him. In a period of six months, he achieved significant relief from his presenting symptoms, made a better ego adaptation, and was far less depressed. Jack began to recognize that he, himself, could have some control over his fears and insecurities, that he could effect some change in his relationship to his family members and to his peers. He was able to grieve for his many losses and to move toward a more productive way of functioning in his school and home life. Although further treatment would have been desirable, many of Jack's issues were addressed and integrated in a relatively short period of time.

CHAPTER 11

VIOLENCE AND TRAUMA ISSUES IN HEALING[84]

What is trauma? Trauma covers any situation where the psyche is overwhelmed and the person is unable to use his/her usual psychological defenses. Because of this, he/she is unable to function in the usual fashion. This is known as traumatic stress and is an overwhelming response to violent acts that can lead to dissociation and/or Post-Traumatic Stress Disorder (PTSD). What has been found, however, is that many PTSD victims are often also suffering from Reactive Attachment Disorder (RAD) and this complicates the situation tenfold. This is due to the fact that a poor attachment history makes therapy much more difficult because the child does not trust the adult to be there for him/her. In these cases, it becomes necessary to decide what to treat first – the attachment issue or PTSD.

Some situations that can lead to trauma are those related to the individual and those related to society. For example, children who have been physically or sexually abused, who have been neglected, who are exposed to domestic violence, who have lost a parent, sibling, or other family member through suicide (or divorce or death by natural causes), or where there is severe illness in self or a family member, are a few of the reasons. Emotional abuse must also be considered as another form of violence – subtle violence assuredly, but violence nevertheless. Children are told to "toughen up" or "you're no good" or "what's wrong with you" when the situation may be the real problem, not the children themselves. It frequently happens that they are the scapegoats when their parents separate or divorce, when things go wrong in school or in their

84 Workshop given by Lois Carey, Center for Sandplay Studies, Nyack, NY., Nov. 2010

world – the author is sure the reader knows what is meant. The problem appears to be escalating exponentially.

Children who have been exposed to societal traumas such as school shootings, 9/11, earthquakes, wars, and news reports are other examples —not to mention computer games and web surfing. No wonder that trauma and violence are such major issues today.

History reveals numerous examples: the Conquistadors, the Salem Witch Trials, numerous wars, the mythologies of the Greeks, Romans, Egyptians, etc., all are filled with violence and trauma. Some of the readers have grown up exposed to a great deal of this and have managed to cope, while many children today seem to be seriously affected. The problems seem to be escalating as more and more children are brought for therapy, many with aggression towards peers, bullying, poor social skills, etc., as their presenting problems. The author truly believes it is overexposure to news on TV, computer games, family break-up, overly programmed activities, two working parents, single parents, grandparents as parents – the list can go on and on. Also, children have forgotten how to PLAY. Instead, they are enrolled in Tai Kwan Do, soccer, T-ball, dance, swimming, football, wrestling, tennis, horseback riding, etc. There is absolutely no time for idling away a day by playing alone with dolls, soldiers, making mud pies, dressing up as a king or queen, etc.

Therapists cannot possibly hope to change the violence in our world or to alleviate traumatic situations. What can be done is to be prepared to deal with the world as it is and as it affects today's child – a very tall order. This is difficult because in addition to treating children, our personal stresses need to be handled and to be handled in a way that does not interfere with the work with clients.

Some of the symptoms shown by traumatized children are fear, anxiety, depression, anger, hostility or aggression, precocious or aggressive sexual behavior, low self-esteem, difficulty maintaining or establishing relationships. There can also be physical symptoms such as bedwetting (enuresis), encopresis, tics, heightened alert or startle responses. When these symptoms occur, many young children do not yet have words to put to the feelings that ensue, so part of the job as therapists is to help children find words to match the feelings. This is why Play Therapy is the treatment of choice for these children because playing immediately lessens the child's anxiety and hastens the child's ability to trust the therapist. Some children may demonstrate signs of what Eliana Gil[85] called "Posttraumatic Play." It is a stylized form of play that includes unique characteristics – it is repetitive, literal and rigid; there is an unconscious link between the play and the event. It often fails to relieve anxiety and it usually depicts danger. There is a lack of spontaneity or fun and the child is often immersed in the play to the exclusion of the therapist. This kind of play clearly signals that attention must be focused on the trauma material; otherwise the child may feel more deeply traumatized and experience feelings of vulnerability and increased helplessness.

The study of PTSD became quite prevalent after the Vietnam War when combat veterans came back with a wide variety of symptoms. Rape victims were also found to suffer from PTSD, which was far worse if the victim had a history of childhood sexual abuse (a re-experiencing of the original trauma). Core PTSD symptoms are numbing, intrusive thoughts, hyper arousal. Several years ago, the issue of "false memories" came up. This was in those cases where the memories that came up were not actual ones, but a fantasy state. Therapists were accused of encouraging these memories during treatment and the patient, wanting to please the therapist, came up with the "memory." There have been some malpractice suits related to this issue. On the positive side, according to van der Kolk,[86] the therapeutic relationship is the cornerstone of effective treatment. Both the therapist and the patient are confronted with intense emotional experiences that can range from helplessness to revenge, from vicarious traumatization to vicarious thrills. This is an extremely difficult area and is central to trauma studies. This type of situation is a good example of when to seek expert supervision.

According to Van der Kolk, traumatic memories are stored in a state-dependent fashion. They are often dissociated and stored outside of ordinary experience making them inaccessible for verbal recall for long periods of time. The research has also found that children of Holocaust survivors were at risk for PTSD because they had unconsciously picked up the parents' traumas whereas the actual victims had been able to use their own coping skills. The symptoms of these groups ranged

85 Gil, E., 1994

86 Personal notes

from depression, to anxiety disorders, to dissociation, and to substance abuse. Somatic symptoms are also prevalent. In women, menstrual disturbances can occur, as well as fibromyalgia and/or chronic pelvic pain. In both men and women depression, irritable bowel syndrome, and chronic headaches can occur. PTSD can be missed because of the multiple symptoms, which means that a very careful trauma history should be taken.

One finding in recent brain research reveals that in major depression, there are increased cortisol levels while in PTSD there are low cortisol levels so that these levels could cancel each other out, making diagnosis extremely difficult. It has also been discovered that there are persistent, profound alterations in stress hormones that are secreted in people with PTSD. They tend to respond to reminders of the trauma with increases in heart rate, blood pressure, and skin conductance. The brain, the body, and the mind are linked inextricably as has been proven over and over.

Trauma reactions run the gamut from disbelief and horror to grief and rage. Regression can occur as well. Children become overly clingy, suffer from bedwetting and/or school phobia. The first 24 to 48 hours after an event is usually the most difficult time and victims are encouraged to try to resume a normal schedule as soon as possible, to talk to others (often by repeating a description of the trauma a number of times, the impact can be lessened), to not overuse drugs or alcohol but to exercise and to use relaxation techniques. Trauma survivors need to feel in control of their own treatment – whether it is psychotherapy or medication.

One of the biggest dangers of PTSD that occurs in adults "after the fact" is substance abuse. Some of the medications used are antidepressants and SSRI's. Medication was found to be helpful in some cases of dissociation, but not for PTSD, per se.

We need to differentiate Acute Stress Disorder (ASD) from PTSD. They are not the same. ASD shows up almost immediately following a traumatic situation whereas PTSD takes longer to develop. For those who have had secure attachment bonds, this serves as a primary defense against trauma-induced psychopathology in both children and adults. If there is a long history of severe neglect, combined with abuse and trauma, there is a poor long-term prognosis.

For those victims where psychotherapy is the treatment of choice, it is important to face the memory rather than fleeing from it. This needs to be treated like anxiety through desensitization. Cognitive therapy that counteracts negative beliefs is one method. Another technique often used (mostly with adults) is EMDR[87] but it seems no one is sure why or how it works, but that it does. Journaling is helpful for some patients, as it allows the self to feel the feelings – they will decrease in time. Most research is time-limited but most patients are not cured in 10 – 15 sessions. One thing noted by all the researchers is that it is important NOT to rush the talking too soon.

It is important to talk to children at a level they can understand, to assure their physical safety, and to limit TV viewing. Those under eleven are most at risk. Be aware of any behavior changes, nighttime fears, or fear of loud noises, wind or rain. Some children refuse school, suffer headaches, stomachaches, vomit, and run a fever. Some things that can help are to draw, to paint, to write a story of the event; or they can be offered clay, Play Doh, music, puppets – anything that can enable them to talk about the event. Some symptoms in adolescence can reveal that earlier sexual abuse has occurred. Symptoms such as self-mutilation, suicide attempts, eating disorders, substance abuse or dissociation require special attention.

Van der Kolk[88] has found, through research that dissociation can be adaptive at the moment the event occurs but not when it is constant. This can sometimes signal a complex form of PTSD. Kluft,[89] for example, found that some patients were extremely adept in some areas while abysmal in personal relationships.

When the event is a sudden crisis, the things to be concerned are how recently this occurred, how near the person was to the event, how near to the family, to physical safety, etc. The goal is to stabilize, mitigate the acute signs and symptoms of distress and restore their adaptive qualities or else help them access a higher level of care. Basic principles in a crisis:

87 Eye Movement Desensitization Response

88 Van der Kolk, B.

89 Kluft, R.

1. Intervene immediately.
2. Stabilize.
3. Facilitate understanding.
4. Focus on problem solving.
5. Encourage self-reliance.

When dealing with children in crisis, it is important to recognize that their age affects their ability to understand. Children under seven or eight have no clear conception of death, but react to the reactions of the adults around them. (Adults model the behavior.) Examples cited by Nancy Webb[90] about 9/11:

1. A four-year-old saw a plane hit the tower and later asked her mother why the plane flew into the building.
2. Some other young children saw people jump from windows and asked if there was a trampoline to catch them.
3. A ten-year-old feared a terrorist would crash into her building and kill her.
4. A 16-year-old honor student saw no point in studying – "We'll all be dead in a war or by anthrax."

A loss of words and symbols often occurs in "terror states." When reminders of the event were presented to subjects, PET scans showed that people with PTSD had an increase in activity in the right hemisphere of the brain that is associated with emotional states and autonomic arousal. There was a simultaneous decrease in oxygen utilization in Broca's area in the left frontal cortex that is responsible for generating words that match internal experience. This can lead to "speechless terror" and leads the emotions to appear as a dysfunction of the body through psychosomatic symptoms. Van der Kolk[91] found that when traumatic experiences were verbalized, the psychosomatic symptoms decreased. Verbalizing helps one regain a sense of self. This is all extremely complex and requires more study than is illustrated here.

90 Webb, N., 2004
91 Van der Kolk, B.

In sexually abused children, van der Kolk[92] found that during EEG's there was a disruption that was particularly prominent in the left hemisphere, the area of language development that also revealed some learning disabilities. Adults who were abused as children have great difficulty recalling historical information – probably related to the fact that traumatic memories are stored in a different area of the brain.

In many recent studies,[93] somatization, dissociation and abuse are all significantly associated.

Negative behaviors usually ensue when trauma has not been made conscious and verbalized. Patients often express their internal state more in physical movements or in pictures than they do in words. Drawings and psychodrama may help them develop the necessary language. Group therapy is also beneficial because they can hear others express what they may be feeling. It helps to put words to their experience.

For children, one of the principal tasks is to learn to negotiate relationships with others. Studies of traumatized children have shown that they often have serious problems in their capacity to play.[94] Traumatized children tend to either be excessively shy and withdrawn or to bully and frighten other children. They often lack social skills so it is extremely difficult for them to be attuned to their environment. Some of these children have also mastered the art of dissociation – making their ability to discriminate almost non-existent. Without such skills, these children do not have the capacity to get comfort from others that points to a poor attachment history. As mentioned above, in this type of case, the therapist must address attachment issues prior to dealing with the crisis.

All traumatized individuals, children or adult, are often fixated at the stage when the trauma occurred, making therapy an involved task, especially for the older patient. Safe attachment is the key to resolution of trauma and is especially important in the therapeutic relationship. It must FEEL safe in order to be effective.

This chapter does not encompass all the aspects of violence or trauma, but it is hoped that the reader will be encouraged to study further in these areas.

---

92 Van der Kolk, B.

93 Van der Kolk, B.

94 Terr, L., 1983

CHAPTER 12

CASE OF BD[95]

This case is that of a 12-year-old boy, that I will call BD, who lived with his natural mother and his stepfather. He was in the sixth grade in school and was a very high scholastic achiever. The reason for the referral was that he had been drawing sexually explicit pictures in school of oral and anal sex. The school called his mother to advise her of this. Further history revealed that BD had been sexually abused by an uncle (mother's brother) from ages five to nine. This had been discovered about two years earlier when a five-year-old cousin told his mother that BD was touching his genitals. His family had had some brief therapy at the time when BD's abuse was revealed, and the uncle apologized to the child for the abuse. He (the uncle) was 16 or 17 years old at the time of the abuse and had spent one or two nights in jail after it became known.

Part of the abuse was related to a time when BD had caught his uncle cross-dressing. His life and the life of his parents were threatened should he tell. It was that incident that led the uncle to seduce the child. The child was having nightmares related to chopping up women when the abuse was going on and he showed quite an interest in knives and swords. The uncle also forced BD to undress, and took pictures of him. Those pictures were supposedly destroyed.

BD's parents were divorced when he was one-and-a-half years old. There was no contact with his natural father. However, it was believed by his mother that his father and the uncle/perpetrator had also been involved in homosexual sex.

The family of BD's mother was rife with alcoholism and incest that went back at least three generations. Her new husband of four years turned out to be a sexual predator who cruised local bars at night in at-

95 Excerpted from Carey, L., 2006

tempts to pick up young males. This was learned through the referring colleague who treated the mother, the uncle, and several of the aunts.

The stepfather was over-involved with BD's treatment process, which was later understood when his (stepfather's) problem behavior was disclosed. On the first interview with BD's parents, the stepfather said that he wanted to take the child to a urologist to check out the size of his penis. He felt that the child's penis was extremely small. He was told that taking him to a urologist was unnecessary and would only put further focus on his (BD's) problems. Later, due to the stepfather's intrusion into the process, the child's treatment ended - about six months' duration and just at the point when it seemed that BD was about to talk to the therapist about his problems.

The communication throughout most of the sessions thus far had entailed the therapist commenting on how BD might be feeling, followed by either a nod of acquiescence or a shake of his head that it was wrong. This was probably the most non-verbal case this author had ever seen, but his pictures will illustrate some parts of the process. Descriptions of some of the other scenes will be included as well.

BD's first picture consisted of knights riding on horseback, who were charging a dinosaur. There is also a half-buried snake and two wizards that are also half-buried. It is often seen that in sexual abuse cases, figures are half buried and almost always in dry sand. The wet sand seems to be too uncomfortable at this early stage for the child to use. Two scenes were produced while a history was being obtained from the parents in another room. In the second picture, BD showed that T-Rex was devouring an alligator. One could surmise that this was an expression of his rage at his situation.

The next picture (Figure 12.1) shows another major battle being set up. This time a work truck has been added. That might symbolize that we are about to dig into the problems in this case, and that there is mechanized energy available to do so. BD very carefully covered much of the scene with sand (as can be seen in Figure 12.2). This type of half-covering of things is something he did often with his scenes.

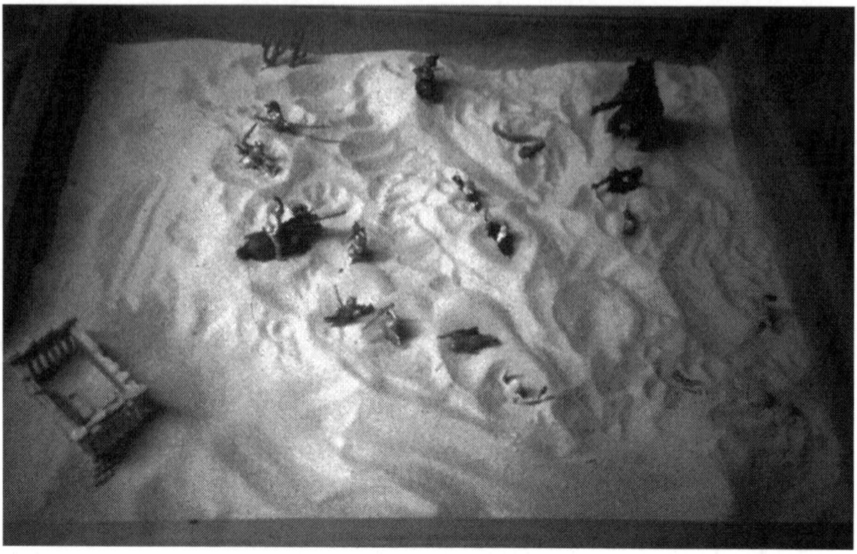

Figure 12.1

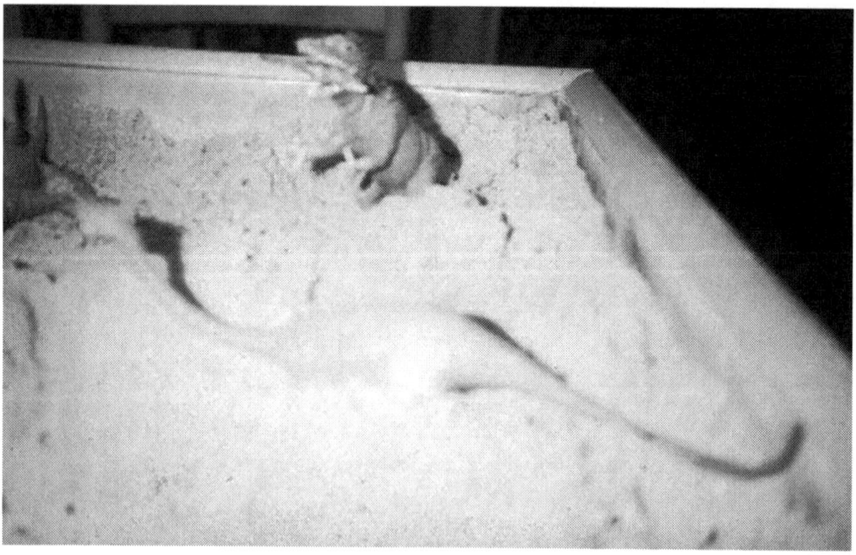

Figure 12.2

The following week another battle was illustrated, this time with soldiers. One can see that the transition from his use of very aggressive animals to soldiers was made relatively quickly. This is considered a move towards more human representation. Once again, he carefully covered most of the figures with sand.

BD found matches and candles during another session that were part of the equipment in the room. Lighting the candles and burning them became an integral part of several sessions. He also burned the genitals of the dinosaurs and the soldiers. The black smoke that filled the room from the burning plastic was too much for both the therapist and BD, therefore, the burning had to be limited, so the therapist brought in popsicle sticks that he could burn instead, if he needed to. There have been numerous questions about this but it was believed that this boy's wounding was so deep that it was important for him to symbolically burn the hurt away. The next scene was another battle where he buried many of the soldiers in the sand.

After a lengthy summer vacation break, BD produced a scene that was similar to what he had made on his first and second sessions. It was as if he had to go back and redo some of the earlier stages. Next, he produced Figure 12.3 which I later understood was an attempt to disclose that there was something evil in his house.

Figure 12.3

First he constructed a house out of Lincoln Logs that had a fenced-in area in the front yard. He surrounded the house with dinosaurs, snakes and large ants. This was one of the most troubling scenes that this therapist ever witnessed and one that communicated his pain in a way that words could not have expressed. The information about his stepfather's activities had not yet been revealed at the time this scene was made. BD was trying his best, without words, to let the therapist know that "something was rotten in the state of Denmark." Attempts to encourage him to verbalize his concerns about "what was going on in the house" were met with his usual stony silence. Shortly after this scene, the therapist asked for a parent conference and tried to probe into what might be occurring. This seemed to be what pushed the stepfather to want the boy to terminate therapy with me.

Following this, BD used soldiers, a dinosaur, and a mummy in a scene. The hopeful sign to me was a wishing well that was perched on the edge of the box. This might have signified his hope that some of his wishes would be granted. In addition, he placed a wounded soldier on a gurney. The hurt soldier often signifies that the child is aware that therapy is a place for wounds to be healed. In the upper-right corner of the scene, a bunny hutch was used as a jail. The therapist asked if that was supposed to be the jail that he wished his uncle to be in. He nodded his assent.

In his next picture, he constructed two jails and was able to verbalize, on his own, that this was where his uncle belonged (also his stepfather?). On another level, however, this might also have signified just how bound up he felt, or that he had managed to split, or dissociate.

The soldier that is seen in the pop-stick enclosure (Figure12.4) was a toy that had been burned previously and was discovered through questioning to be another image of his uncle (and perhaps his stepfather).

This could be interpreted as an attempt to illustrate how he would like to punish the offender(s) and an attempt to symbolically eradicate his own wounds.

The use of fire can be viewed in several ways. Fire has many aspects, both positive and negative. Its place in the alchemical process is certainly unquestioned, as the early alchemists attempted to change base metals to gold by the use of fire. The sandbox is often viewed as an alchemical vessel, the place where change can occur; therefore BD's use of fire could be interpreted as curative, at the same time that it served to illustrate his trauma.

Figure 12.4

During the next session a battle with soldiers took place, many of whom again were buried in the sand.

One day it was suggested to BD that perhaps he might want to draw a picture instead of using sand, and all the art materials were laid out. He said he wanted to use all of them, which he methodically did, one stroke at a time and using one type of color at a time, tempera, colored pencils, markers. The therapist asked him when he finished, what it looked like to him. "A waterfall" was his response. To her, it certainly looked as though the picture represented all the fire that he had been involved with for the past couple of months.

Several weeks after BD made this drawing, his stepfather decided that he should terminate. He wanted to take BD to a "more directive, confrontive" therapist. So a premature termination occurred. The therapist was not at all happy with this parental decision, but this is one of the troublesome issues that therapists who work with children have to contend with. All attempts to reverse this decision were rebuffed.

The therapist did, however, get some feedback from the colleague who had referred the child to her. BD and his mother and stepfather moved to the South about a year or so after he had been treated. The mother apparently knew of her husband's addiction to young boys, but decided to stay with him nonetheless. She gave birth to a second son after the move. BD was then about 17 and doing extremely well in high school. Reports said that he had a girl friend and seemed quite happy and well adjusted. The parents never took him to another therapist, so it can only be surmised that through the experience with Sandplay he had been able to discharge enough of the rage from his abuse to carry on with his life.

He may be plagued again at a future time with some remnants of his very serious abuse. This therapist hopes that the positive experience he had with Sandplay will help him seek appropriate help when that time comes.

CHAPTER 13

ATTACHMENT AND LOSS[96]

THE BEREAVED CHILD IN SANDPLAY THERAPY

Attachment and loss have been major areas of study in psychology and psychiatry for many years. Dr. John Bowlby's[97] work has been noteworthy in the profession with the publication of his first book in a series - *Attachment*, published in 1969, the second, *Separation*, in 1973, and the third, *Loss*, in 1980. Numerous other researchers have followed his lead and there have been extensive studies made of all these issues, some of which can be found in the bibliography.

Some of the results of these studies will be reviewed in order to pinpoint the importance of this subject and then to examine how Sandplay can be an effective tool in helping to resolve and heal the wounding that occurs when the attachment to the mother or mothering figure is broken.

When one speaks of the bereaved child, there are many forms of bereavement, not just the child who has lost a parent to death. The bereaved child is one who has suffered any form of loss to an attachment figure, i. e., the child of divorce, the foster child, the adopted child, the child of substance-abusing parents, as well as those who have been deprived of their childhood, such as the sexually abused child or the child who has witnessed violence. In other words, most of the children who are brought for therapy are suffering from bereavement issues.

The major thrust of much research today is subsumed under the title of "Attachment Disorders." Researchers have been able to illustrate the vast importance of a child's attachment relationships that, when dis-

---

96 Presented at Center for Sandplay Studies, Dec. 2004

97 Bowlby, J., 1969, 1973, 1980

turbed, can impede the developmental process. The question needs to be asked, then: "Why is attachment such an important area to understand and what does it have to do with the developing mind and body of the child?"

In order for a child to develop into a healthy, well-functioning adult, certain critical events must occur in order for healthy attachments to form between child and mother or mother/figure. Attachment is often referred to as "bonding" today, and refers to a child's ability to feel secure in relationship to his/her environment so that he/she is ready to proceed with normal developmental tasks. Attachment is the basis for everything that follows and is solely related to the interactions that occur and the relationship that develops between mother and child from the time of conception onward.

One is led to recall the experiments a number of years back that linked the ability to attach as being possible only during critical periods of development.

The studies by Konrad Lorenz[98] examined the imprinting (or attachment) of geese to humans as only occurring at a certain stage of development in the goslings. In his laboratory, he observed that at some point in development the geese attached themselves to the humans who were caring for them and followed them around as if they (the researchers) were mother geese. This point is not to be belabored; however, the role of the mother or caretaker is critical to the development of attachment and to the well-being of the child - most especially during the holding and feeding of the infant that must occur within the first few hours after birth.

Attachment for the human infant begins at conception – from that moment when the sperm first unites with the egg attachment is being formed and continues to solidify, at least through the first two years of life. A book of recent vintage, *Ghosts from the Nursery,*[99] outlines this process thoroughly and suggests that the critical period for attachment development is from conception through the age of two – the first thirty-three months of life. When there are disruptions or environmentally

98 Lorenz, K.

99 Karr-Morse, R. and M. Wiley

caused intrusions on the brain or emotional life of an infant and/or mother, disastrous consequences can ensue.

The birth process itself is a significant moment in solidifying attachment because the newborn child is often laid on the mother's stomach as soon as possible after birth as a way to begin the extrauterine bonding process that began in utero. There are some circumstances that do not allow for this early relationship, such as with premature infants who must be immediately placed into an incubator or those who are given up immediately for adoption, or in those rare instances when the mother dies during childbirth. For such children, there is a variety of outcomes, not always positive. Consider adopted children. Statistics support that the numbers of adopted children on the rosters of child therapy clinics far surpass others– something like four to one.

What has been learned over the past number of years related to attachment is that infants who have not had early experiences of bonding or those who have been neglected or abused in any way, most often suffer from later attachment disorders and often grow up to neglect or abuse their own children and are unable to form positive attachments. The problem is truly all-pervasive.

The major issues surrounding every child with an attachment disorder, regardless of the cause, are related to bereavement issues such as abandonment, loss, low self-image, low self-esteem, physical and sexual abuse, and depression. Therapy with these children and their families must be geared to both repairing the loss and developing appropriate attachments while being careful to include the stages of mourning that are similar to the treatment of bereaved children. Treatment must, of course, be geared to the developmental age of the child.

Many children who have an Attachment Disorder, also display signs of Separation Anxiety that is usually extensive. Many of these children develop severe clinging behavior. Some of these children develop severe detachment reactions and cannot interact with others at all. Each child's intellectual ability to deal with these issues is age-specific that will be discussed shortly.

Grief and mourning are NATURAL processes that everyone goes through in adapting to situations that entail loss in any form. Children who have experienced loss have many issues to resolve and much of it has to do with their age when the loss occurred. There are significant stages that transpire for grief resolution. The primary thing to remember is that grief and mourning MUST occur after a loss; otherwise, at some future time, it will be exhibited in relationship to some other event that is not always recognized as a grief reaction.

Common wisdom leads us to believe that the child under two or three, the infant and toddler stage, has no conception about adoption, death, divorce, or serious illness in a parent or child; however, he/she is definitely affected, which is often illustrated behaviorally. This is the age when separation anxiety can be paramount. For example, if one considers the studies done years ago by John Bowlby,[100] among others, it was proved that young babies, some as young as two weeks of age, go through a period of mourning when the primary caretaker disappears. Babies can, even at this young age, respond quickly if a substitute caretaker is presented. This is one of the main reasons that direct, honest answers to children's questions needs to occur as soon as possible when a loss has been experienced. This does not mean that the questions or behaviors will cease immediately, but it will mean that the child will be able to pursue feelings about the event from time to time. All children take their cues as to how to handle the loss of an attachment figure from the adults around them. It is important that the adults be open with their feelings so that the child will not feel that he must hide his. This is true of all age groups.

From the ages of about three to five or six, the child, in a natural situation, has the ability to conceptualize the parent. He or she has gone away but will be back later. The child is in the "magical thinking" stage. From everything they've experienced thus far, death has no permanency and children have a distorted view of death; however, they do have a great deal of fantasy about it. The children have witnessed on TV and in the movies that the superhero never dies, the cartoon character is killed and comes back to life. Ghosts and Freddie Kreuger, however, have the power to terrify them. This is an active period of a child's fantasy life, especially when one considers the fantasies related to the Oedipal stage, that of killing off Dad and claiming Mom for one's own. This is the developmental task during this stage. If a young boy loses his father at

100 Bowlby, J., 1969, 1973, 1980

this time, either through death, divorce, or illness, his guilt can be overwhelming. He believes that his wish had caused the loss. Or, perhaps, consider the small child who has been reprimanded by the mother and he or she says to him or herself, "I wish she was dead!!" When a mother's death actually occurs during this period, it is compounded and made far worse by the fantasy. An excellent teaching opportunity for the parent can arise if a child has witnessed the death of a pet or found a dead bird on the street. Incidents such as these can be used to help a small child understand loss, even if they have not yet experienced one.

If a child has had a solid attachment by five or six, he may be at less risk to develop an attachment disorder than a younger child. However, when a child is adopted or loses a parent to death or divorce, it remains a traumatic event. The tasks for these children are multi-faceted. They need to grieve their loss as well as accomplish adjustments to a new family constellation in order to form new attachments. This is a tall order when one considers the numerous insecurities that exist normally during the Oedipal stage. The hope, probably unfounded, is that many children today are being helped to cope with these events at the time they occur, rather than waiting years when entrenched behavioral symptoms invariably crop up and demand attention. Schools and other agencies are more attuned to children's needs today than was the case in earlier times, however, much more needs to be done.

From age six to eight, death is seen as irreversible, but "it only happens to others, those who are old, or bad or sick." For the child of this age who may also have an attachment disorder, the scenario could be that this is just one more incident of loss. If the child has been in several foster homes awaiting adoption, for example, or one whose parents have had major problems since they were born, related possibly to substance abuse, or witnessing violence, and a significant death occurs, much therapeutic work needs to be done. These children have the need to grieve all the previous losses, such as living in numerous foster homes, in order to ever experience positive attachments to other human beings.

Children begin to have the cognitive understanding that death is final around the age of eight or nine, but for the attachment disordered child, defensive negative behavior patterns have often developed by this time that causes rejection from those around them, behaviors that are usually quite entrenched. It is almost as if they reject any overt attempt to help them attach. This can be a VERY difficult age at which to adopt such a child and requires extreme patience, understanding and love from the adopting family.

The child has finally accepted that death is forever by the age of nine or ten and he/she now has the capacity to understand it. This does not mean, of course, that they fully accept it, just that it is more cognitively understood. The magical-thinking stage of the toddler has ended and the period of concrete operations leading to abstract thought is in place according to Piaget's[101] studies. Any traumatic event is a major crisis for a child with an attachment disorder and everything that has been said before about the need to mourn is critical for such a child.

Just briefly, there are certain predictable stages that occur in so-called normal reactions to grief, no matter what the cause.

1. There often comes denial - refusal to believe that anything has happened.
2. Shock and anger follow when the denial ends.
3. There can be a disorganization of the personality with intense emotion - fierce separation anxiety and depression can occur - the younger the child, the more intense the reaction can be. However, these reactions are not always solely based on age. It can be much more difficult if the child has any other handicapping condition.
4. After these stages have been more or less worked through, some adaptation to the loss occurs.

These are the stages for an expected death or for a parent's abandonment for any reason for children who have previously had positive attachment relationships. As one can imagine, each situation is different and requires different treatment planning dependent on all of the variables.

The normal mourning process in children is very gradual and differs from that in adults. Children can tolerate only small doses of painful feelings at a time and, as mentioned earlier, they look to the adults

101 Piaget, R., and B. Inhelder, 1955, also see http://www.wikihow.com/Make-a-Genogram

around them to provide guidance and give them permission to grieve openly.

It is ESSENTIAL that every child be told the reason for any loss in order to counter thoughts that he or she was "bad" or in some way caused the loss - at least to the level that they can understand. Of major importance, in all situations, is to keep the lines of communication open between the caretaking person and the child.

For children who have suffered a loss and show signs of attachment disorder Sandplay can be an effective treatment method. This is not meant to say that it is better than other forms of play therapy or family therapy, just that it is another tool to consider. Most of these remarks have been looking at bereavement issues as a normal process that must be worked through with the long-term goal being to assist the child to form healthy attachments to significant others.

One book mentioned earlier is *Ghosts from the Nursery: Tracing the Roots of Violence*[102] by Robin Karr-Morse and Meredith Wiley. *Ghosts* focuses, among other things, on prenatal influences that contribute to a child's propensity to violence that these authors believe is the number one problem facing society today. Many would have to agree with them since the violent person most often has many issues related to lack of attachment and loss. Much of what these authors say is intended to alert us to the issues of prenatal conditions of the mother, particularly the use of drugs and/or alcohol, and the effects on the brain of the developing fetus, especially at critical periods of development. This is not a new idea, however, as discussed earlier.

In today's vocabulary, most of the children that were studied by Spitz[103] and Bowlby[104] would be termed "Attachment Disordered."

The role of touch is a required element in healthy child development. Harlow's[105] studies focused on the effects of maternal touch on the later socialization of monkeys. The experiments involved monkeys that were fed by either a "wire mother" (a robot-like construction) with nothing soft about it, or a "wire mother" that had a soft cloth draped over it.

102 Karr-Morse, R. & M. Wiley, 1997
103 Spitz, R.
104 Bowlby, J., 1969
105 Harlow, H., 1963

These studies demonstrated that the monkeys that had been fed by the cloth-draped monkeys related much better to other monkeys as they matured. This confirmed his hypothesis that the sense of touch is vital to later socialization.

As the mental health field progressed, it was discovered that the sense of touch, in and of itself, could be either healing or destructive dependent on the purpose of the touch. The terms "Good Touch and Bad Touch" have been quite prevalent in educating children about issues of touch. There is a third form of touch, however, called "Secret Touch" that applies directly to the sexually-abused child. It is in this category that we find many attachment-disordered children. Touch is resisted for these children because many of them have learned to dissociate or detach in order to survive psychologically. Part of their healing entails grieving the lost innocence of childhood and recognizing that not all touch is bad or secret.

On the more positive side, it has been found that the sense of touch has been linked to a child's early maternal experience and touch sometimes becomes the agent used to heal. It is certainly vital for any child with a label of "attachment disorder."

Patterning is one of the techniques used for children who have certain neurological disorders. The treatment consists of helping the child to develop motor skills – especially in cases of cerebral palsy, or other delays in development. The physical therapist is trained to move the child's body in certain patterns that helps the child learn how to move, to crawl and eventually to walk. The children are treated with a hands-on approach that addresses physiological as well as psychological ills.

There have been successful outcomes for people with different types of massage for healing – healing of bodily aches and pains, which, as it turns out, has the pleasant side effect of healing the mind. There is nothing quite like a deep, relaxing massage to take one's mind off of one's troubles and to really heal the soul. There are many different forms of massage such as Swedish, acupressure, Rolfing, Alexander Technique, Osteopathy, Therapeutic Touch, chiropractic and many more.

Viola Brody[106] used the sense of touch with children that she treated. Her techniques were expanded by Ann Jernberg,[107] and Theraplay was born. Theraplay is especially useful with children who suffer from the negative effects of attachment issues such as the "failure to thrive" infant, the autistic child, the sexually or physically abused child, the adopted or fostered child. Theraplay treatment is one of short-term design and includes all forms of touch such as the therapist holding the child, playfully tickling the child, kissing the child's toes and fingers, etc. The treatment is geared to assist the child in developing healthier attachments and uses touch to accomplish this – much like a so-called 'normal' child might experience during the early years with his/her own birth mother.

How does Sandplay fit into all of this? It has been shown that there are very strong connections made between the mind and the body when one engages in Sandplay Therapy. By reconnecting the mind and the body through the medium of sand, the child has a much better chance of repairing faulty attachment issues. A child's kinetic movements are also involved in play therapy, of course, but the addition of sand is what differentiates the two methods. It is difficult to fully explain what happens when one is immersed in a Sandplay process, but all one's senses are involved. Just as verbal therapy cannot explore the entire realm of problems in one session, neither can Sandplay. Just as verbal therapy is sometimes accompanied by intensity of affect, the same is true for Sandplay – in both these approaches there can be connections made that bring insights.

In Sandplay, not every session is intensely moving, but on those occasions when certain aspects of the psyche are touched, one is immediately aware that a very deep level has been reached that affects the body as well as the intellect. A grounding phenomenon occurs that words cannot do justice to. This can best be described as the "Aha!" experience that is sometimes achieved in verbal therapy. The therapist can observe the non-verbal affect of the child and see the relaxation in the whole body. An overall lessening of tension is apparent. What is reported by parents and teachers is that they begin to notice improvements in all areas of the

106 Brody, V.
107 Jernberg, A., 1989

child's life – from better focusing on school work to improved relationships with parents, siblings, and peers.

The medium of sand is unique to this technique and is absolutely necessary for this kind of mind/body connection to occur. Sandplay is not the be-all and end-all of child therapy, it is another tool. There are some diagnostic categories where it can be contraindicated. This is particularly true in severe cases of obsessional disorders where even touching the sand can cause extreme anxiety. One needs to move slowly in cases such as this because Sandplay is something that is never forced. To do so would undermine the process. A refusal to use Sandplay can be a resistance that must be honored. It is rare that a child refuses to use sand, but when he does, alternative forms of treatment are offered such as art, puppetry, clay, games, etc.

Since most cases of poor attachment stem from difficulties within the Mother/Child dyad, it is helpful to consider these ideas in the overall understanding of these children. As Jung and others have told us, many disorders of adults and children stem from a break in the Ego/Self[108] axis. Today we would term this break in the Ego/Self axis "Detachment," a Mind/Body split.

Archetypes[109] are really non-definable, as they are, most simply, a concept. The best that one can do in attempting to describe an archetype is to recognize that it is virtually impossible to describe and that we can merely approximate what the meaning might be.

To summarize then, it is proposed that archetypes are part of an invisible world that no one has ever seen and that they reside in the deepest level of the psyche. They are represented differently in each one of us and are found in all peoples worldwide. We know them through myth, fairy tales and stories told the world over. If we use the Mother archetype as an example, She has been shown in numerous fairy tales – both in her positive and negative forms. What can be a better example of a negative mother than the witch or the wicked stepmother who has the ability to terrorize so many children? On the positive side, we have the old woman in the shoe or the good fairy godmother – the list can go on and on.

---

108 See Chapter 1

109 See Chapter 28

It is useful in Sandplay Therapy when the therapist has some understanding of the archetypal meaning of the miniatures chosen because this knowledge can enhance and deepen the therapeutic process. In addition to the child's (or adult's) own interpretation of the scene produced (discussed when a scene is completed) the therapist's understanding is critical. Jungian Sandplay Therapists believe that a great deal of the therapist's understanding appears to be transmitted to the patient on a non-verbal, non-rational, unconscious exchange through the medium of sand. The sand tray, then, is the vessel through which the child and the therapist can connect physically, intellectually and emotionally. Dora Kalff referred to this as the "free and protected space," by which she meant that a child is free to use anything in the room in constructing a scene while being protected by the presence of a caring therapist.

Sandplay is sometimes more of a "felt" experience than one that can be verbally described, again, demonstrating the link between mind, body and attachment. At those times when the archetypal level is illustrated in a sandplay session, one knows that it is an important moment because of one's sensate bodily reaction that is primarily a "felt" experience. The patient can experience this sensation, if he/she is at least partly conscious of a relationship to the archetype, as children usually are, because of their familiarity with fairy tales and myth. The therapist's understanding seems to be the key to deepening the process, because such understanding serves to enhance and expand the patient's unconscious, even without verbalization.

I recall one 12-year-old girl who produced a very moving sand picture that depicted a lotus blossom, just opening up (Fig. 13.1). This child had never used wet sand before and she poured one cup of water into a corner, then carefully scooped it up and moved it to a different area. She then used shells to portray the scene. There was no verbalization expressed, but there was a sense of awe that accompanied the end result. This child had been sexually molested by a stranger some years earlier and this picture seemed to indicate that there was now an opening in her psyche that would allow her to proceed with appropriate adolescent development. She had developed detachment as a defense that soon gave way to more appropriate forms of relating.

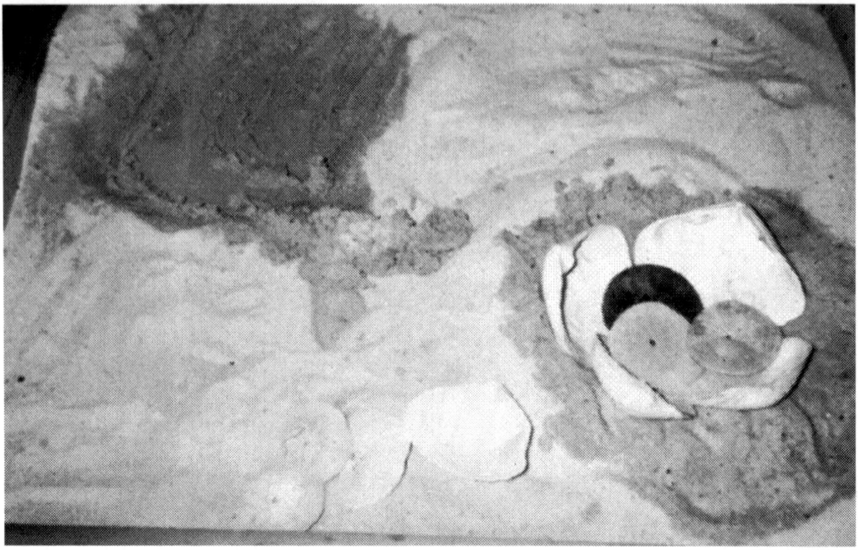

Figure 13.1

For anyone who desires to use Sandplay in his/her practice, it is important to have some experience with the medium on his/her own personal issues. Otherwise, the procedure is like a therapist who uses verbal therapy with no personal experience of his/her own in a therapeutic process. One can work without experiencing either therapy or Sandplay, however, it is like working with blinders on. The untreated therapist or Sandplay practitioner can only go so far. One can never take a client farther than one has gone him/herself. Sandplay is not practiced solely by Jungians who have spent years in exploring archetypes and Jungian theory, but one must have a connection to some theoretical orientation.

How does one know that the mind and the body are being connected for the child who is producing a sand picture? It is partially related to one's observational skills as well as one's overall play therapy skills. Children often spend the first few minutes of every session letting the sand slip through their fingers or bury their arms in the sand as far as possible. Then, when they feel that a connection has been made, they move towards selecting miniatures that they want to use in the tray. It is as if the connection with the earth (sand) is the medium that helps them to focus and to attach themselves to the healing process. Their bodies and minds are fully engaged. If one tries to divert the child with comments or questions, one is often met with blankness, almost as if the child hadn't heard anything that had been said.

Sand can be a deeply healing experience for those children who have attachment disturbances when they are given the opportunity to deal with a bodily trauma in such a grounding way. For the sexually-abused child, touching the sand and being fully grounded in his/her body - he/she is able to begin to heal the deep wounding and shame that accompanies such an intrusive, traumatic act. These children often cannot talk about their pain verbally, at least when the trauma is fairly new, but can express it in this non-verbal form. These sexually-abused children will often unconsciously reveal the abuse. For example, in many cases of sexual abuse it has been noted that the child buries the miniatures from the waist down. The child may be communicating that the pain and the shame need to stay partially hidden, at least for now. Eventually, as therapy progresses and the figures are allowed to be fully visible, the time comes when the bodily experience and the intellectual understanding can be assimilated and verbalized.

Children who have learned to detach through dissociation are then able to form more appropriate attachments once their grief work has been accomplished.

CHAPTER 14

A DOG CALLED SWEETHEART[111]

After 9/11, this author was one of the New York Association for Play Therapy volunteers at Kids Korner at Pier 94 in New York City. The site had been set up for families to receive assistance that was needed as an aftermath to the September 11th tragedy. This ranged from financial assistance to housing assistance to job assistance and more. Kids Korner was coordinated through the Association for Benefiting Children and enabled parents to drop off their children while they were taking care of the myriad details that had to be attended to.

A number of Therapy Dogs made rounds at the Pier and visited various sites, including Kids Korner. One time, the author saw a very bedraggled looking, small black-and-white dog that was named Sweetheart and that seemed to have some sort of skin disorder. Much of her small body was bereft of fur, especially around her hind quarters and stomach. The hair she did have was insufficient to cover the many large bald spots. The woman who was escorting the dog was asked if the dog had eczema or something similar. She told the author the dog's story; one that brought her very close to tears. A teen-aged girl had set the dog on fire and her present condition was the result of many skin grafts (about $7,000 worth) that had kept her alive. The woman said that Sweetheart had then been trained to be a Therapy Dog and visits many burn units to give hope to the victims there. She assured the author that the dog was very happy and committed to performing her acts of mercy. The trainer had driven here from California with another dog and trainer to provide this service. This dog's story gives one hope that out of something horrible, some good can emerge – it is a paradigm for healing. The author asked the woman what had happened to the perpe-

---

111 Reprinted with permission from the Newsletter of the NYAPT (2012) and the East Coast Journal of Sandplay Therapy (2012)

trator of such a heinous act, but she did not know. Sweetheart was not this woman's dog but had been lent to her to bring to New York and offer her services.

This entire experience was one of the utmost challenges that this author has ever encountered and she is thankful that she was able to provide some small contribution; however, it did cause her untold pain as well, as she realized how truly vulnerable we all are. Sandplay was not one of the healing modalities offered there, although it was suggested. The concern was that there wouldn't be enough trained professionals to provide proper guidance; however, the art that was produced was quite effective and consisted of innumerable American flags being drawn and depictions of the twin towers being struck, bodies falling, and the utter devastation that ensued. It was like a mass catharsis, if there can be such a thing.

This author also treated a couple of children in her private practice for whom Sandplay was definitely part of the experience and, here too, themes of towers being struck by planes with firemen and police to the rescue were the norm.

This author's countertransference reactions were compounded by her family concerns. When 9/11 occurred, her husband was in a rehabilitation hospital recovering from a minor stroke. She cancelled her clients that day (9/11) and went to be with him; however, everyone there, doctors, nurses, aides, patients, were living in dread that Indian Point Nuclear Plant might also be on the "hit list" and Indian Point is directly across the Hudson River from this site. This experience, coupled with the volunteering was more than she had bargained for. During the ensuing weeks, she found herself bursting into tears at the smallest incident or raging for no apparent reason that could be figured out. It became so intense that she recognized that she had better get herself some supervision – fast – and so she did. It helped immeasurably to get her back on track. Anyone having similar reactions to crisis work is urged to seek out whatever support system is available. One possibility for Sandplay therapists is to think about pairing up with one another and sharing these deep feelings in this marvelous non-verbal milieu that is so much a part of our lives.

CHAPTER 15

SEXUAL ABUSE: HISTORICAL COMMENTS

Sex abuse has always been there - at least as far back as Greek mythology.[112] When Cronus married Rhea, an oracle told him that one of his children would overthrow him and take his crown. In order to prevent that from happening, as each child was born to Rhea, Cronus grabbed it and swallowed it whole. In this way, he devoured Hestia, Demeter, Hera, Hades, and Poseidon.[113] This angered Rhea, as you might well imagine, so when she gave birth to Zeus she played a trick on Cronus. She substituted a stone for the newborn Zeus whom she wrapped in swaddling clothes and hid from his father's sight. Cronus immediately grabbed what he thought was the infant and instead swallowed the stone. This made Cronus quite sick and he immediately threw up all the previous children.

The child was a major threat to the old order. Consider this in psychological terms, it is really child murder and it was solely for the purpose of maintaining one's own status - a strict ego need.

Jumping ahead a few years, it is said that Zeus married Hera after an engagement of 300 years. Hera was Zeus's elder sister - an early example of brother/sister incest. Such a practice was common among the Greek gods as well as the Romans and the Egyptian Pharaohs.

In addition to brother/sister incest, incest also existed between mother and son that is detailed in the Oedipus myth. An oracle had foretold this event, but the eventual incestuous act was done purely in innocence. The Queen had no idea that the young man was her son, nor was the son aware that she was his mother. The natural parents had ordered Oedipus to be taken out and left to die so that he wouldn't grow up to kill his father and marry his mother, as the oracle had predicted. But,

112 Kerenyi, C.
113 Kerenyi, C.

fate intervened, he was not killed, he did not die, but he grew up and unknowingly killed his father and unknowingly married his mother.

Alice Miller, however, questions the validity of the Oedipus myth because it was a totally unconscious act by all the parties concerned.[114]

In the Greek myths (as well as other myths), there are repeated stories of child killings, incestuous unions, etc. These are almost all related to attempts to preserve the old order and not to make way for the new.

Alice Miller questions Freud's theory of Infantile Sexuality[115] and presents the idea that a child's sexuality is a direct response to the adult's sexual interest in the child. She illustrates how, in the 17th century, a child had no privacy about his own body, being at the mercy of the adult's sexual excitement. In this way, she believes that Freud "missed the boat" through his own background and the times in which he lived, a time when there was so much sexual repression - at least overtly.

What is witnessed today is not a new phenomenon - it is as old as Cronus himself (Cronus = Father Time). It was always felt (and in some cases, still is) that a child was nothing more than a possession of the parents to be done with as they pleased.

When did a change begin to occur? Fairly recently, it would seem. Child labor laws were drawn up in the late-19th Century; the first reported case of actual child abuse goes back to about 1872 when neighbors of a family found a 12-year-old girl chained to a bed in an attic when her parents went to work. She was unclothed, filthy, had no food or water nearby. The neighbors tried to find an authority to report this situation, but there was none available at that time to protect a child. They did, however, go to another existing organization, the Society for the Prevention of Cruelty to Animals. Child Protective Services was finally born out of this case. So, it is only in the last 100+ years that the plight of children has been addressed. Given this history, is it any wonder that from Cronus to the present child abuse is still prevalent?

These examples, however, are the extremes. Alice Miller goes on to illustrate many other subtle ways that children are mistreated, made to feel unworthy, are guilt-ridden, etc., all of which are directly due to the injustices heaped on them by their elders - the ones who attempt to

114 Personal notes from Miller lecture (1987)
115 Personal notes from Miller lecture (1987)

maintain the status quo. She claims that parents and teachers are guilty of "soul murder" and it is at this level that reparation must be made. These children who have experienced "soul murder" often grow up and inflict the same thing on their children. It is imperative that this be stopped immediately as a way to eventual world salvation. In spite of the most horrendous form that abuse can take, the child usually blames him/herself and is convinced that the parent acted this way "for the good of the child." In every child-centered agency this can be witnessed many times over. No matter how badly abused a child has been, if given the choice, he/she will almost always want to return home.

Today, with widespread child abuse in evidence, it seems that what is indicated is that the adults themselves are disconnected from the positive, creative aspect of their own inner child (a shadow state). A part of their psyche has been split off and they envy the actual child or else they project their own unacceptable impulses onto the child. This is a VERY serious split in the human psyche.

In psychological development, according to Erich Neumann,[116] the basic need for development is the mother/child unity that allows the Self to constellate and that can always be returned to. One cannot forget that this ALL takes place within the context of the family, society, and culture into which the child has been born.

In the "normal" state of development, all developmental systems progress in an orderly fashion most of the time. However, many things can and do affect and disturb the best integration in any one of these systems. For example, a birth injury can occur or genetic factors can play a part, all of which affect a child's physical and cognitive development. These factors, in turn, have an effect on a child's personality development. Problems may also arise within the family, such as substance abuse in the parents or a sibling, a catastrophic illness, a death or divorce - all such problems have a direct effect on the child. The parental handling of the child spurs him/her to become either shy and retiring or demanding and aggressive in attempts to gain parental attention.

Problems can interfere with psychological development at almost any age and are directly connected to ego development that determines and can interfere with the reparation of the ego/Self axis (see Chapter 2). Just

116 Neumann, E., 1973

as the body strives to heal itself when ill, so does the psyche. Jung tells us that the psyche can be self-healing just as the body is, given the space and time for this to occur. Sandplay therapists believe that the sand tray provides the medium in which this can effectively occur. The purpose of any symptom, then, is to call attention to the fact that something is out of balance or is disconnected. To rebalance such disturbances, one very much needs the sense of play and a connection with fantasy.

The author has come across several young children in the past few years whose parents describe them as "sexualized."

a. One was a girl of five who engaged in sex play with another girl in her class – French kissing was the practice and also pulling down each other's underwear.

b. Another was a boy of six who, with two of his friends, engaged in touching the private parts of each other. This child also admitted to having oral sex with one of the others. In exploring the roots of this further, he was asked if he or his friend had seen this activity on TV, or on the Internet, or in magazines. He said that his friend had seen it in a magazine. In both of these situations there was no apparent overexposure to sexual material in the families; however, these children were getting the information somehow.

CHAPTER 16

SEXUAL ABUSE DEFINED

Sexual abuse is most often considered to be the perpetration of a sexual act by an older person upon the body of a younger child, the intent being to provide sexual satisfaction for the perpetrator. The act is sometimes accepted willingly by the child, at other times it is resisted. Sex abuse does not necessarily involve penetration. It can mean things such as fondling a child's genitals in a manner that makes the child feel uncomfortable or having the child touch the genitals of the adult. There are occasions, of course, when it is necessary to handle a child's genitals such as when a parent changes a diaper. When a child has an infection or irritation in the genital area, it is necessary to cleanse that area in order to apply medication

Sex abuse happens to both boys and girls and can be perpetrated by older boys or girls as well as by adult men and women. Sex abuse knows no boundaries, which is why it is so pernicious in our society today. One of the more frightening facts today is the proliferation of incidents in which children have been introduced to perpetrators over the Internet, as well as by priests, school coaches, etc.

A few years ago in Switzerland this author had the opportunity to hear Alice Miller[117] lecture on the general topic of child abuse and some of her ideas will be discussed in this chapter. Alice Miller was Freudian-trained but differs from the Freudians on several themes.

1. Infantile sexuality - she sees this as a defense that is related to the child's reaction to the adult's sexual feelings towards him/her. In other words, the child is mirroring the adult's attitude and, in many cases, complying with what the child thinks that the adult wants from him or her.

117 Personal notes from Miller lecture (1987)

2. Oedipus complex - Miller believes that this theory makes the CHILD responsible for misdeeds rather than what the adult has perpetrated on them - the child is "put out in the woods to die."
3. Miller discusses all this with reference to her work on child abuse, which has become a much more critical issue than it has ever been. One case she cited was a boy called Jurgen Burtsch who was kissed and hugged one minute and beaten the next – he received totally inconsistent handling.
4. In her book, *Thou Shalt Not be Aware,*[118] Miller discusses writings from the early Victorian age and illustrates how Louis XIII was subjected to what would be considered today severe sexual abuse during the earliest years of his life. He was encouraged to show his penis to everyone in the court and much giggling and playing with it ensued by members of the court. It is appalling to consider this today.

How has this state of affairs developed? The perpetrators can be anyone – someone who is known to the child or someone who is a stranger. Many times it is a favorite relative – a dad, a mom, an older sibling, a grandparent, an uncle, an aunt, a cousin, a neighbor, a teacher, and/or as mentioned above, clergy, and the latest news (2011) reveals that several football coaches have been named as perpetrators.

The problem today has become so widespread that children need to be educated at a very early age about what rights he/she has with respect to his/her own body. Much has been written about Good Touch/Bad Touch but there is another kind that is called Secret Touch – when an older person tells the young child that the experience is "secret" and no one ever tells anything that is a secret between two people. What a dreadful situation this is for the child who really loves Dad, grandpa, or uncle. Children need to know how to protect themselves if an older person touches them in any way that makes them feel uncomfortable. They should be educated to immediately tell another responsible adult. One hopes, he/she will choose an adult who is in a position to listen and to help him/her. In some situations, however, the child is not believed and

---

118 Miller, A., 1986

is made to feel that he/she is "bad" for saying such things. How awful that must feel to a vulnerable child.

It is necessary to consider some of the other contributing factors as to why this particular child is being victimized. It is known that sex abuse happens far too often when drugs or alcohol are being used by the perpetrator. Can anyone stop drug and alcohol abuse? Of course not. The only thing that can be done is give good solid education to these young, vulnerable members of our society as to how they can best protect themselves.

Another much too common contributing factor is that sex abuse is often practiced by adults who were also abused as children, and who often came from drug-addicted or alcoholic families themselves. When the perpetrator is a stranger, one must need to consider whether or not he/she is a known offender or perhaps someone who has a psychopathic personality.

Our understanding of the dynamics of sex abuse has come a long way, but there is much more that is needed. When dealing with cases of substance abuse, sex abuse or violence it may be helpful to read a book that was recommended to this author that has been mentioned in previous chapters, *Ghosts from the Nursery: Tracing the Roots of Violence.*[119] The authors take a long, hard look at why violence is so prevalent in our society. They believe that violence is rooted far earlier in life than we had previously thought. In fact, they go so far as to suggest that the critical period (for a predisposition to violence) is during the first 33 months of life, including the nine months of uterine existence. They cite numerous studies that cover things such as the effects of drugs on the fetus that the mother may have consumed during certain critical periods of development. These are not necessarily "street drugs," but can also be prescribed medications. Interspersed with the factual material these authors present are heart-breaking anecdotal stories that they have encountered either personally, or that they have read about or seen on TV, which they later researched for this book. It is a very upsetting book to read, but a definite MUST!!

Certain symptoms that develop and that give clues to parents, teachers or professionals that sex abuse is occurring or has occurred in the past

119 Karr-Morse, R. and M. Wiley

are an obvious change in behavior, such as a child who becomes oppositional, one who becomes withdrawn, one who develops poor sleeping patterns, one who becomes clingy or whiney, one who suddenly exhibits enuresis or encopresis. Today, with more recent research, it is found that many of these children show signs of attachment disorders (discussed in Chapter 13). There are also those children who have learned to dissociate and that can later develop a multiple personality disorder. Therefore, sexual abuse is an important area for all therapists to be cognizant of.

CHAPTER 17

ASSESSMENT OF THE SEXUALLY ABUSED CHILD

First and foremost when one is asked to treat a sexually abused child is to conduct a thorough assessment of the situation consisting of such basic information as to what happened from the child's perspective, the family's perspective, etc. It is also essential to explore whether or not the case has been reported to the authorities, whether or not there has been a physical examination of the child, and the reports of other professionals who have had contact with the child/family. Additional information consisting of the child's age, developmental stage, family constellation, any unusual behaviors, school performance, peer relationships, who the perpetrator might be, and how the child's behavior has changed since the issue of sexual abuse has been revealed. The parent(s) can be interviewed first in order to get the relevant history and then the child can be included on the second session. During that next session when the child is included, the parent(s) are asked to tell the child the reason he/she is coming to see a play therapist. This is vitally important so that there can then be open communication with the child when he/she is seen in individual sessions. This also helps to reduce the issue of "family secret" because that is often the reason that sex abuse occurred in the first place.

Following these two meetings, the child is seen alone three or four times, with the understanding that after the assessment is completed, a session will be held with the entire family to develop a case plan.

On the first session with the child he/she is asked to tell the therapist what he/she remembers from the family session. This is important so that the child and the therapist are both focused on the presenting problem. Unless the entire family had been shown the play space with all the various activities that can be chosen to play with the child is introduced to the play room. The child is then told that he/she is free to use whatever toys or art materials appeal to him/her. Sometimes the choice is to draw, sometimes to use the dollhouse, at other times, to play with puppets, at still other times, he/she elects to use Sandplay. (Sandplay is this author's primary therapeutic tool.) The therapist observes what is chosen and how it is used (tentatively, aggressively, inquisitively), and asks the child some neutral questions pertaining to his/her choice. If one sees a bear looming behind a small child in the sandtray, one could ask what the child might feel when he/she sees the bear. Or, the therapist might inquire whether the bear was friendly or dangerous. These kinds of questions reveal how a child might view threatening material and begin to open him/her to verbalizing some of his/her fears.

CONCLUSION

Play Therapy is a necessary tool for anyone who treats children, no matter what the diagnostic category. This therapist has been using various techniques of play with children for over 35 years and needs to stress its effectiveness in reaching all children, not just those who have been sexually abused. Anyone who treats young children or adolescents, either individually or in families, needs to explore the many facets of this approach. Play can reach areas that are simply not available to verbal recall, and can eventually help mend the broken parts of a child's psyche.

CHAPTER 18

THE ACTING-OUT CHILD

This is a case from which this author learned a great deal, and, probably made some errors along the way. However, it is only from one's errors that one is forced to grow as a therapist and so this is presented for whatever help may be provided.

The case is that of a four-year-old girl who presented with multiple problems such as temper tantrums, poor peer relations in nursery school, and mutilation of her favorite dolls. She beheaded them and smeared lipstick all over them. She was the only child in this family. Her mother was a psychotherapist and her father was a teacher. They both had had many years of therapy and didn't want to make the child the Identified Patient, "If it's really our shit."

During the intake, it was noted that the father appeared quite depressed while the mother was possibly bulimic (she was a therapist who treated eating disorders). Both gave a somewhat odd impression, almost as if they were left over from the hippies of the '60s.

The parents reported that the child lived in fantasy and changed her identity from time to time. At that time she called herself "Rudolph the Red-Nosed Reindeer" and would get extremely angry if the other children taunted her about this. Her nursery school teachers felt that her reactions were beyond the norm. This was the extent of the information that was received on intake. Much more came later.

The first meeting with the child called 'Evelyn' was very positive. She warmed up to the therapist almost instantly. She was a very pale blond child with blue eyes and a fairy-like quality about her. She liked to play in the sand and it was noted that she often used two of everything – two Miss Piggies, two owls, several dwarves, penguins, etc. She buried many of the figures in the sand and then cleaned them in a ritualistic fashion. She seemed to show improvement during the first couple of months of treatment until one day Mom called and said that she was again decapitating her dolls. She had cut off the hair of one, and she had again experienced renewed episodes of nightmares. At school, however, she continued to improve. Evelyn and Mom came together for a session after this phone call, but nothing came to light as to what might be troubling to this child. Possible sexual abuse was explored, which the child and mother denied.

About this time, the therapist took a planned, two-week vacation that was followed by the family's vacation, so there was a lengthy break in treatment. Here is a replication of a scene that she made after the return from vacations.

Figure 18.1

She placed fences around a couple of dragons and she placed a giraffe lying down in a box. At this time, the only association that could be made was to that of a giraffe. The giraffe, with its very long neck, might indicate the unconscious wish to keep the head and the body separate – a dynamic seen in many cases of sex abuse.

During this period, she used giraffes frequently, either placing them in boxes such as this or having them lying down on beds. Reports continued to be positive other than the fact of continued nightmares; however, both Mom and Dad suffered from nightmares as well so there was not alot of concern. She reported one dream to the therapist:

> A friendly alligator was in the river. Mommy and Daddy's car overturned, and an alligator saved everybody.

She continued to focus on giraffes and brought one from home, as well as using the ones that were available in the play room. She also illustrated several dolls sleeping together in beds.

At this time, Mom requested that we stop for the summer and that the therapist should be the one to tell Evelyn. This was one major mistake. The therapist did not feel comfortable doing this, (telling the child), but somehow, given the therapist's inexperience at that time, she did so. Evelyn's reaction was one of anger and she refused to play out any possible good that could come from this. Finally, she put several items in jail, that seemed to illustrate how powerless she felt. Right before the summer break, she brought a dream wherein she said she had drowned. Mother called to say that she had reconsidered termination. Evelyn was vehement about the need to continue.

The following week a frantic call was received from Mother. She had come home early from work and found that the babysitter had drawn all over the child's body with lipstick prior to giving her a bath. This sitter had been employed since the child began nursery school in the Fall. This was the next July. The sitter was a neighbor's child and was only twelve years old. Evelyn's parents also knew that this child (the sitter) had been sexually abused and was hospitalized not too long before they hired her! One has to wonder at the lack of parental wisdom!

During the following emergency session, Evelyn was asked to show the therapist on a doll how the babysitter had used the lipstick. She denied being touched anywhere else but on the stomach. She was asked how this made her feel. She looked up and placed her hand over her chest as she replied, "It hurt my heart." This therapist nearly cried in response. The father called later and reported that the child complained of a burning pain in her genitals while she was in the bathtub so they were taking her to the doctor. A couple of days later, another frantic call came from Mom saying that she had suspected sexual abuse from the beginning and why hadn't any attention been paid to that. She decided to take the child to a "sex abuse specialist." Reasoning with Mom led nowhere. She again wanted the therapist to tell this to the child; however, she had already taken her elsewhere, unbeknownst to this therapist, for an intake. There were only two or three sessions granted to terminate the case and it ended a couple of weeks later. This left the therapist with a wide array of feelings – loss, anger, rage, insecurity about her abilities, etc., etc. The therapist reconnected with a supervisor to help sort through this. He asked if, had all this been known, would anything have been done differently. In all honesty, the process was evolving and it did feel like there was positive movement with the work that had been done. Since this therapist is non-directive, she doubted that she would have moved directly into the sex abuse material. She certainly knew that it was there and that it would evolve in its own time, however, she was not given that opportunity.

There is a follow-up to this case. About a year later a phone call was received from Mom with new information and a request that she come for a session to look at the child's sand pictures. This was precipitated by her own therapy wherein she was diagnosed as a Multiple Personality, stemming from her own childhood abuse. Her parents were involved in some sort of satanic cult and she was subjected to their machinations. The same thing had been perpetrated by the grandparents on Evelyn – ergo, the many giraffes in boxes. (Part of the ritual was being enclosed in a coffin.) Mom and the therapist closely examined Evelyn's pictures and there was a definite correlation between weekend visits to grandparents and the scenes that followed by giraffes in boxes. The mother had a court-ordered injunction against the grandparents so that they could have no more contact with Evelyn. The family then moved to the far West and nothing further was ever heard.

As was mentioned in the beginning, this case was a very deep learning experience. What was learned, primarily, was that the process needed to be honored along with this non-verbal technique. The sexual abuse issues were appearing and the therapist's intuition was activated as she had discussed with Evelyn and her mother. This was denied at the time by both of them. The therapist believed that the facts would evolve in time once the child felt fully accepted and trusting of both her and the process. She was especially disturbed at the ending of this case as she was aware how devastating it must have been to Evelyn to end so abruptly. It was devastating for the therapist as well because she struggled to regain her objectivity to an impossible situation. This therapist was also amazed that these parents, one of whom was a therapist, could entrust their child to someone with the known history of this sitter.

As a post script and mentioned above, this case became so intense that supervision was sought that helped immeasurably to get this therapist back on track. Any therapist who might have similar reactions to a difficult case should not hesitate to seek out whatever support system is available. Sandplay therapists would do well to share these deep feelings with a trusted colleague or supervisor who is familiar with this marvelous non-verbal milieu that is so much a part of our lives.

CHAPTER 19

POST-TRAUMATIC STRESS DISORDER

What exactly is "post-traumatic stress disorder?" According to the Diagnostic and Statistical Manuary-IV[120] definition (consolidated) first, the person has been exposed to a traumatic event in which the following were present:

1. The person experienced, witnessed, or was confronted with an event or events that involved actual or threatened death or serious injury, or a threat to the physical integrity of self or others.
2. The person's response involved intense fear, helplessness, or horror. In children, this may be expressed by disorganized or agitated behavior.
3. The traumatic event is persistently re-experienced in one or more of the following ways:
    a. Recurrent recollections; in young children, repetitive play may occur in which themes or aspects of the trauma are expressed.
    b. Recurrent, distressing dreams of the event, (in children there may be frightening dreams without recognizable content).
    c. Acting or feeling as if the event were recurring (includes a sense of reliving the event, illusions, hallucinations, and dissociative flashback episodes). In young children, trauma-specific re-enactment may occur.
    d. Avoidance of the stimuli associated with trauma, numbing may occur.
    e. Persistent symptoms of increased arousal that were not present before the trauma, such as problems with sleep, concentration, hypervigilance, exaggerated startle response.
    f. Duration if the disturbance is more than 1 month.

120 Diagnostic and Statistical Manual of Mental Disorders-IV

There is often a loss of words and symbols in "terror states." Positron Emission Tomography (PET[121]) scans have shown that people with Post-Traumatic Stress Disorder (PTSD), when reminders of the event are presented, had an increase in activity in the right hemisphere of the brain that is associated with emotional states and autonomic arousal[122]. This is one of the primary reasons that non-verbal methods that reach the right hemisphere of the brain are so useful in these cases.

There is also a simultaneous decrease in oxygen utilization in Broca's area that is located in the left frontal cortex and that is responsible for generating words that match internal experience. This is the area where symptoms that seem like "speechless terror" exists and leads the emotions to appear as a dysfunction of the body through psychosomatic symptoms. This is all extremely complex, as the reader can see.

Van der Kolk[123] found that when traumatic experiences are verbalized, the psychosomatic symptoms decrease. Verbalizing helps one begin to feel in control and to regain a sense of self. Negative behaviors ensue when trauma is not verbalized. Patients often express their internal state more in physical movements or in pictures than in words. Techniques such as drawing and psychodrama can help the victim to develop the necessary language (of expression). Group therapy is also beneficial because the members hear others express what they may be feeling. It helps them to put words to their experience.

For children, one of the normal developmental tasks is to learn to negotiate relationships with others. Studies of traumatized children have established that they often have serious problems in their capacity to play.[124] Traumatized children tend to be either excessively shy and withdrawn, or to bully and frighten other children. It is extremely difficult for them to be attuned to their environment because of the lack of social skills. These children have mastered the art of dissociation which makes their ability to discriminate almost non-existent. Without these skills they do not have the capacity to get comfort from others, which often

---

121 These produce 3-dimensional, color images of functional processes within the body

122 Disorder characterized by persistent or recurrent symptoms

123 Van der Kolk,,B.

124 Terr, L., 1983

points to a poor attachment history. Another finding of all the research is that persons who have had a secure attachment history are far less likely to develop PTSD.

For all traumatized individuals, they can be fixated at the stage when the trauma occurred and that makes therapy an involved task, especially for an older patient. Safe attachments, once again, are the key to resolution of trauma and safety must exist, especially in the therapeutic relationship, for healing to be possible. It must FEEL safe in order to be effective.

Trauma consists of those things that are impossible for the psyche to absorb, things such as sexual abuse, rape, or serving in combat when one fears for one's life and witnessing others' deaths is frequent. Vicarious trauma can also occur by watching TV news reporting: 9/11 and the tsunami are good examples. Internal reactions run the gamut from disbelief and horror to grief and rage. Regression can occur, especially in children, who become clingy, resume bedwetting, or cry uncontrollably.

The first 24 to 48 hours after trauma are virtually important in treatment, in order to prevent PTSD from developing. Prior to an actual PTSD diagnosis, what is usually encountered after trauma is Acute Stress Disorder. The difference in diagnosis is primarily the length of time after the occurrence and the severity of symptoms. Acute Stress is usually seen in the days immediately following an event, whereas PTSD is often not seen before six months to a year after the trauma.

When there is almost immediate contact with victims, they need to be encouraged to exercise, practice relaxation techniques, structure their time, keep busy, and talk to others about what happened. For adults, they need to be advised against the overuse of drugs or alcohol and to resume their normal schedule as quickly as possible.

One time this author was called in to a bank that had just been robbed for crisis work. The employees were visibly shaken because they had been held up at gunpoint. One of the women had been locked in the vault. This was certainly an example of "on-the-spot" assistance that allowed some processing of this incident right after it had occurred and thus alleviated some fear. Each person had time to tell his/her version of what happened and how they had been able to aid the one who had been locked up. By processing this experience so soon after it occurred, the employees were able to see that each had had an important role to play and helped to put their feelings in perspective – they had been able to feel partially in control, in spite of their fear.

Post-traumatic stress was first discovered as a disorder in soldiers after the Vietnam War when the veterans came home with symptoms such as depression, dissociation, recurring dreams, anxiety and/or substance abuse. Research was begun as a way to ascertain the causes and possible treatment for these men since there were so many of them presenting with the same symptoms.

As the research progressed, it was extended to include women who had experienced sex abuse as children. Many women displayed somatic symptoms such as irritable-bowel disorder, chronic pelvic pain, fibromyalgia, orgasmic dysfunction, dissociation, multiple-personality disorder, etc.

Another group that was discovered as suffering from post-traumatic stress symptoms was the adult children of Holocaust survivors. It appeared that they (the children) had introjected the pain of the parents, parents who had been able to submerge the trauma and showed no obvious symptoms, but their offspring did. The symptoms were often a sense of unease or anxiety from no known cause.

One woman who was treated a couple of years ago had severe anxiety symptoms. Her presenting problem was an overwhelming fear of cancer. She had had a small cyst removed from her thigh and was certain that she was about to lose a leg. It was far beyond her actual condition. Her mother, a Holocaust survivor, was still living and was apparently quite healthy at 72, but this client was obsessed with cancer fears. The author was not certain how this came to be, unless it was the symbolic cancer of the Holocaust, but it can be attributed to her deep-seated, but unrecognized, fear that must have been internalized from her mother. Instead of focusing on the mother, however, this client's fears were focused on this small cyst of her own. Nothing could reassure her. She had consulted several doctors and all assured her that this cyst was not cancerous.

Another dynamic that existed in this case was that she was completely over- involved with her daughter and her daughter's every move. They had a symbiotic or co-dependent relationship, although the daughter was then 25. Thus, instead of being concerned about her aging mother, she transferred her fears to both her possible "cancer" and her own daughter. She and her daughter communicated by cell phone at least five or six times a day. The daughter had graduated from college and was working in a different city. One or the other would call on rising, mid-morning, lunchtime, mid-afternoon, dinner, bedtime – quite excessive. This client was especially involved with her daughter's dating behavior and the daughter complied by giving her every single detail. This client was treated for over a year, but only with verbal therapy, because she was quite obsessive and "couldn't get her hands dirty" with sand or art.

Her daughter had one or two sessions when she was home visiting her parents and she, too, exhibited anxiety symptoms as well as having severe relationship problems. She was referred to a therapist in her area that she only saw a few times.

At the conclusion of this woman's therapy, her cancer fears had lessened and she and her daughter had cut down on the frequency of their contacts, but this was definitely a case of post-traumatic stress disorder.

Many times PTSD can be missed because of the multiple symptoms (anxiety, depression, substance abuse, etc.) which is why a thorough history is so important. One important finding of Bessel van Der Kolk is that when cortisol levels were examined in major depression, there was an increase in these levels (that are found in the adrenal glands), whereas in PTSD, low cortisol levels were found, so that these two conditions can seemingly cancel each other out.

As far as treatment and prevention of PTSD goes, several things must be implemented. First, there is verbal psychotherapy during which one faces the memory rather than fleeing from it. The survivor must give him/herself permission to "feel the feelings" and to be reassured that the strength of these feelings will decrease in time. They must also be urged to rest, to eat (even if they don't want to), and to learn deep breathing techniques. This condition can be treated like anxiety, through desensitization or cognitive therapy that is designed to counteract the negative belief system; EMDR (Eye Movement Desensitization Response) has been especially useful in cases of PTSD. In this method, the patient/client is instructed to visualize the images related to the trauma and to replace negative thoughts with positive ones, which helps one find an acceptable response to the trauma.

The biggest problem with most of the research that has been done is that the research is time-limited and most people are not cured in 10 or 15 sessions. This is the case with the combat veterans on which much of the research has been conducted. Various medications have been used; some are helpful, some not.

The most important thing to consider when treating any form of trauma is that the survivor needs to feel in control, as in the bank robbery described above, no matter what form the treatment takes.

When the victim is a child, it is essential to talk to them, assure them of their physical safety, limit their TV viewing (example of 9/11). Children under eleven are most at risk, because by age eleven there is more intellectual understanding. Parents must be aware of behavior changes, and especially any nighttime fears. Children may develop an intense startle response, be afraid of wind, rain, storms. They may regress and refuse to attend school, develop headaches, stomach aches, vomiting, or develop a fever. Things that can help children are activities such as drawing, painting, writing a story of the event, using clay, Play Doh, making music, using puppets – really any technique that can help a child process the experience, both non-verbally and verbally.

When called upon for crisis intervention, the important aspects are:

1. Immediacy – how long ago did this happen?
2. Proximity – how near was the person to the event?
3. Expectancy – how life-threatening was it?
4. Brevity – how can the effects be shortened?

The goals are:

1. Stabilization – as quickly as possible.
2. Mitigation of acute signs and symptoms of distress.
3. Restoration of adaptive independent functioning or facilitation of access to a higher level of care.

Five basic principles:

1. Intervene immediately.
2. Stabilize.
3. Facilitate understanding.
4. Focus on problem-solving.
5. Encourage self-reliance to the extent that the child can begin to function as he/she did before the trauma.

This is a very brief description of a very complex diagnosis that requires further study than what is presented here. Further Information can be found in the bibliography.

PART III

FAMILY/CULTURAL/SPIRITUALITY

CHAPTER 20

FAMILY SANDPLAY THERAPY

Presented at the Center for Sandplay Studies-1989, 1995

This technique combines family therapy and play therapy with the addition of sand. The reader will be given a brief history of these two methods before proceeding to family sandplay therapy.

Family Therapy goes back at least 100 years and had its beginning when pastors visited their flock. Many issues were uncovered during those visits such as illness in one family member or another, an impending death or separation, or extended family concerns. It was about that time that community centers were founded such as the Young Men's Christian Association (YMCA). As time progressed, various "schools" of Family Therapy were explored with different therapists associated with different schools. Some of these later became known as:

1. Structural (Minuchin) – focus was on how power was assigned in the family.
2. Strategic (Palo-Alto group) – focused on strategies that were employed to keep the "status quo" in the family.
3. Behaviorists (Skinner) – focused on what behaviors needed to be addressed.
4. Communicationists (Satir) – focused on how family members communicated (non-verbally; over-verbal; aggressive, etc.).

Play Therapy began around the same time, but it was not formalized until later –around the 1920s. The founders are discussed elsewhere in this book. However, various "schools" of play therapy were also developed such as:

1. Child-centered/non-directive (Satir[125], Landreth[126]) – the entire therapy revolves around the child's actions and wishes.
2. Directive (Schaefer[127]) – the therapist is in charge and directs the session depending on the dynamics of the case.
3. Object relations (Scharff, J. S.[128]) – best understood in the context of the family.
4. Jungian (Kalff[129], Jung[130]) – based on the theories of Jung and Kalff.

There are other "schools" such as Gestalt, Behavioral, etc., but those listed are more well-known.

"Family Sandplay Therapy"[131] was a seminal article that effectively combined the techniques of sandplay and family therapy. This chapter demonstrates how sand can be an effective, healing milieu with families and stresses the differences of approach when one uses sand with an individual or with a family.

Sandplay, as a Jungian technique, was spread primarily through the work of Dora Kalff, a Swiss Jungian analyst as discussed in Chapters 3 and 5. The focus in Kalff's work was on the individual child and his/her journey to wholeness.

When a child is the Identified Patient who shows symptoms after a family breakup or a death in the family or for any other cause, more and more therapists are finding that it is beneficial to include the family in the child's treatment so a Family Therapy method is used.

Family Therapy views the family as the "Identified Patient" and is designed to improve communication and respect among the family members in order that the family can reach a more optimal level of functioning.

---

125 Satir, V.
126 Landreth, G.
127 Schaefer, C., 1993
128 Scharff, J. S.
129 Kalff, D. M., 1980
130 Jung, C.G., 1959, 1969
131 Carey, L., 1991

When a sandplay therapist is consulted for treatment, a full examination of the presenting problem is held and a decision is made whether the case is best treated with the individual child or with the family. When the decision is to treat the family, they are asked to first make a genogram (see Chapter 21) for assessment purposes. The sandplay therapist can quickly see some of the family dynamics just by observing how the family pursues this task. For example:

1. Is the family cooperative or argumentative?
2. Does one person overrule the others?
3. Do they talk or do they work silently?
4. Does everyone participate or does someone stay in the background?

The answers to some of these questions can be apparent to the family members as well as to the therapist. Some families can see almost immediately what needs to change in order for their relationships to be strengthened. In other families, the needs are not so apparent and the therapist, by keeping his/her remarks in the metaphor of the tray, can influence the family to move in a more positive direction. For example, he/she may suggest that the family give individual associations to the animals used. One may say that an elephant is helpful, another may find the elephant as aggressive.

The major problem for play therapists is that they are not always comfortable with the families of their young patients and, conversely, family therapists are not always comfortable with either play or young children.

It is widely believed that for some families, Sandplay Therapy can be more effective than verbal therapy just by virtue of the tactile nature of the medium.[132] This brings to mind the old adage that "a picture is worth a thousand words." Additionally, recent brain studies by Van der Kolk,[133] Siegel,[134] and others, have demonstrated that many nonverbal therapies such as art, drama, and Neuro-Linguistic Programming

132 Personal notes, D. Kalff workshop, 1986
133 Van Der Kolk, B., 2002
134 Siegel, D., 1999

(NLP), can tap into the area of the right brain (where symbol formation is located) and thus reach a deeper level more quickly than with verbal therapies alone. This theory would extend to Sandplay Therapy also because positive results are much more attainable in less time than when words and reasoning are used as the primary method.

Sandplay and family therapy, when combined, offer a variety of possibilities for further study.[135]" Some of these are:

1. Because of the dimensions of the sandbox, limits are both physically and symbolically set. This can provide a containment for families where boundaries are a problem. Members can learn to particularize their own dilemma while, at the same time, learn a new way to accomplish integration and communication.
2. Family alliances can be observed by the therapist through the choices made, such as who chooses to work with whom, which miniatures are selected and by whom, and so forth. These choices can offer an opportunity to intervene by re-structuring destructive alliances into healthier ones and can thus provide a more objective view to the family.
3. Unconscious contents are rapidly revealed to the therapist as well as the family and make it possible to discuss some of the patterns as they emerge. In this way, more conscious choices are suggested and can be implemented within the therapy.
4. Sandplay appeals to the children in a family and offers reparative work to the "inner child" of each parent as well.
5. The uniqueness of each family can be revealed in the sense of the family as a life force as these are seen in each individual as well as in the family unit."

Needless to say, this author is a firm believer in the possibilities inherent in a Family Sandplay Therapy approach and something that should be a part of every sandplay therapist's repertoire.

135 Carey, L., 1991

CHAPTER 21

FAMILY GENOGRAMS IN PLAY THERAPY

Family therapists frequently do not include young children in family therapy and are thus excluding a most important part of the family. In addition, many family therapists are uncomfortable with "play," an essential component in work with children in a family. A genogram[133] is a familiar technique for family therapists and can help ease the transition from an adult treatment approach (verbal) to one that includes an attitude of "play" for all family members, young and old alike. It has been found that play is the language of children and when families can see the value of communicating with their children in this symbolic way, significant improvements are possible. When one makes a genogram "come alive" through the use of objects, it may be possible to see, depending on placement and type of objects used, who may be the scapegoat, who is the identified patient, who is the leader, who is the controller, who is the follower, is there a "family secret," are there alliances, etc. A wealth of information about the family may be revealed through the use of the genogram, combined with three-dimensional objects. It is also important to notice who may have been left out and ask the maker why that person(s) is/are not included. This is especially helpful if the case is one of death or divorce or in step-families. This technique is suitable to diverse types of cases – families that are intact, single parent, homosexual/ Lesbian, death or divorce, sex abuse, ADHD, depression, and many others. This technique can be used not only for assessment, but also during the treatment process by addressing the problems that have been revealed by the genogram.

The purpose of the genogram is to engage the family while, at the same time, assessing the problem.

133 McGoldrick, M. and R. Gerson, 1985

There are several goals that are important:

a. Include the young children in family therapy (the youngest this therapist had ever had was 5 days – an early delivery and a surprise for her).

b. To understand the family dynamics.

c. To observe the communication patterns in the family.

The necessary materials to have on hand are drawing paper, crayons, markers, air drying clay, miniature animals (if available), puppets (if available), natural objects (shells, rocks, acorns, etc.).

It is important that the therapist "set the stage" before the family arrives such as,

a. Provide a large table for work space.

b. Provide supplies on the table.

c. Miniatures need to be available for making the family genogram.

d. Set up an example of a genogram that covers three generations.

When the family is present, explain the use of genograms to the family, using the example that has been arranged previously. Tell the family that it will be useful for them to see themselves and each other in relation to the others and will also help the therapist to understand what some of the underlying problems may be. Describe what they will do.

"First, I would like each one of you to show me what your family is like compared to the one I illustrated for you. I have laid out a large piece of paper and I will ask you to draw the family – squares are for males, circles for females. You can put the age of the person on the symbol, if known. Please include all of the children, the parents, and grandparents; and any other significant relatives (aunts/uncles/cousins). The whole family can contribute to the making of the genogram. After the genogram is drawn, I would like you to think about each member and then select an object from those that are available and place it on the genogram where that person is shown. It is important that the maker select an object for him/herself as well."

NOTE: Depending on the size of the family (more than three or four), it is possible that each one of them have a separate piece of paper (in the interest of time). When the large one (or the individual ones) is/are complete, the therapist will ask questions such as:

- "Why does so and so remind you of that figure/animal/etc?"
- "Did you learn any new information about your family?"
- "What made you the most curious?"
- "How did you feel when you described your choices?"
- "Where do you see the strengths in the family?"
- "What do you think needs to be changed?"

Following the question period, the family can use the chosen objects and make a scene with them. If sand is used, the scene can be portrayed in the sand tray. If not, it can be shown on another large-sized, clean piece of paper as a base. It does not matter whether the scene is made in sand or on a piece of paper, but it is important that each family member tell a story about what has been portrayed. The therapist can give a simple instruction such as, "Now I will ask that the family make up a story of what you see in the tray. The important thing is that only one person speaks at a time; otherwise, I won't be able to comment." After the story is completed, the therapist can add his/her comments to what has been produced and said.

This sounds like a lot of material to cover, but once this technique has been used, it becomes easier each time.

CHAPTER 22[134]

PUPPETRY IN FAMILY THERAPY[135]

The use of puppets in therapy provides an approach to which many families easily respond. Puppets offer a way to break down resistance and are especially helpful in cases of sex abuse or where there is a history of domestic violence. Anatomical puppets (for sex abuse cases) make it much easier for children to reveal the trauma. Puppets are also helpful in physical abuse cases because the child can learn that other parents treat their children differently from how he/she has been treated. In cases of domestic violence, puppets can tell the story far more easily than through verbal means. Denial, as a defense mechanism, is very easily broken through when puppets are used, because then the puppet is in denial, not the person. Puppets are also productive with the verbally deficient; sometimes selective mutes or stutterers will talk through puppets.

Advantages of Puppets

Puppets are useful with any theoretical approach. They are active and immediately engage the person (or family) verbally and physically. Puppets can be of great help in externalizing an internal conflict, for example in describing things like nightmares, internalized anger and/or fears of abandonment. These conflicts can be revealed through various parts of the puppet story. "The puppet is angry, not me." The puppets provide a bridge between fantasy and reality.

The child's (or family's) emotions can be owned or disowned onto the puppet, although it is a very thin line and one must be very careful

---

134 Presented by Ruby Koppelman at Center for Sandplay Studies, Nov. 1997

135 Personal notes; Diane Frey, Ph.D. and Ruby Koppelman, MA., ATR

to observe the limits. Puppets can help to verbalize thoughts and feelings and teach coping strategies.

Puppets offer an opportunity to master a situation: it is the actor who creates the scenario while the child can generate new and different solutions. A puppet is, after all, only a head and a costume to a child.

When puppets are compared with other media, they are not as flexible as clay, not as structured as dolls, not as ambiguous as art. They do, however, have shape, form and other attributes. They are often useful in the early stages of therapy for rapport-building.

Puppets are extremely useful in family therapy play; they make it possible to dialog with the child. Children tend to replay themes throughout any form of play therapy, including with puppets. There may be times when it is helpful to videotape the action, especially in family therapy, and later play it back. This is a most effective and poignant way to communicate with parents.

Another interesting aside is that when a child (or adult) is prepared with puppets for a medical procedure, research has shown that recovery time is improved.

Puppet Advantages over Dolls

There appears to be more of a possibility of transference onto puppets than dolls, as well as more identification. Puppets have a diversity of movement, many dolls are not as flexible. It is possible to make one's own puppets using either styrofoam balls or pet balls with holes cut in the bottom into which pop sticks can be inserted. They can then be personalized with facial expressions and dress, yet, at the same time, maintain anonymity.

Uses in Family Therapy

1. Provides the ability for all members to express inappropriate, unwanted thoughts and feelings through the puppets.
2. Can be used between two conflicted individuals or with an entire family system.

3. It is often helpful to discuss how and why each person selected his/her specific puppet.
4. Projection can be utilized quite effectively.
5. Families often accept puppets more easily than art or sand as they are more commonly known to the general public.

Irwin and Malloy[136] have worked with puppets for many years. They tell families that they are to make up a TV play that is to be a made-up story, not one that the family has heard, seen, or read. Each member then selects one or two puppets to use in their dialog. Through watching the family process, some insight is gained, such as who is the organizer, who dominates, who is the scapegoat, the victim or the pacifier. Much is learned about the family style in just this way and in a much shorter time than is possible with verbal therapy.

When a family appears to be "stuck" and not able to move, one can ask if they would like to try puppets. After making their selections, each family member introduces him or herself through the puppet. If the family is hesitant about how to start, the therapist may say something like, "Let's see what happens in the opening scene, where does it take place, who is there, what time of day is it, and what is going to happen."

One needs to be quite specific that the puppets do not TELL the therapist, but that they SHOW him/her. Then, the action can be continued by talking directly to the puppet. After the story is concluded, time is spent for each person to associate to the story. For example, each one might think of a title, a theme, which character was liked, which one was not liked, why they chose the puppets that they did.

This method is a very sound technique for families where communication is difficult. It is also effective for highly organized, rigid, intellectualized families.

Patricia Ross[137] uses puppets in pairs, quite often mother and child, which is very helpful with single-parent families. Her instructions are to show her a recent event using the puppets. Some mothers are quite resistant and need reassurance that many families feel this way about using

136 Irwin, E. & E. Malloy, 1994

137 Ross, P, 1994

puppets in the beginning. If puppets are too strongly resisted, one does not insist on continuing because strong resistance is always there for a reason. (In Ross's method, the therapist is only the observer or the audience and does not take part in the action as in some other methods.) After the pair has completed the scene, the therapist can ask that they reverse roles - child plays mother, mother plays child. The final step is to resume the original roles and to reenact the scene as each one would have WISHED that they had acted or spoken.

What is seen using these methods is the PROCESS of Family Play Therapy. While the content is certainly important as well, it is the process that sets the stage for healing. Sometimes, one can observe subgroups forming: all the females, or all the children, or one child with one parent. The therapist can also observe the patterns of interacting, particularly the verbal and non-verbal exchanges.

One stumbling block in using puppets according to Gil[138] is the clinician's hesitancy to engage the families in puppet work, probably because of their own discomfort with the use of play. Gil believes that clinicians often stifle their own creative energies, as well as their capacity to have fun and communicate through symbols rather than words. "Asking questions can help the clinician to better understand the story's potential meaning; and once clinicians allow themselves opportunities to practice this technique, they will feel more comfortable to hypothesize regarding the meaning inherent in puppet selection, themes, and interactions within the story.[139]"

Uses with Chronic Psychiatric Populations[140]

Ruby Koppelman used puppetry with chronic schizophrenics and found that puppets helped to expand the patients' expressive responses, initiated creative thinking and improved interpersonal relationships. Clients who usually had no impetus to interact with others were thrown into situations where they could make social contact, puppet to puppet.

138 Gil, E., 1994

139 Gil, E., 1994

140 Koppelman, Ruby, The Arts in Psychotherapy, Vol. 11, pp. 283-288, 1984

Puppetry allows many of the creative arts to be used together: art and drama, music and creative movement, all are used in making a puppet show.

Koppelman developed a program where she taught clients to make puppets and then use them to create a drama. Changes were seen through the colors used when the heads were painted, or the materials that were chosen for the clothing. Koppelman used Celluclay to make the heads; later clients were introduced to paints. Clients who maintained strong controls while sculpting a head might obliterate or exaggerate those features with the application of paint. Applying color to the head was exciting and stimulating, but it also produced anxiety for many of the clients.

Once the puppet was made, the next step was to enable it to reach its full potential by giving it "life" in a scenario. Koppelman taught the clients how to make use of hands and arms to portray various emotions.

She believed there was an important difference between using a table and using a stage for puppet plays and skits. Tables involve direct confrontation between participants, as both the puppet and its manipulator are visible. Stages offer more protection and provide clients with greater freedom to express his/her feelings through the puppet's character. Koppelman moved from single puppet scenes to those that allowed for two or three puppeteers which added to the client's socialization skills.

Puppets are projective representations and the puppet is used as a kind of alter ego, expressing himself/herself in ways that he/she usually does not do. The puppeteer is protected and unseen behind the puppet "stage." Koppelman found that timid clients allowed their puppets to express affection, anger or rebellion, even without words. Those clients who were more non-verbal sometimes began to converse through their puppets.

Most clients tend to identify with any puppet character they use, but especially with puppets that they themselves have made. The puppets embody their makers' feelings of strangeness, alienation, and grotesqueness through their id, ego and superego representations.

The possibilities are endless when one chooses to use puppets. This method is especially useful if one has the time and materials available for the client to make his/her own puppets. This method is extremely useful when incorporated into a therapy group, whether it is with a chronic schizophrenic population or with a higher-functioning client group.

Other Group Uses

Puppets are a tremendous asset in certain types of groups, for example, groups of abused women and their children, possibly in shelter situations. They are also useful for groups when families are being reunited; for adoptive parents, etc. Perhaps the reader might think of even more uses.

CHAPTER 23

ONE FAMILY'S SANDPLAY JOURNEY

Early Parental Loss and Multiple Diagnoses[141]

The family discussed in this case was presented to the 2000 conference of the California Network. This was a case that the author had been involved with for a number of years and covered various developmental stages of the two children involved.

The case began with the cancer death of the father who left his wife, that I will call Melinda, and two young children - a daughter, called Sally, who had just turned three years of age and a ten-month old son that will be called Johnny. Some other relevant family history was disclosed at intake as well.

The father had suffered from Hodgkin's Disease as an adolescent, been treated, and eventually recovered. Research demonstrates, however, that adolescent sufferers of this disease often develop cancer in their adult years. This was the situation for this young man because he developed cancer throughout his system, probably around the time that Sally was born. He underwent numerous hospitalizations, surgeries and chemotherapy. The mother of these children, at age ten, had been badly scarred by a fire. She had been making something on the stove and she splashed an enormous amount of grease over her body. In addition, she had been molested by her grandfather before then. The scars from the burns were quite visible on her face, arms. and legs.

Shortly after Dad's death, Sally, just three years old, began to experience severe nightmares, regressed to diapers and asked for a bottle. She also began to bite her classmates in nursery school. Her situation was compounded by the fact that children often regress to an earlier stage when a new sibling enters the family. Her mother had contacted several

141 Presented by L. Carey to the California Network, March 2000

other therapists before she called this one. They all advised her that they would treat her, the mother, in order to help the child, but that they would not see such a young child. This therapist told her honestly that she did not have experience with a child that young, but that she was willing to try as long as that was agreeable to her.

Family sessions were begun first with mother and child and later moved to individual sandplay therapy with Sally. The reason for starting with Sally and her mother was because of Sally's severe Separation Anxiety which was quite understandable, given her age and the trauma of her father's death. Children of this age have no intellectual understanding of death and, as has been proven, grieve differently and at different times than adults do.

Sally was attending nursery school and after her father's death tried to talk about it in school, but was forbidden to by the staff, because "it might upset the other children." On Open School night, she had dictated a poem to her mother about her loss that was to be posted for all the parents to view. She was not allowed to put her story up with the others. The mother immediately found another nursery school (with the therapist's help) that was the exact opposite experience for her, one that was nurturing and supportive and allowed her to grieve when she needed to. Sally's treatment lasted for approximately three years and her slides clearly illustrated Neumann's stages of development - her beginning chaotic state, the conflict, and the ultimate acceptance of her loss. Dora Kalff's theory regarding the Constellation of the Self was also depicted. She experienced severe rage reactions that were eventually demonstrated in her play. She used dinosaurs to express the rage and, at the therapist's suggestion, fed and toileted them to keep the rage contained. In addition, she routinely included her father and God as part of the play. She expressed her anger at Dad for dying and at God for taking him away. She also began to express other fears of death - her mother, her grandmother, herself. One night when her mother went to the movies with a relative, Sally stayed up until midnight when her mother returned home.

Mother was treated by another therapist during this time for her own mourning issues, in addition to those sessions when she was included in Sally's treatment.

Sally experienced another VERY difficult period around her birthday as she and her father had shared the same birthday. In essence, she had to understand and to separate for herself that it was Daddy who died and not she.

After approximately eight or nine months, Sally produced a very intricate burial scene. It consisted primarily of shells that were lying on top of other shells. She described it by saying that the shells were covering people who had died and the top shells were their souls in heaven. This type of comment never ceases to amaze - that a child of four could have this kind of spiritual conception.[142]

Sally continued to produce sand scenes, but she eventually tired of that and began to ask to hold her sessions in the "big" room. Many sessions were spent there where games were played, stories were told and illustrations were drawn. Her favorite story was "Cinderella" and it had to be enacted every single week using dolls that were in the office. Then, as part of the story, she would draw the characters and make changes of clothes for them.

Sally's therapy continued for a total of almost three years when there was an appropriately-timed termination, although a tearful one, when considering all that she had experienced during those years.

Johnny, the baby in the family, was another story. During the time that Sally was being treated, Mom often brought Johnny along. He did not seem to be developing normally and when Mom discussed it with this therapist, it was recommended that he be tested. He was three at that time. The test results indicated that Johnny had speech and language problems, including echolalia, and was developmentally delayed. He entered a therapeutic nursery at that time. Later there were additional diagnoses of Obsessive/Compulsive Disorder, ADHD, Tourette's Syndrome, possible Seizure Disorder, and Learning Disabilities. He also experienced numerous allergies and many phobias. That pretty much covers the gamut of his diagnoses. He was placed on varying combinations of drugs - some agreed with him, others did not. Mom asked me to treat this boy when he was in a special-ed kindergarten and this was continued for a number of years. He seemed to be doing much better

142 See Fig. 24.2 on p. 183

in a 7th grade contained classroom although what the future might hold for him was a question.

The problems were legion with this child. He suffered from many phobias, severe learning problems, difficulties with peers, extended family problems, separation issues, sleep disorder, etc. He also had numerous adverse drug reactions. The paternal grandparents were particularly difficult with regard to Johnny because they overtly rejected him in favor of Sally. This was related to his mother because she refused for a long time to apprise them about all of his problems. For several years, all that they were aware of was that this was a child who didn't appear "normal" like their other grandchildren. He was an attractive child but there was no eye contact whatever and much of his behavior was bizarre. He continually chewed on his shirt, had numerous tics and his head was usually on his chest. Many of those symptoms did improve during the time that he was treated.

When Melinda first brought Johnny for therapy at age five-and-a-half, his speech was extremely difficult to understand so it seemed that Sandplay could be an effective way for him to communicate. However, the therapist was unaware at that time of the Obsessive/Compulsive (OCD) diagnosis. This OCD included his refusal to touch his penis when he had to urinate. He had numerous accidents because he could not control the flow. He continually left a mess in the bathroom that he refused to clean up. His mother had her own issues around obsessiveness and his refusal to urinate in a way that directed the flow made her most irate.

When Johnny first came to therapy he wanted to use Sandplay, but it was immediately apparent that this would prove almost impossible for him at that time. He had an aversion to even touching the sand. If he accidentally touched it, he immediately would scrunch up his face and violently try to brush it off of his hands. Instead, he preferred to build scenes on top of the box, which he did for some time. Much later he moved to the use of dry sand and, eventually accepted and used wet sand effectively.

One comment that is needed is how excruciating it was to watch when he finally did build some scenes. He could never get things to perform the way he wanted them to and he would struggle and struggle until he got it "right." He was allowed to struggle, yet he knew when it got too difficult for him that help would be there and he occasionally did take advantage of that, but only after he had given it a valiant try.

Johnny's treatment was primarily child-centered because he desperately needed his own space as he struggled to reach a better level of functioning. By now, Sally had become a top-notch student and Johnny felt his inadequacies intensely. The times that his mother was included in his sessions were those occasions when there was a major incident that she needed to address with him, such as when her own parents divorced or when there was some sort of incident on the school bus or with a friend at school. He constantly asked her about why they didn't have a Daddy, couldn't she get him one, and why not. She really felt that she had run out of things to tell him. He, like his sister, went through the Neumann and Kalff stages of development. He was continued in treatment on a supportive basis until all felt (Johnny, Mother and therapist) that he needed to see a male therapist as he approached adolescence.

The mother of these children was included in various ways throughout the children's treatment. In the early stages, as mentioned earlier, she was involved in verbal therapy with her own therapist. However, when she took part in either of the children's sessions, she was an active play participant.

The normal stages of grief resolution were accomplished with Melinda, but because she was only 33 when she was widowed, she had very much hoped that she would find another mate. This never happened during the time that this family was treated. She went to a number of singles events where she was either the youngest person present or else she would be overlooked. Also mentioned earlier was the fact that she was badly scarred from the early fire and does not present an outward appearance that would attract male attention. She was quite intelligent, however, but the men she met did not seem to be interested in that aspect of her personality. She dated no more than three times that this therapist was aware of. One person with whom she felt she could have had a relationship was discontinued because he was of a different religious faith and that was unacceptable to her. Another disturbing factor for this mother and the children has been numerous ongoing physical problems. Melinda has rheumatoid arthritis and has had knee surgery twice from a fall she had taken at a company party. She also had a hysterectomy, cystic breast disease, asthma attacks, etc. Each of these incidents caused the children a tremendous amount of fear because she was, in fact, their only parent. Her major ally was her own mother who was able to fill in when the need arose. She has two sisters but they each have families and responsibilities of their own.

A series of Nannies were engaged when these children were younger. Not one of them met Melinda's expectations and each lasted for short periods of time. Each departure renewed the separation fears, particularly of Johnny. This mother has worked sporadically since Johnny was about four, but his needs, combined with her own physical problems took precedence. She left several jobs as she felt that things ran more smoothly at home when she was present.

This case, with all its complexities, was also one of great learning. It necessitated learning about the different medications as they were tried, as well as some of the side effects. The various diagnostic categories that were applied were studied and a deeper understanding of many issues was achieved. Sally was immediately adored. She brought up the therapist's own bereft inner child, the child who had lost her father through divorce. With Johnny, the therapist's "Great Mother" issues predominated. The struggle with him was how to connect emotionally with this multi-diagnosed child. Many times, the therapist was plagued with the thought that she didn't know enough, she needed to do more, etc. He brought up a major savior complex. With these children's mother, the therapist had to help her become less rigid in some of her expectations while supporting her through numerous traumas. She was empathized with fully and it was discussed how very difficult this situation must be for her - to parent two children effectively, each one having different needs. Her determination was valued as she got the best services possible for both of these children. She went to great lengths and great expense of emotional (and physical) energies to obtain the proper services for Johnny. She frequently had to fight school personnel and state agencies in order to achieve this. Earlier, she had fought to obtain the best nursery school situation for Sally.

There came a time that Johnny's mother decided to take him off of all medications in order to see "what the real boy is like." This decision was precipitated by the fact that he experienced seizures that seemed to be epileptic in nature and that could have been related to medications that he was taking at that time. He was hospitalized for numerous tests and nothing was revealed. With the cessation of medication, there was an outstanding transformation in him. In order to confirm her own intuition, Melinda arranged that Johnny be re-tested. A full-scale battery of educational and emotional testing was performed. From an I.Q. of 72, in April 1994, he tested at 96 in May 1999. His tics continued for a couple of months after the cessation of medication, but became quite minor most of the time. Eye contact that was always avoided by this boy was still evident at times, but it was no longer a significant problem.

In Junior High, Johnny was mainstreamed in a couple of minor subjects. He truly became a different child. Whether this was due solely to the absence of medications, the school program or therapy is anyone's guess. It is rather suspected that it was all of the above along with a very intelligent mother who went to great lengths to get both of her children the help that they needed.

CHAPTER 24

DEATH OF A GRANDPARENT OR A PARENT[143]

1. Introduction

This chapter will focus on the use of Sandplay in treating young children (under eight) who have experienced the death of a grandparent or a parent. For many children, the loss of a grandparent or a pet is their first experience of death and, for some, this can be a very traumatic experience. Other children experience death through the loss of a parent. In either case, the child's age and the reactions of other family members are significant as to his/her overall understanding and eventual resolution of such an event.

Children under the age of seven or eight have not yet developed a mature understanding of death because they are in the Preoperational Stage of Development, as described in the theories of Piaget.[144] This is the stage where fantasy is paramount and children view death as temporary. They have seen countless cartoons and videos where the superhero returns to life after death and have thus gained an unrealistic understanding of the true meaning of death. This type of fantasy can confuse a child when an actual death occurs in a family.

The death of a grandparent is often the first loss encountered by a child so the reactions of those around him are paramount. Children look to their elders to understand what this loss is evoking in other family members. This helps the child to either express or repress his/her own feelings. Too many times the child's emotions are discounted when a survivor remarks, "He/she is too young to understand."

One such incident was observed with a child of five. Her mother's grandmother (her great-grandmother) and her mother's mother (the

143 Excerpted from Webb, N.B., 2010

144 Piaget, J. and B. Inhelder

child's grandmother) had both died within six months of each other. This double loss had caused a severe depression in the child's mother that left her unable to fully attend to her child's needs. To complicate matters even further, within a year the mother's only brother (the child's uncle) died at a very early age. The five-year-old child felt completely helpless. She commented during the uncle's funeral, "I think my mother is the saddest one here." Her other grandmother, who recognized the child's unspoken grief, held her tightly to give her whatever support was possible. Later that day, she and the child talked about how very sad she (the child) was.

Children who are as young as one year of age experience loss in ways that can undermine their coping capacities and retard their overall development. This was studied many years ago by John Bowlby[145] who found that infants, when separated from their mothers, suffered what he identified as "anaclitic depression." Further studies led to efforts to help these children; the reader is referred to that early work for a fuller description.

Sandplay has an innate appeal for all children (Kalff, 1981; Lowenfeld; Carey, 1999) because while the scene is being constructed it can be totally non-verbal. Once the scene has been constructed, the child usually tells a story about what has been created and evoked. This verbalization allows the child to relate his/her concern through the story's use of metaphor. Metaphor is the technique that allows the child to reveal feelings in a disguised form. For example, a child of four or five might say, when he/she relates a story about a bear, "the bear has gone away, but it will come back later." This kind of statement is age-appropriate (for a four-year-old) because the child is firmly convinced that the dead person will return.

The young child of today can be further confused about death when he/she sees characterized figures continuing their superhuman activities even though they are supposedly "dead." Cartoons achieve somewhat similar goals. The author remembers seeing movie cartoons of "Daffy Duck" and "Tweetums" when she was a young child. They were caught, thrashed and sometimes killed, yet somehow got the last laugh on their abusers by the end of the episode.

145 Bowlby, J., 1969

II. Sandplay Therapy – discussed in Chapter 3

III. Sandplay Equipment – also included in Chapter 3

However, it is important to note that each therapist's collection is unique, and reflects his/her interests and experiences. Mrs. Kalff always stressed (personal notes 1980) that a therapist should never have any item in his/her collection that he/she has no relation to, otherwise the item is just an item and, as such, is useless. The personal meaning of each item is where the healing potential lies. For example, the author has a coffin and several headstones because she often sees children where loss is an issue.

IV. Process

When individual therapy with the child begins, the instructions are kept simple. First, he/she is encouraged to feel the sand in both boxes in order to decide which one he/she wants to use. The therapist then says, "Please select as many objects as you would like and make a scene in the sand." Children under four or five will often take an inordinate number of figures at the first session and then will become more selective after the third or fourth session. A child is told that he/she will know when the scene feels complete and then a picture of the scene will be taken. On completion of the scene the child is asked to tell a story about what has transpired.

One of the guidelines that is discussed with the parent and the child during the intake session includes the reason for pictures (record keeping as well as possible future use in a publication). The parent is asked to sign a permission statement that covers the possibility of future use of the pictures in an article or a book. (See Appendix) Confidentiality issues are also discussed at that time and the child is the one to decide if and when he/she wants the surviving parent to view the scene. There is a great deal more than these few remarks can provide that is involved in

Sandplay, so I would refer the reader to several other sources. (Kalff;[146] Carey;[147] Bradway[148])

V. Age of Child when Death Occurs

Any death of a significant figure is usually traumatic for a child and, as noted earlier, is affected by the age of the child when the loss occurs. Children under the age of eight or nine have very limited understanding of death, and a major loss during this time can cause a great deal of confusion for the child and his/her caretakers. Children from two to seven do not have the reasoning power that they develop during a later developmental stage. Fantasy predominates at these early ages and the child may believe that the person is simply away and will return. For this reason, it is helpful that the surviving relatives understand mourning stages for variously aged children so that they do not expect more than is possible for either a toddler or a teenager.

VI. Typical Mourning Behaviors of the Young Child (under eight)

1. The child may cry sporadically and then go back to play with their friends.
2. There may be complaints of stomach aches or headaches from no known cause.
3. They may regress to an earlier stage of development.
4. Quiet, well-behaved children can become aggressive and outspoken.
5. Aggressive children may begin to withdraw.
6. Children have great difficulty in telling their friends what has happened because they fear that they will be seen as "different." Friends, also, are often at a loss as to what to say to the child, and may withdraw and no longer want to play.

146 Kalff, D., 1980
147 Carey, L., 1999
148 Bradway, K., et al

Any of these behavioral changes are clues for the survivors or the child's teachers that the child might benefit from therapy.

VII. History Taking

When one is consulted about a child's treatment after loss, it is important to obtain a thorough history, including the period prior to the death. Dr. Nancy Boyd Webb,[149] in the first volume of *Helping Bereaved Children*, developed the Tri-Partite Assessment of the Bereaved Child (pp. 29-42), which is invaluable to the practitioner in helping these children. Briefly, to sum up the critical issues, one needs to explore the cause of death: if the death was expected, sudden, accidental, a suicide, a drug overdose or a community disaster such as 9/11, a school shooting, an earthquake, a cyclone, etc.

Every child deserves to know the details of the death and these must be presented according to the child's age and ability to understand. The details cannot be minimized because the child's questions will continue to come until he/she can make sense of it. The details cannot be ignored or glossed over because, if they are, these issues will surface later and may be more difficult to resolve because of the earlier confusion. As is common to all mental health issues, early intervention is the optimal time for treatment to ensue.

VIII. Genograms in the Sand – Please see Chapter 21

IX. Benefits of Sandplay for Children Suffering a Loss

What are the benefits of using Sandplay with a bereaved child?

1. A child can be readily engaged with this method that has shown positive outcomes for many children who have lost a close relative. (Carey, 1990)

2. The younger the child, the more difficult it is for him/her to verbalize feelings. The feelings can be illustrated instead, through the

149 Webb, N.B., 1993

construction of a sand picture and the storytelling about the scene that follows. This is especially true for the developmentally delayed child or a child who is on the Autistic Spectrum.

3. For a child who has witnessed the funeral and burial, he/she has the ability to replay that painful, leave-taking event that will provide some catharsis. If he/she has not attended that ritual, he/she has the means at his/her disposal to make up a satisfactory answer to his/her (possible) confusion. This is where the skill of the therapist is paramount, to help the young child make sense of the insensible.

X. Case Vignettes

(Cases are composites and names have been changed.)

1. Alana S., a six-year-old girl, was brought to therapy by her father because her mother had died about one year earlier. The child showed absolutely no reaction to this loss until shortly before her father called. She was the youngest child in the family; she had two teen-age brothers. Alana began to experience problems at school, both with her educational progress and her lack of social skills. She would suddenly burst into tears with no apparent precipitant and could not self-soothe. The history revealed that her mother had been struck by a car and was killed instantly.

   Mr. S. had been quite depressed since his wife died, so part of the healing was in a family therapy format that consisted of Mr. S. and Mr. S.s' mother, Alana's caretaker. This set of grandparents helped out with necessary baby-sitting arrangements. Mr. S.'s mother prepared dinner each night for them and Alana was allowed to sleep in whichever house she chose. This pattern continued for about the first six months of therapy, after which Alana slept in her own home.

   The teen-age brothers in this family had different fathers and spent week-ends and holidays with them. After their mother's death, the boys were returned to their natural fathers.

   Cultural issues were important to consider with this child as well. Part of the relevant family history was that Alana's Mom was from the Caribbean while her Dad was of Scottish descent. Her Mom was in recovery from drug and alcohol abuse at the time of her death. Both of Alana's parents had severe drug histories.

This child chose to use Sandplay almost exclusively during her individual therapy hours. Her favorite animals were lions, entire families of them. She repeatedly played out the story of *The Lion King*.

In the picture lions and other animals are coming to pay their respects to the dead Father Lion that is buried beneath a headstone. She owned the video of this story and often watched it at home, until she felt secure enough to move on.

Family sessions that were held with Alana and her father utilized therapeutic board games. Their favorite game was "Talking, Feeling and Doing," developed by Dr. Richard Gardner. This intervention was chosen as both of them seemed to suffer from an undiagnosed Expressive Language Disorder. This proved to be the case for Alana when she had to be tested for learning problems and required extra support in school.

One time during a family therapy session, Alana asked her father to give her Mom's cross. It had hung on the wall by the parents' bed. She began to sleep with it each night thereafter, which contributed to a part of her healing. This allowed her to feel close to her Mom and the cross served as a transitional object for her. Eventually, she asked that it be hung over her bed. She was able to feel her Mom's presence in this way. Her grandmother was not in favor of allowing this, feeling that it was "too morbid." It was supported as a way for the child to feel some connection to her mother.

2. The second example is that of a three-year-old girl, Sally (discussed in Chapter 23).

This was the case of an expected death, as mentioned above. However, for a three-year-old, it was much more than that. Her father's death precipitated severe reactions in this child. She was experiencing nightmares, having temper tantrums, her toilet training had regressed, and she was demanding a baby bottle several times a day and also to help her sleep. She was attending a religious nursery school that would not allow her to talk about her loss. On Parents' Night, the staff refused to post the story that she had written (dictated to her mother) because "it might upset the other children and their parents." We found another nursery school soon after that. This was another loss for this child, but it was indicated nevertheless because of the long-term advantages.

Sally continued to have sleep problems that were permeated with monster fears. One scene she replicated a number of times in her sessions. A decision was made to switch to a more directive approach and it was suggested to her that she could pretend that the dinosaurs were her fearsome monsters that came to bother her at night and, if they were fed here, that might make them content to stay on the shelves and not pursue her at home. This "clicked" with her and a ritual for her loss was developed. She made "food" for the dinosaurs and fed them. They were then taken to the toy bathroom set (that had been placed in the sand), where they were toileted, bathed and put to bed. This ritual took place for several months.

Figure 24.1

Of particular interest was that she always placed two other dinosaurs on top of the other sand box. She said that one was "Daddy" and the other one "God." (She had been told that Daddy went to heaven and was now with God.) This ritual resolved most of her regressive behavior after several months. She no longer experienced tantrums and she had given up the bottle and the diapers. This next picture was another way in which she attempted to understand death. She placed many large stones with other stones placed on top. She placed small figures between each of the stones. She said that this scene represented "All the souls in heaven." This was quite an illustration for a 3-and- ½ year-old child!

Figure 24.2

Sally was a very bright, verbal child, but Sandplay allowed her to express her fears far more effectively than any words could ever do. Sally, at three years of age, had no way to put these deep-seated fears to rest, but she was able to concretely address these issues in the sand.

A few years after therapy ended with Sally, her mother sent me a copy of a story Sally had written for a school assignment when she was in the fourth grade. This is taken from Carey[150] (pp. 183-4).

150 Carey, L., 1999

A Special Helper and Friend

> After my dad died, I was very sorrowful. My mom took me to a special Sand Play Therapist for kids and this helped me to learn to cope with his death. My dad died of cancer when I was three years old. It was very sad! I was just devastated and confused.
>
> My mom took me to a psychologist that practices Sand Play Therapy. Her name is Lois Carey and her husband's name is David Carey. My dad's name was David too. David Carey is a musician. Since Lois works at home, when I went there, I sometimes got to hear music.
>
> Lois has a room with a sand box of wet sand and a sand box of dry sand. When I went there, I played in the sand and made a scene with my choice of little figures and props. She took pictures of my scene, and I told a story about my scene that explains feelings. Sometimes I went into the office-type room, and played games, colored, or just talked and told stories.
>
> After my dad died, I started going to Lois. I had fun with Lois and she took my mind off my dad and convinced me that everything would be okay! She made me feel a lot better and helped me to understand what was going on and what had happened!
>
> Death is very difficult for a little kid to understand. I am glad that there are special people like Lois to help you get through it.

3. Tom, a six-year-old boy, was brought to therapy by his clinically depressed 32- year-old mother. The woman's mother had just died from a sudden heart attack. The grandmother had been the sole caretaker for this boy because his single mother was employed and they lived with her. The boy was withdrawing from all of his friends, had lost control of his bladder functioning and had no focusing ability in school. This child was in a frozen state with no support from his depressed mother. There were no other close relatives; his father's whereabouts were unknown.

This case appeared to be one that required a family systems and play therapy orientation and was presented to the mother that way. She refused at first, saying that she didn't have time to "just play." The rationale was explained to her, by saying that this format could help her, as well as the child, and would help in restructuring their family, now that Grandma was dead. Reluctantly, the mother agreed. In order to assure the mother's cooperation, it was suggested that they try a short-term contract of six sessions, with the option to continue should that prove necessary.

A family genogram was completed on the first session with mother and son together. Mother chose a dragon for her mother, a soldier for the boy, and a kitten for herself. The boy chose a bear for Grandma, a wolf for his mother, and a lion for himself. Mother described her choice of a dragon for her mother saying, "She was always angry and I could never find a way to please her." Her son was described as "a brave little soldier," and for herself, "the kitten was all soft and fuzzy."

The boy, in describing his choices said, "Grandma was like a great big, loveable bear who hugged me lots." Mom was described as a snarling wolf, always angry at him and he, as the lion, was "like the boy in the Lion King story who had lost his father."

The theme of anger was picked up from both parties and the therapist said, "You two sure have different views of Grandma! Mom sees her as very angry and Tom sees her as loveable. Tell me about her as each of you saw her." In talking about Grandma, anger and tears were elicited from both mother and son and the discussion helped each one to see Grandma in a different light. When it came to talking about themselves, Mom was able to see how deep the grieving process was for her son and she was able to be more effective in nurturing him. The absence of a figure for the father was noted. The boy's mother said she had no idea where he might be, and the boy had never met him. I asked each of them to pick a figure that might represent him. Mom chose a large cobra and Tom chose Superman. A comment was made about these choices: Mom sees the Dad as a large poisonous snake; Tom sees him as a Superhero. These choices, and the later discussion, helped them both see the father in a more realistic light.

Mom's choice, the cobra, represented all that she had ever known about him. He was a one-night stand and both were high on crack cocaine when Tom was conceived. (This fact was withheld from Tom in order to not tarnish his view of Dad. Tom was told that the father was on leave from the Army and that he had been killed in action.) She never did see the father after that; however, it was the pregnancy that sent her to rehab. This information saddened Tom and made him wonder what his father may have been like. His fantasy life had selected Superman as a hero father which seemed appropriate for his developmental stage. (Mom was advised to tell Tom the truth when he was older and better able to understand these facts.)

The experience with the genogram in that first session enabled this family to use the information gleaned to help mother and son rebuild their lives without Grandma. Mom's depression was reduced so that she was able to be more nurturing to Tom. Tom quickly regained control of his bladder and was again interacting positively with his peers. Grandma had left a small estate that Mom inherited and, with this added income, she was able to hire appropriate child care for Tom when she returned to work. This was a short-term contract where the set goals were achieved:

- To relieve some of Mom's depression.
- To restructure the family without Grandma.
- To allow both mother and son to mourn their loss.
- To help Tom regain control of his bodily function.
- To help Tom and his mother bond as a unit.

4. Another case is one that began when a phone call was received from Mrs. W., mother of a five-year-old girl, Gail, another example of an expected death. Mrs. W. said that she was dying of brain cancer and asked me if therapy could be provided for her daughter. Mrs. W. was bedridden and could not come to the office for an intake, so a home visit was arranged to meet her and to see the child. She was, indeed, in the final stages of cancer. She was very frail, she had no hair and her head was wrapped in a scarf. The visit lasted less than half an hour because she became exhausted.

Mrs. W. was a very brave woman, who had taken the time to write notes to her daughter, that were to be given to her at appropriate times: birthdays, graduations, sweet 16, etc. The notes were kept in a special place and Gail's father, Mr. W., was instructed as to when they were to be presented. This woman was setting up the process whereby the child could continue to be connected to her, even after death. The actual death occurred less than one week after that first meeting.

Therapy was begun with the child shortly before Mrs. W's. death. Family members were also included in treatment: Mr. W., the child's father, and the maternal grandparents who were suffering from the loss of their daughter. This case is a good example of a family that had done a great deal of anticipatory mourning and had effectively planned for this young child's bereavement. Gail used sand very effectively in her individual sessions and was able to verbalize her concerns through her stories. Her stories, like those of the other children cited, were about her missing the dead parent, being angry that she no longer had a mother, and finally an eventual acceptance of the situation.

Gail's therapy might have ended within the first year except that her father re-married within six or eight months of being widowed. This meant that the child needed additional treatment in order to accept a mother-substitute so soon after her loss. She not only needed to resolve her bereavement issues, but she had to adjust to a new family constellation. This new family also received family therapy as part of the adjustment.

This particular case was a number of years ago. Her grandmother kept me apprised of Gail's progress by sending me a new photo of the child that she included with a Christmas card. The most recent picture was that of a young graduate who had just completed a master's program at a prestigious university.

XI. Conclusion

The challenge to help young children with the healing process after the loss of a parent or grandparent is a major one. This can be doubly challenging if the therapist has had a similar loss at a similar age. It is hoped that the therapist has dealt with his/her issues before treating a bereaved child; otherwise, one might be faced with difficult counter-transference issues.

It has been illustrated through the previous examples how these families dealt with death.

The first child, Alana, was cross-cultural – Puerto Rican and Scottish. These two cultures are widely divergent in their customs. Her mother was Latino, where the rites can continue for several days and the religion is Roman Catholic. Her father's family was Protestant and was much more reserved in handling any crisis. In both of these cultures there is resistance to the whole idea of therapy. Therapy is viewed as "you must be crazy if you see a therapist."

Alana was negatively impacted because of her grandmother's feelings towards Latinas. She discouraged the child from having any contact with the mother's family. This had a very undesirable side effect because Alana knew and understood that she was bi-cultural and that part of her was being rejected.

The second and fourth cases were Orthodox Jewish. There is an extended period of mourning in this community; beginning with the fact that the burial takes place within 24 hours. The family then sits "shiva" for seven days after the burial. That is the intended time for friends and family to go to the home of the deceased to express their condolences. A gift of food is offered to the family by the visitors. The final ritual occurs one year later when a headstone is provided for the grave.

The case of Tom illustrated a short-term contract to deal with the loss of a grandparent. This family had no active involvement with the grandmother's Catholic background, but one part of the termination session was to enroll Tom in a religious education program. Mom was able to agree with the understanding that this could benefit him in further healing this loss.

These few examples comprise part of this author's professional experience in providing therapy to bereaved children. The reader may have other cultural examples from his/her own practice; but no matter what the religious background of the child, it behooves everyone to pay particular attention to the cultural and religious background of each family. This is a necessity in order to best help the child to incorporate the strengths found in his/her family of origin. It is doubly important that the therapist does not impose his/her cultural values and/or religion into the treatment but is instead empathic and supportive to the child.

This chapter has focused on the use of Sandplay Therapy for a bereaved child, primarily because that is the specialty of this practitioner. However, other play therapy methods can be equally effective. Techniques such as art, puppetry and story-telling are well-utilized with a grieving child because they do not require extensive verbalization, but keep the treatment in a metaphoric milieu. This is especially true for the child under eight years of age because he/she has not yet reached the age for a more intellectual understanding of death. This understanding can come later; in fact, the child may need to address various issues pertaining to the loss at different stages of life.

The most important function of therapy with a young child is to help him/her to process what has occurred, at his/her level of understanding. By achieving some early resolution of the significant death, a child can then proceed with the rest of his/her developmental, educational and social needs that certainly will lie ahead, without unresolved loss issues that can be a major hindrance.

CHAPTER 25

A CASE OF SUICIDE

Suicide is a topic that sends chills down the spine of most play therapists and it is assumed that is the case for many other professionals. At times, there is a hint that the client is contemplating suicide, while at other times it is a complete surprise. The case to be discussed is the suicide of the mother of a child who was in treatment with this author.

This family will be called the "D" family. The children will be called Eunice, age ten; Tom, age seven; Billy, age three.

Tom had been treated for two years for ADD and Depression. He was in Kindergarten when he first came for therapy. Tom and his mother came for the intake; his father was unavailable at that time. Tom had a history of moderate hearing loss and he wore a trainer in school and two hearing aids. He was resistant to wearing the trainer and the hearing aids because they made him feel different from the other children. Mrs. D. informed me that there was also a suspicion of sexual abuse during his pre-school nursery school years. This was eventually verified through the art work he produced while in treatment. Tom acted out frequently at school and impulsively attacked other children. He was treated on a once a week basis with parent consultations once a month. The parent meetings were most often with the mother, as the father seldom attended.

Tom was referred for a psychological evaluation that determined that he "shows signs of poor short and long-term memory, graphomotor immaturity and a tendency towards disorganization. He continues to show signs of language delay. His academic achievement is somewhat below his potential and he shows an overall unevenness of functioning. Emotionally, he is a depressed boy preoccupied with fears of loss and does not experience the environment as supportive. He fears bodily harm and feels helpless about his poor muscular control (which includes enuresis).

He attempts to avoid his fears and puts forth a "good boy" façade, but aggressively acts out when fears overwhelm him."

After two years Tom had made limited improvements; his behavior in school had stabilized, but he was not ready for termination. However, it was agreed that there be a summer break with the intention of resuming sessions in the Fall. In August the mother was called to arrange the schedule at which time she advised me that they had decided not to continue. She was told that this was premature, but she was adamant. That was the last time she was heard from.

In October of that year, a call from the police was received because Mrs. D.'s body had been found about 100 miles from home. The therapist's business card was the only thing that was found in her jacket pocket. The police had identified her by the license plate on her car. Few facts were uncovered, there was no note. She had stopped in at her work that morning, although she was not on duty that day. Her wallet was found in a drawer there and it had some money in it and all of her credit cards. She was a nurse and had procured, from the hospital drug supply, the substance that the "Death Doctor" used on assisted suicides and had injected a sufficient quantity that caused her death.

Mr. D. telephoned me the next day because he had no idea what to tell the children. I coached him with some guidelines so that he could handle it as well as possible under the circumstances. The therapist attended the wake and funeral because she felt it would be useful for these children.

Mr. D. agreed to start family sessions and individual sessions for himself as soon as the funeral was over. The children suffered this major loss in confusion because he believed they were too young to understand the truth. This continued to be the case when there was a termination some six or eight months later. The children (Eunice and Tom) believed that their mother died "because she smoked." Billy, the three year old, was unable to verbalize his thoughts at that time and became a selective mute at school. Knowing his brother's history, the therapist is of the opinion that Billy's mother, when she dropped him off that morning, probably said something like, "be good at school, not like your brother." She had taken him to school that day and then drove off to her death. The boy's grandfather was called when she did not pick him up at the usual time and this started the police search for her. Billy's selective mutism lasted approximately three months; however, he continued to stay to himself during the school day. Tom's earlier acting out was resumed; Eunice seemed to be the one best able to cope.

Mr. D. moved himself and the children into his parents' house within two weeks of the mother's death that was another loss for these children – they had to attend a new school, be in a new home and lose their friends. As if that were not enough, within six months, the father married a woman who had two children, both of whom also had emotional problems and they all moved again.

Mr. D.'s new wife would not attend family sessions here because her sons were in treatment elsewhere. It was she who determined that these children should see a different therapist and so treatment ended in about eight months. At that time the children had never been told the reason for their mother's death.

This case was a very involved one, partly because of the age difference of the children. Mr. D. believed that he might be able to tell Eunice, but "not until she is a teen-ager." He said he would have to wait and see if and when he could tell Tom (the child I had originally treated) and Billy. He was advised that it was best not to wait as they were sure to overhear something and then they would be quite angry at him for not telling them. It is not known if and when any of this information was transmitted to these children.

Several years later, a relative of Mrs. D. came for therapy and told me that Tom had attempted suicide in his teens, but was now in college and seemed to be doing pretty well. Eunice was married and had two children. Bill was in high school, still a "loner" and isolated. She did not know if the children had ever been apprised of their mother's suicide.

Needless to say, this was a case that caused the therapist much angst but one that also taught her a great deal. She needed to draw on her own inner spirituality in order to help this family to the best of her ability. She was inwardly angry at the mother and needed to sort through her feelings in order to treat this family. This was a case that prompted her to return to supervision.

CHAPTER 26

CULTURAL DIVERSITY

This topic is an extremely vast one that calls on all therapists to expand and deepen their knowledge in this area.

Our country was originally founded by persons from a variety of nationalities, cultures, races and religions and, unfortunately, most persons continue to be more or less ignorant about the wealth of experience and knowledge that each group can provide. One can only think of our present dilemma in the Republican Primary (2008, 2012) where the issue of race has become paramount. It will be most interesting to see how this plays out and whether or not it will expand our vision about contributions that can be made from so-called minorities (black, Middle-Eastern, and female).

The author grew up in a suburb of Pittsburgh, PA, where there were no black residents. There was one Chinese family that owned the local Chinese laundry, but that was the extent of her exposure to non-whites. The major division was religious – Protestant and Catholic, with a very small percentage of Jews. In the author's town, the Protestants refused to allow a Catholic church or a Jewish temple to be in the community, so the Catholics and Jews had to attend a church or a temple in a neighboring town.

This author was one of the Protestant majorities, but during high school she began to date a young man who was half Jewish and half Irish. Her parents had no objection, but her grandparents certainly did. She has now been married to him for 66 years! This couple raised three children that produced five grandchildren and three great grandchildren.

Divisions within cultures can be as challenging as divisions across cultures. For example, among Protestants there are major divisions depending on whether one is Baptist, Presbyterian, Lutheran, etc. Among

Catholics, there are those churches that continue to provide masses in Latin, while others have switched to English. Among Jews, there are the Orthodox, the Conservative, and the Reformed. There is even one group called "Jews for Jesus."

In spite of all these major religious and cultural differences, mental health issues do not discriminate. Mental illness is found across the country, across social class, across religions and across cultures. According to the World Health Organization, in developed countries like the United States, mental health concerns rank second only to cardiovascular disease as a leading cause of disability. When addressing cultural diversity in mental health, therapists need to consider access, definition, and communication. If the language or the cultural values of our clients are not understood, therapists will not be well-equipped to diagnose or treat the client's personal issues.

So, while this therapist's own personal journey has enabled her to understand at least the Christian and Jewish cultures, she is not quite as adept at the black experience in all its various forms, or the Muslim, or the Islamic.

In our country one of the greatest difficulties is in the area of social class and income levels. It has been widely studied that those families who live on a poverty level have very few opportunities for a good education, which leads to numerous social, occupational, and mental health issues. In the poor areas of any large city, one finds easy access to drugs and weapons of all sorts. The treatment issues for those persons are huge as any therapist knows who works in the inner city of New York.

This therapist has been fortunate to have treated many persons from faiths other than her own. These include those from the Catholic faith, the Jewish faith, blacks (these are also diverse, depending on whether they are Afro-American, Jamaican, Dominican, etc.) and a few Asians (also diverse, such as Chinese, Japanese, Taiwanese, Pakistani, etc.).

It is important to mention that Sandplay has its own cultural bias. It was developed by Frau Dora Kalff in Switzerland. She was very much influenced by her Swiss/German background as well as her interest in Zen Buddhism and Jungian theory. These influences certainly affected the way she interpreted sand pictures, because they were viewed through her particular lens. Each therapist has his/her own lens through which he/she peers. This is the reason that practitioners need to pay particular attention to a serious study of cultures and religions other than one's own in order to broaden their observational skills.

European Sandplay has different cultural attributes from the American (or the Asian). For example, in 1992, Martin Kalff hosted the first Sandplay conference after his mother's death. The format was that there were five European presenters who all presented the "perfect case." I have never seen a "perfect case" in my practice. Martin's presentation was one that seemed to all the Americans present to be one of sex abuse. This was vehemently denied by all the Europeans as they could not recognize that sex abuse happened in Europe. Needless to say, all the Americans were sure it was a case of sex abuse. At that conference, everyone had the opportunity to present a "new kind of case" that he/she may be struggling with. This therapist chose a family example and, at the conclusion, a German analyst was aghast that she had four people in one sandbox. These were all Jungian analysts (who have their own culture biases) and could not envision the use of Sandplay other than for an "individuation process."

Jungian theories appear to be consistent, no matter what cultural group you may be dealing with based on Jung's theory of archetypes. One of the major tenets of Jungian psychology is that all persons, no matter what their race, national origin, or culture may be, have an archetypal level of the psyche. The archetypes vary from culture to culture but each group has its own images of great mothers, great fathers, beginning of the world, hero's journey, etc. Particularly important are the various religious symbols of each culture; while they are different, they all have elements of God, Allah, the Devil, good and evil. The last section of this book discusses archetypes.

All therapists, of whichever cultural or religious background, are urged to study this topic thoroughly in order to prepare for future clients that may appear in their practices.

CHAPTER 27

SPIRITUALITY IN SANDPLAY THERAPY

This topic is a vast one and one that this author hopes to do justice to. Every person has his/her own interpretation of spirituality. Some persons recoil at this term since spirituality and religiosity are often confused. Each one of us has different views about these terms, so the author is presenting her idiosyncratic view of this most complex subject.

These two words can be synonymous, according to the dictionary, which is where some of the confusion begins. However, it can be suggested that religiosity is more related to things connected to a specific church or religion, whereas spirituality is taken in a much broader sense that suggests that one can have a very spiritual attitude without having an association with any organized religion. True spirituality includes respect for ALL human beings, no matter what their creed or belief system, what color of skin they possess, or in what part of the world they live.

What does one's personal history have to do with the spiritual experience in Sandplay? Jung has written and said repeatedly, that to do any kind of psychotherapeutic work, one must have done one's own soul work in whatever form that has taken. This does not mean to imply that one needs to belong to an organized religion, but that one honor the innate spirituality in him/herself as well as in the client that one is called upon to treat.

It has been found that spirituality can often be seen in one particular symbol or another. For example, in one sandplay article, the symbol of the red rose indicated a deep spiritual experience, in another, it was the rainbow, in still another, it was comparing the sand box to an inner garden. The possibilities are legion.

When thinking of one's own Sandplay experience, it might be that one or more symbols predominate and that seem to "speak" of the individual's own spirituality. It might be a miniature of one sort or another or it might be a natural substance like a seashell or a pine cone. It could also be simply the shape of the sand which has been molded. But over and above the end product, one's personal spirituality is portrayed in the process of constructing a sand picture. The process itself is a meditative, deepening experience which touches each individual in varying ways. Many adults when first using sand feel uneasy and sometimes intimidated. This is occasionally the case with children, however, much less frequently than with adults. Not too long ago, an adult woman who has been in treatment for some time expressed the wish to use the sand. Her first picture is Figure 27.1

Figure 27.1

The following week the woman reported how much the experience had "shaken her" and had stimulated an intense period of dreaming. The dreams took her to a much deeper level than she had touched previously and were truly "archetypal" in their make-up. The therapist's reaction to this picture was that of feeling a positive movement in her process. She used primarily natural substances (shells, rocks, trees) and one miniature that represented a pond. In the center she has cross-hatched a wide path that leads to the pond. Since this was her first sand experience, I did not offer any comments.

Dora Kalff's tape on the *Symbolic Images of the Self in Sandplay*[151] illustrates many different possibilities for a reconnection to one's spiritual experience. The aim of ALL therapy and Sandplay, in particular, is to reconnect the ego with the split-off, spiritual center of the psyche (the Self) in order to provide the deepest healing possible. In Kalffian terms, this is referred to as the "Manifestation of the Self" and is the signal to the therapist that the ego and the Self are now in a positive relationship. Jung has said that the most prevalent problem of modern man is that he/she has been cut off from his/her deepest spiritual core. This means that most persons are operating primarily from the ego level rather than being connected to and able to utilize that deeper Self symbol that provides them with access to their innate spirituality or wholeness. Jung believed that individuals are only partially fulfilled as humans and that each one's potential is far greater than what is actually used. That is the reason Sandplay is so effective - it provides the opportunity for such an ego/Self connection to occur. It does not ensure it, of course, as Estelle Weinrib[152] points out, but it does set the stage. It is like a drama in some respects - the play may be written, the actors engaged, the theater lit up, BUT a director is needed to orchestrate the work before life can be breathed into it.

This is similar to Sandplay - one has sand, miniatures, a client/patient - but without a therapist present to honor the process, to reflect, to understand and empathize - all one has are sand, miniatures and persons. How many times have the words been heard from parents: "Well, we have a sandbox in our back yard so he can do this at home." When these remarks are heard, most therapists cringe because they reveal the parents' unwillingness to relinquish their authority and it is possible that they will undermine the therapy in some way. How does one circumvent this? Parent education is the answer and is a definite "must." However, therapists need to remind themselves that parents, too, are cut off from their spiritual core and, when aware of this, the situation can be handled adequately. Admittedly, it is extremely difficult to explain

151 Kalff, D. 1980
152 Weinrib, E.

to parents what is different about Sandplay therapy than other forms of play therapy, but it behooves all therapists to find ways to do this.

One case comes to mind where, during a parent consultation, the child's mother asked for clarification. This was quite a difficult question and it needed to be answered with extreme care in dealing with this particular parent. The parent is already in unconscious competition with the therapist and ways must be found that support the parent's position as well as the therapeutic one. This Mother said that what her son did with the therapist was just what she observes all little boys of his age doing - having wars and always being the victor. The therapist agreed with the mother that this was a normal developmental stage and that through observing the process and intervening when it was appropriate, this child was able to resolve some of his numerous conflicts. This was an adopted child with severe speech and language deficits. When he first began therapy, it was impossible to understand him. He also suffered from severe separation anxiety and wore a diaper at night, (age six). He had many fears and very poor peer relationships. All of his sand pictures until then were illustrative of wars of one kind or another. Several times dinosaurs were portrayed swallowing up babies. By the time of this consultation, some of the presenting problems were partially alleviated. Mom wanted to know if it was from his school placement, his speech therapy, or therapy here. She was told that it was probably all three and that she deserved credit for paying attention to all these very serious issues. She was hoping to cut back on the frequency of sessions (she had no insurance), but it was suggested that the therapy continue for another two months and be reevaluated at that time. Fortunately, she did agree, which may have been possible because of her being given some of the credit in handling these various issues. As an aside, there was another adopted child in the household, a daughter, age 12, who was quite bright and competent.

Up to the point of this consultation, there was no indication of centering or wholeness in the sand pictures of the child. This brought up the adoption issue because there was no history relating to this boy's early weeks and his attachment history was unclear. His early mothering experiences were unknown. He was six weeks old when these parents adopted him. Whether his natural mother suffered from drug or alcohol problems was unknown, so the aetiology of his condition was also unclear. The task for the therapist was to find ways to keep Mom engaged long enough to allow further development for this fragile child, with the hope that those early, unknown weeks of his life would have some chance of resolution.

During the Christmas break and many snow storms, there were lengthy absences. He said that he didn't want to come to Sandplay anymore. He said this at the very end of one session. His mother had apprised me of his resistance also. He was told that it could surely be talked about the next time because the therapist did not want to "make" him come, but that she wondered if perhaps he was angry at her since there had been such a long break. He said nothing to that comment. The next week, shortly after the session started, the subject was broached. His response was, "Oh, I changed my mind, I don't want to stop."

In summary, the author needs to stress that Sandplay is the ideal milieu in which a child's spiritual issues can be visualized and expressed, often non-verbally. Jung and Kalff, as well as most Sandplay therapists that have been known over the years either personally or through teaching and consultations, have very strong connections to their own spirituality. This would seem to be a prerequisite in order for true healing to occur with the clients that are seen.

PART IV

A BRIEF INTRODUCTION TO SYMBOLS AND ARCHETYPES

CHAPTER 28

SYMBOLS AND ARCHETYPES IN SANDPLAY THERAPY[153]

This article is written in order to acquaint the reader with an understanding of symbols and archetypes as they are portrayed in Jungian Sandplay Therapy. A brief description of Jung's psychic structure that enriches the Sandplay process on one's journey towards individuation will set the stage for why this knowledge, when added to the therapist's repertoire, will deepen and enrich the process (see Chapter 2). Differences between symbols and archetypes will be discussed and illustrated. Archetypes[154] have both positive and negative poles; some of the archetypes (they are countless in number) to be illustrated are the Great Mother, the Wise Old Man, the Hero/Heroine, Anima/Animus, Ego/Self and the archetype of Evil. Representative examples will be sand pictures of both children and adults.

An archetype is nothing more or less than a model - often a model of an idea. For example, when someone thinks of "mother," he/she may have several ideas in mind. One thought, of course, is one's personal mother, but the archetypal mother is the ideal that no human can ever measure up to. An example of this might be Mary as Christ's mother—the idealized saint. Then, as archetypes are two-sided, one needs to consider the Negative Mother Archetype—Medusa is a good example of this one.

A symbol often points to an underlying archetype. For example, a dove is a symbol for peace. Churchil held up two fingers during World War II which symbolized the letter "V" for victory. Symbols are also found in music and mathematics, i.e., notes on the scale symbolize what keys to play on an instrument. In mathematics, addition, subtraction,

153 Reprinted from NYAPT Newsletter, 2011

154 *Webster's New World Dictionary*

division, or multiplication signs demonstrate what process should be undertaken.

Jungians believe that dreams are the most common place where one's own personal symbols are encountered – those that are connected with one's own psychology. This topic is pertinent to Sandplay because Sandplay is often referred to as a "waking dream."

Webster,[155] writing about "symbol," says that it is a token by which one infers something else, i.e. the "dove of peace." He goes on to say that in psychoanalysis, a symbol is an act or object representing an unconscious desire that has been repressed. Prior to 9/11, the World Trade Center was thought of as a symbol of the power of the United States and the flag symbolized our unity as a nation.

Dreams happen spontaneously and are the main source of knowledge about symbolism and how they can point to an underlying archetype, but the symbol is not the archetype itself. The author will present a personal example that was discussed more fully in her memoir, *A Salty Lake of Tears.*[156]

Several years ago I had a dream where my husband and I were confronted by a buffalo that first sniffed at him and then made his way towards me. I awoke at that moment, quite frightened. However, in analyzing that dream, I discovered that there were several aspects to this particular symbol. The image of the buffalo directly linked me to a pleasant childhood experience while, at the same time, encouraged me to draw on the strength of the buffalo at those tense moments when I was just beginning to deliver lectures. This is a dream that has stayed with me for many years. I also added many buffaloes to my miniature collection after that dream and often carry one with me when I lecture.

My family's Sunday drive usually led us to a large herd of buffalo that lived in South Park in Pittsburgh. This was a very pleasant memory of a not-so-pleasant childhood. I studied up on this symbol to gain further insight into this unusual dream image. I found one passage in the Medicine Cards'[157] that says "Buffalo medicine is a sign that you achieve nothing without the aid of the Great Spirit and that one must be

155 *Webster's New World Dictionary*

156 Carey, L., 2011

157 Sams, et al

humble enough to ask for that assistance and then be grateful for what is received."[158] This was a very positive connection with a dream symbol that led me to the Power Archetype and that the buffalo was a sign of my own inner power. Naturally, not all symbols are positive as, like archetypes, they can have both positive and negative aspects.

Jungian therapists seek to locate connections between the conscious mind of the patient and the unconscious archetypes or symbols that cause personal suffering to the client. The danger that arises when this material remains unconscious is that the client can become IDENTIFIED with the archetype and this can cause much suffering. In those situations, Jungians believe that the archetype has power over the person rather than the person having power over the archetype.

In order to assist the reader with the balance of this article, please refer to the three illustrations and descriptions in Chapter 2, pages 17-20.

An archetype is a model by which an idea is referred to, for example, the Great Mother, the Hero, and the Inner Child. An understanding of the Jungian concept of archetypes can enhance the therapeutic benefits that are inherent in Sandplay. One example of a major archetype is that of the Great Mother. One of the symbols for the Great Mother is a cave, an interior place, deep within the mountain.

Erich Neumann[159] produced an entire volume on different aspects of the GreatMother. In Her positive view, She is the caretaker, the nurturer, *par excelence*. One of her negative sides can be represented as Medusa who turns men to stone.

The Goddess, Demeter,[160] in Greek mythology, is a prime example of the Great Mother. Demeter was the mother of Persephone and when Persephone was abducted by Hades (King of the Underworld), Demeter went into a deep depression. Following this event, Demeter dictated the change of the seasons as a result of her grief at separation from her daughter. (Her name – Demeter – means The Mother.) During those times of the year when Persephone was with Demeter, Spring and Summer reigned. The fruits of the Earth came to life, bloomed and produced

158 Sams, et al

159 Neumann, E., 1955

160 Kerenyi, C., 1979

fruit. When Persephone was with Hades, Fall and Winter ensued, representing Demeter's sadness because of the separation. Much of what is seen today about wintertime depressions can be directly related to this myth.

The negative side of the Great Mother archetype is that She can also try to control every relationship. She is the mistress of guilt: "See all that I've done for you, how you can possibly do this to me?" The negative controlling side can become so extreme that it totally denies the personhood of the other. In this aspect, Medusa is a good example – Medusa was the goddess that men could not look in the face or they would be slain – she could only be approached from behind (the unconscious).

Sandplay is particularly suited to problems with the Great Mother simply because of the use of the earth element of sand that symbolically has the potential to link a client directly to the realm of the earth mother. "Mother Earth" is a direct reference to the numinous power of the archetype and often alludes to these issues, issues that have existed from the earliest of times and across all cultures. Because this archetype holds so many varied characteristics and is depicted by so many symbolic representations, one cannot say "the Great Mother archetype is . . . ." She is many things and that is the essential reason that Sandplay therapists consciously employ Her in Her function of Nurturer and Healer. Many persons, both men and women, find themselves caught in the clutches of the Great Mother archetype and nurture others to the complete exclusion of everything else.

How does one learn about this archetype in Sandplay and the many diverse forms that indicate the presence of the Great Mother? Needless to say, this is a lifelong process, but there are some beginnings that can be made towards an understanding of the archetype. For example, She (in her positive form) can be most readily seen in formations made in the sand such as mountains and hills. Animals, such as the cow, the pig, the whale, can indicate Her nurturing aspects. In Her negative form, She may be depicted as a volcano, or She might be illustrated as an octopus with its many tentacles. These are just a very few examples.

It is often said that the archetype, or complex, is in charge of the person, rather than the person being in charge of "it." This is often the case with the young man or woman who cannot leave the personal mother, or who cannot maintain a relationship with the opposite sex. The "mother complex" can also exist in young children when there is an attachment disorder stemming from an early separation from or loss of the personal mother. The search for a positive Great Mother substitute can last for a lifetime. The characteristics of the Great Mother archetype are quite complex, yet when one is able to contact and mediate with Her, She holds the potential for a deeply healing experience. Therapists must pay special attention to this archetype because its power can sometimes reach epic proportions.

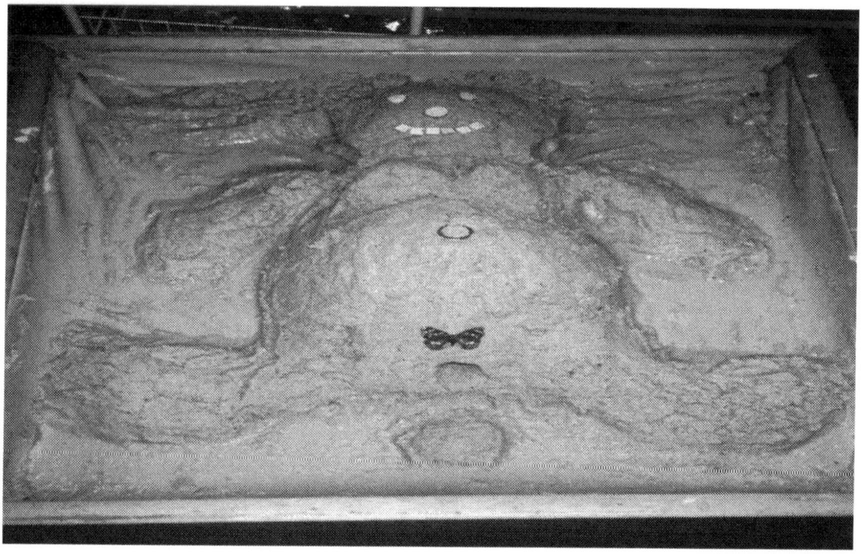

Figure 28.1

This is one of the archetypes that can control the unconscious of the therapist and often leads him or her into this field in the first place. It is vitally necessary, therefore, for the therapist to contact this archetype during his/her training and learn to mediate with Her so that this does not contaminate the work with the patient or lead to burn-out of the therapist. This archetype can be seen in therapists who arrange appointments at inconvenient times for themselves or who take phone calls at all hours of the day or night. The deep issues that surround the Great Mother archetype are one of the prime reasons why every Sandplay therapist needs to have the experience of his/her personal process. There is simply no substitute for this. Figure 28.1 was discussed in Chapter 6 (Figure 6.1) but is a good example of how the author struggled with a Great Mother issue.

The second example is that of a Negative Great Mother that was made by an eight-year-old-boy who was in the care of a personal mother with suicidal ideation.

Figure 28.2

The archetypes of the Wise Old Man, the Hero/Heroine, and the Inner Child follow. Sand pictures that portray some of these archetypes will be included as well.

The Wise Old Man, often known as the Senex, is particularly relevant to the work of Sandplay. The male therapist (and often the female) embodies this archetype for the client who views him/her as all-knowing, as wise as Solomon, a guru, a savior, etc. He is the masculine representation of the Great Mother. He can also be Zeus or God. This aspect is often projected onto an analyst (just as the Great Mother archetype is) and it has nothing to do with the sex of the therapist. The patient will use the analyst as whatever is needed for psychic health at the moment. The therapist must carry the projections until the patient eventually gets in touch with his or her own Great Mother or Wise Old Man. For those who have ever been in therapy, this may have been experienced with one's therapist, analyst, etc. The opposite, negative side of the Wise Old Man is the Inner Judge, the one who is constantly critical. These are all inner figures, all a part of the dreamer or Sandplay patient. Miniatures that are often chosen to represent the Wise Old Man can range from animals with male-like characteristics such as the bull or lion, to rabbis or priests or other power-filled male figures.

The picture below is that of a ten-year-old boy who was struggling with the aftermath of 9/11 as discussed in Chapter 7. It is repeated here to illustrate how physical symptoms occasionally come into sand pictures. He suffered from severe migraine headaches (note the dragon in the upper left corner).

Figure 28.3

Note the large dragon in the upper left corner. The dragon also represents his Inner Judge that urges him on in spite of the assault on his head. I believe all the warring figures represent many of this boy's concerns.

The following picture is that of an adult woman who was pressuring herself to identify her Wise Old Man. She had projected the archetype onto an artist from her childhood and replicated this picture from a dream she had. She had not as yet internalized her own inner wisdom figure.

Figure 28.4

The negative side of the Wise Old Man is the Puer, the eternally youthful man who refuses to grow up, but who lives his life in a "devil may care" fashion. He is often the adventurer in stories such as Robin Hood or Peter Pan or, in real life, like Lawrence of Arabia. He seems to have frequent accidents and often an early death. These are often the patients who are beset with alcohol and/or drug problems and who live in constant denial. They are usually brought to therapy by others because of continuing relationship difficulties. Figure 28.5 is that of an adult male with an obsessive/compulsive diagnosis who longs not to grow up but to be the eternal child in relationship to his wife/mother. "Puella" is the term for the female who wants to stay youthful and to never grow old.

Figure 28.5

Myths can reveal archetypes in a telling way. One myth that is encountered through all segments of society is the myth of the Hero. The Hero liberates his people from destruction and death, usually at great odds. He is greater than great or bigger than big. The Hero is that aspect of the psyche that dares to venture into the unknown, into the shadow of the unconscious, bringing one in touch with the darker aspects in the soul and in the world. The Hero allows one to figure out what it will take to achieve goals that have been set. Think of the myths of Hermes, of Ulysses, of Christ as prime examples.

Hermes is a good example—he was born with super-human qualities. On his first day of life, he made a lyre from the shell of a turtle and used hairs from the tail of a cow to make the strings and sang songs using this lyre. That same day he played a trick on his brother by turning the hooves on the cattle backward so that it looked as if the cattle were traveling in the opposite direction than they really were. Hermes could also be viewed as the Trickster. All myths have certain things in common—an unusual circumstance of birth, superhuman powers, conquering might with right. One sees this frequently with young boys in therapy as they strive to assert themselves.

The female form of the Hero is, of course, the Heroine—perhaps best explained by the goddesses in Greek mythology such as Athena, Aphrodite, or Psyche. Jean Shinoda Bolen's[161] book discusses many of these goddesses and the reader is referred to this excellent source.

The Inner Child is another archetype that is directly relevant to the play therapist. All therapists need to have an active inner child or it would not be possible to do the work of play. Play therapists need to PLAY with the children that are treated and the best way that can be done is to become like a child again. There is a strong need for therapists to paint, to draw, to read fairy tales, to laugh and sing.

Jung wrote in *Memories, Dreams and Reflections*[162] how, after his break with Freud, he had to become like a child again and simply play – primarily with his imagination. This act of Jung's is often thought to be one of the forerunners of sandplay because he built a miniature village on Lake Zurich out of found objects—sticks, twigs, rocks, etc. He even dammed up one area that he could open and close with a barrier to allow the water to flow freely or to be stopped. This activity led Jung on to stone-cutting, Active Imagination, and the Individuation Process. (This all requires much study of Jung and is beyond the scope of this book.)

Jungians are quite familiar with how the role of the child archetype is expressed. It can be found in many fairy tales, myths, etc. One that is recalled is The Little Prince[163] by St. Exupery. Greek mythology is full of child archetypes as well, for instance, Hermes who was discussed previously. Having recently visited Ireland, the Leprechauns come to mind. In fact, several play therapists from that trip went to the Leprechaun Museum—such fun!!

One or two examples of the child archetype as illustrated in Sandplay follow.

Figure 28.6 was made by an eleven-year-old girl. During a previous session, she had made the tiny figure on the boat that she said was a "unisex" figure. She named the overall picture "The Squall"—the only survivor was the lone figure on the boat. No doubt she was protecting her Inner Child. She was a sex abuse survivor.

161 Bolen, Jean S.
162 Jung, C.G., 1965
163 Saint-Exupery

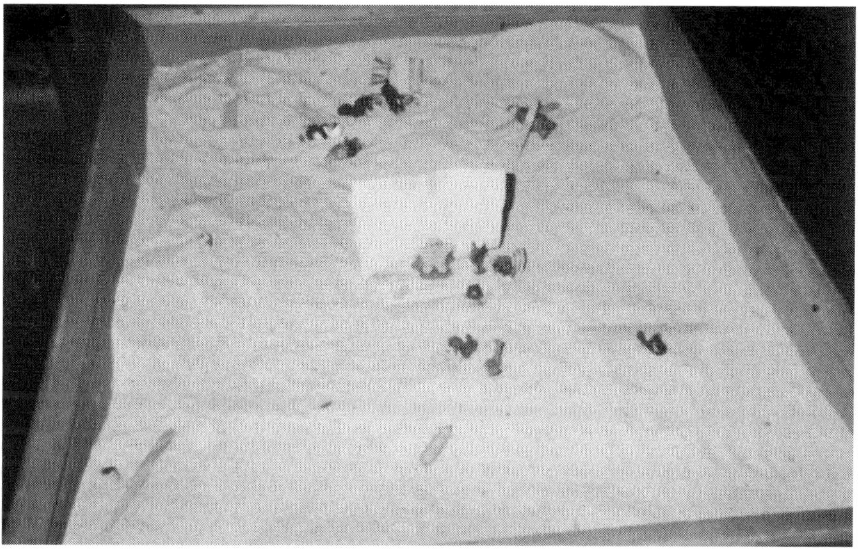

Figure 28.6

Figure 28.7

Figure 28.7 is that of a six-year-old boy who has gathered all of his favorite playmates for a "play date". He is making sure that he stays in touch with his Inner Child. This was a very anxious child who really enjoyed sand and playing!

Next the archetypes of Anima/Animus, ego/Self and Good/Evil will briefly be discussed as this is a vast subject that requires years of study for a fuller understanding of the topic. These archetypes are extremely complex and those that have been chosen are a few examples that have been encountered with child and/or adult patients in Sandplay Therapy.

ANIMA/ANIMUS is a central archetype in Jungian psychology. Anima is the term used for the feminine aspect of male psychology, whereas Animus is the male aspect of female psychology. How are these illustrated in life and in Sandplay? One example: when a man dreams of a woman like Marilyn Monroe or Lady Gaga, who is not known to him, the figure can represent a positive aspect of the dreamer's animus. If, on the other hand, he dreams of a witch stirring a pot, one can surmise that this is a male who may be under the subjugation of his mother and no woman is good enough for him. Or, the mother has so much power over him that he is unable to individuate. The anima, then, can be seen as either a beautiful goddess-type woman or as a nagging shrew/witch.

Figure 28.8

A boy of nine discovers his anima potential in Figure 28.8. This is especially seen in the couple about to be married, as well as in the mermaids near the upper left corner.

Figure 28.9

Another picture is that of a 60-year-old man who was involved with a 40-year-old woman. He was overly kind to older women, but was having erectile problems with the young woman. His sand picture is shown above as he desperately attempts to assure his masculinity.

Her animus picture will be illustrated in the next section.

The Animus in the feminine psyche is viewed as either super-controlling (negative) or else as a helpful male figure of some sort. For example, a woman dreams that she is alone at night on a deserted country road. A man comes and offers to help her, or else, three or four threatening males appear with the intent to rape, rob or kill her. In the first example, this is the positive animus figure while the negative aspect appears in the second.

Figure 28.10 is that of a nine-year-old girl during a resistant phase of therapy and is an illustration of the negative side of the archetype. She had refused to come into the session with her father and, instead, went into the Sandplay room and produced this picture. She has drawn a pouting face in the sand while in the upper right corner (not fully visible) is a G.I. Joe figure sitting on a toilet!

Figure 28.10

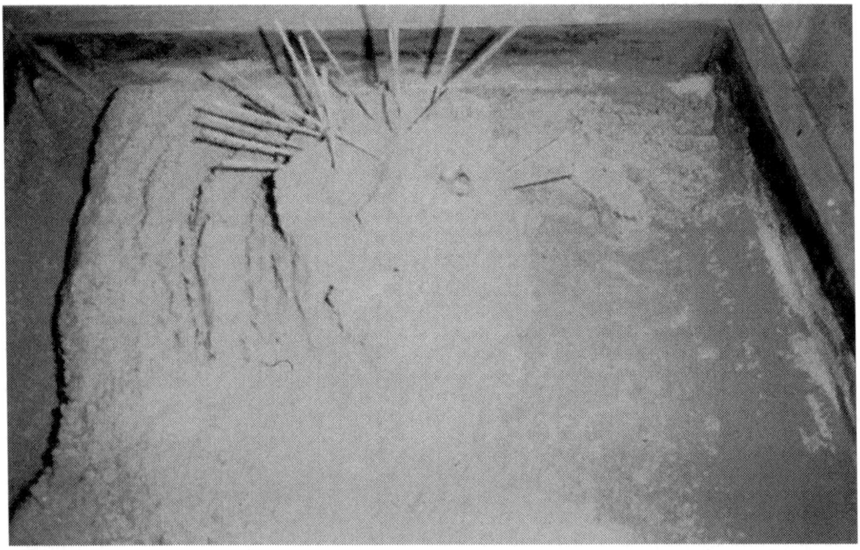

Figure 28.11

Figure 28.11 is another example of a negative animus and is the woman mentioned above. Unfortunately, it is somewhat over-exposed, but it is a gigantic head of a monster that is stabbed repeatedly with sharp-pointed sticks.

Figure 28.12 is a search for the positive animus portrayed by an adult woman. The following week, she brought in a poem that she had written at home. The poem describes the picture that she named "The Man in the Desert." She describes the entire scene and ends with the native woman approaching the hurt man as he asks himself:

> "Will she unwrap the skins from her back to cover me?
> Do I have the strength to tell her not to?
> Or to allow her to?"

Figure 28.12

The Ego/Self archetype is the central archetype in the collective unconscious. According to Jung, the ego is an archetype but it is related to the conscious part of the psyche while the Self (spiritual center) is in the unconscious realm. The Self is considered to be the Central Archetype of Wholeness and Totality. The word SELF does not refer to the individual, but to the whole of the personality. The numinous power inherent in the Ego/Self archetype is the healing factor that comes from the ability to reconnect and to center in order to balance the opposites. The Self appears in dreams, myths, and fairy tales and is seen as the King, the Hero, the prophet, the savior. It can also appear as the Magic Circle, the Square and the Cross; it is the total union of the opposites.

In Chapter 2, it was described how the ego and the Self are connected by an invisible thread that is called the Ego-Self Axis[164]. Any early wounding or trauma to that axis causes a split (or splits) to occur. The task of therapy is to repair the split so that the ego and the Self are again in a connected relationship.

Figure 28.13 is that of an adolescent girl who was repairing a split caused by molestation by a stranger. She carefully added water to the sand, then scooped the wet portion up with her hands and placed it as the reader can see. She then very carefully formed a lotus flower out of shells with the stem also shown. (The lotus is a symbol of the Self.) This picture led both the girl and the therapist to gasp with the beauty that was portrayed.

Figure 28.13

164 See Figure 2.3

Figure 28.14 was made by an adult woman who was on her own individuation journey. The turtle is shielded by an umbrella for protection against the sun. Note the balance of everything in the tray.

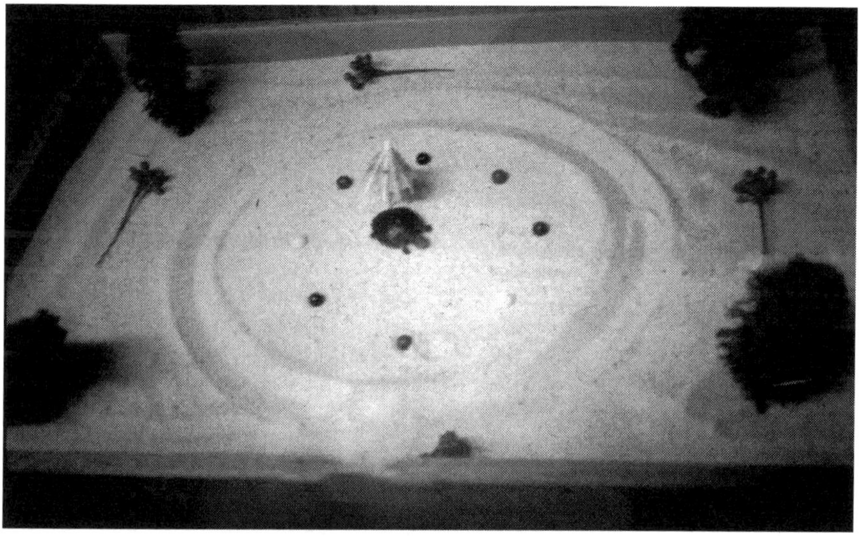

Figure 28.14

Much more could be said about both of these pictures; however, it is hoped that the reader can get a glimpse of the world of the archetypes from these brief examples.

The Good/Evil archetype is the final one to be examined in this chapter. Jungians have found that there is definitely an Evil archetype that needs to be balanced with the Good. Good, as an archetype, does not need a lengthy description but can be viewed in sand as something positive and spiritually uplifting, like Heaven. Evil, on the other hand, is seen as something fearsome, hurtful or dangerous. The events of 9/11/01 certainly encompass the archetype of Evil.

Figure 28.15 was made by an adult woman after 9/11. Her only comment (through tears) was that if there were enough dolls here, they would reach as high as the ceiling.

Figure 28.15

Figure 28.16 is that by an adolescent girl that seemed to come out of nowhere. One side is labeled "Heaven" and the other side "Hell."

Figure 28.16

Harry Wilmer[165] on the Archetype of Evil:

> "In the still depth of the collective unconscious dwells Absolute evil. Its model is hell and purgatory. It is manifest in cruel torture, fiendish torment, and terrorism, in deeds so dark we know they are malevolent, heartless, diabolical. Terrorism and torture are justified by claims of 'cause,' 'belief,' and 'right.' Extermination, holocaust, lynching, mutilation, the collective Shadow bursts like napalm in your face."

This ends a small contribution to an extremely vast subject.

165 Wilmer, H., 1991

CHAPTER 29

SANDPLAY AND THE GREAT MOTHER ARCHETYPE

A growing number of therapists today have chosen to use Sandplay as a method to access the archetypes that lie buried in the deeper, unconscious level of the psyche, in order to bring them to the patient's conscious awareness and thus to provide him/her with a reparative experience. Sandplay offers a temonos or place of healing for this "encounter with the archetypes" to occur, often non-verbally.

The Sandplay therapist provides the client with ready-made figures that hold archetypal significance. The patient can employ miniatures of his/her choosing, such as people, real and legendary creatures, animals (wild, prehistoric, domestic), environmental elements (trees, mountains, stones, shells, bodies of water, etc.) and man-made constructions (buildings, bridges, and vehicles of various kinds). The selection of these pieces and the way in which they are used by the patient can provide the therapist with very valuable insights into the patient's problems. By understanding and using the archetypal meaning of the pieces, the therapist is able to engage the patient in a unique therapeutic process. The finished product is termed a "sand picture" that illustrates and objectifies the patient's inner dilemma, clarifying the situation for both the patient and the therapist.

Some understanding of the Jungian concept of archetypes can enhance the therapeutic benefits that are inherent in Sandplay (discussed in previous chapter).

Wilmer[166] tells us:

"The world of the archetypes is the invisible world that we have

166 Wilmer, H.

never seen; it is hypothesized to be the deepest realm of the psyche, which has the potential to evoke images of a more or less predictable nature. It is these that we see. They keep recurring worldwide in all people's psyche, and they have been reappearing from time immemorial. We know them through myths, fairy tales, sagas, legends, and stories that are told the world over." (p. 56)

The task of the Jungian analyst and other therapists is to seek the connections between the conscious mind of the patient and the unconscious archetypes that cause personal suffering and to help make some of the unconscious elements conscious.

The Great Mother archetype has been chosen for this chapter because of the medium of sand in Sandplay and its relationship to the mother issues one often encounters in practice. Erich Neumann's book, *THE GREAT MOTHER,*[167] is a classic study of the diverse aspects of this archetype. In Neumann's pictorial images, he has demonstrated numerous examples of the Great Mother both in her positive as well as in her negative roles. These range from very early primordial goddesses such as the Venus of Willendorf to the later Greek and Roman goddesses. The book is a wealth of information about the Great Mother and should be a part of every therapist's library.

Sand is an earth element and is a natural milieu where the Great Mother can be constellated. "Mother Earth" is a direct reference to the numinous power of the archetype and often alludes to these issues, issues which have existed from the earliest of times and across all cultures. Because this archetype holds so many varied characteristics and is depicted by so many symbolic representations, one cannot say "the Great Mother archetype is . . . ." She is many things which is the essential reason that Sandplay therapists consciously employ Her in Her function of Nurturer and Healer.

According to Jungian theory, archetypes are located in the unconscious level of the psyche (see Chapter 2) and can pose a challenge to many therapists simply because they are unconscious. A patient often enters analysis with certain symptoms that propel him/her into analysis. When the symptoms are examined by an analyst, it is sometimes said

167 Neumann, E. 1955

that the patient has a "mother complex," which usually indicates that the person is having an inner battle with the Great Mother archetype that is being made manifest by the particular symptom. In such cases, it is often said that the archetype, or complex, is in charge of the person, rather than the person being in charge of the complex. The archetype is being demonstrated in its negative form in this type of situation, i.e. the Great Mother (and perhaps the personal mother as well) holds onto the child (or adult patient) psychologically and/or physically. This often seems to be the case with the young man or woman who cannot leave the personal mother, or who cannot maintain a relationship to the opposite sex.

The "mother complex" can also exist in young children when there has been an early separation from or loss of the personal mother. The search for a positive Great Mother substitute can last for a lifetime.

An understanding of the complex role of the archetypes can enhance and enrich the work of the Sandplay therapist. The more one learns about the archetypes and their role in a healing process, the more effective treatment can be. This benefits both therapist and patient alike. It is not necessary to discuss all of the archetypal understanding that one has with the patient, but some of this information appears to be transmitted to the patient on a non-verbal, non-rational, unconscious exchange through the medium of sand.

This idea is linked to the transference/counter- transference pattern that exists between patient and therapist on both the conscious and unconscious levels. Jung[168] diagrammed a similar procedure in *The Psychology of the Transference* which Hall[169] describes as the situation existing between a male analyst with his anima and a female analysand with her animus or a female analyst, her animus with male analysand, his anima. This idea can be extended to include issues such as those that exist in same-gender pairs.

In Figure 29.1, (adapted from the ideas of Jung and Hall) patient and therapist jointly communicate from the conscious of one to the conscious of the other, from the unconscious of one to the unconscious of the other, from therapist's conscious to patient's unconscious, etc.

168 Jung, C.G. 1954
169 Hall, J., 1983

It is important to remember that when the communications are in the unconscious realm, i.e., to and/or from patient and therapist, the archetypes are free-floating between them and it is essential that these facets be made conscious in order for healing to occur. This is yet another of the major benefits of Sandplay - a concrete space is provided for a symbolic grounding of these issues. It is an interactive field at its best.

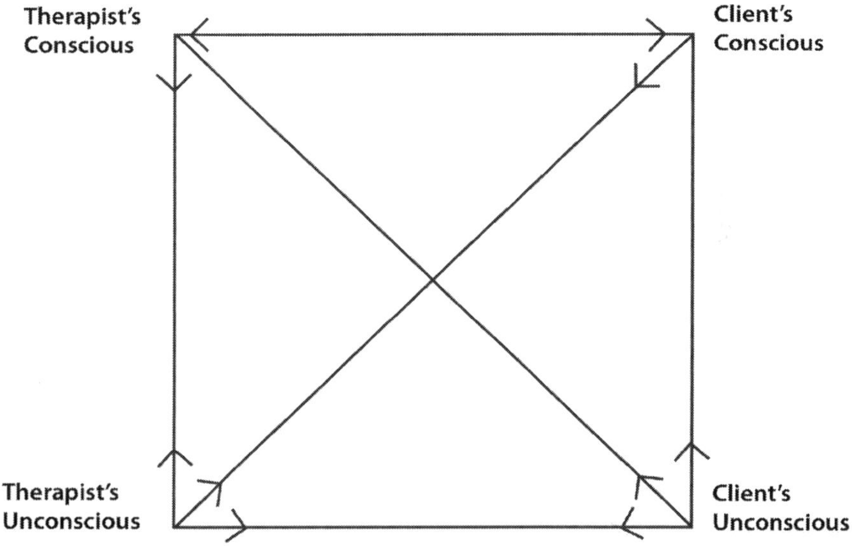

Figure 29.1

When an archetype is experienced in any therapeutic process whether verbal or non-verbal such as Sandplay, it is sometimes more of a "felt" experience than one that can be verbally described. In this situation, one knows that an archetype has been activated by one's sensate bodily reaction. The sensation can be experienced by the patient, if he/she is consciously related to the archetype or, conversely, by the therapist if the archetype remains in the patient's unconscious. This is the point where the therapist, by stating his/her bodily reactions to what has been presented by the patient, can assist the patient with a deeper understanding. It is one of the therapist's best tools for healing – the use of his/her own "felt" experiences in relationship to the material.

The Great Mother archetype has characteristics that are quite complex, yet when one is able to mediate with Her, She holds the potential for a deeply healing experience. This archetype can be a nurturing, all-giving, embracing one. Conversely, She can also devour, destroy, and swallow everything up.

Since the Great Mother has both positive and negative aspects, examples of each follow:

Figure 29.2 is a Sandplay scene by an eight-year-old-girl whose mother had died of AIDS. The child went through many stages of grief resolution and this picture is one example of how she began to adjust to this very serious loss. She had frequently used dinosaurs in prior pictures to depict some of the rage she felt. In this picture, however, the dinosaur has transformed from the negative, rageful one to one who has made a nest and given birth to its young.

Figure 29.2

This scene is a good illustration of the necessity for considering *both* aspects of any archetype, the positive and the negative, because both can be illustrated in a single construction. One intuitively assigns a dinosaur a negative connotation because of its association with rage, but care must be taken to understand each and every situation as a unique one.

The process of making this scene was quite moving and cannot be illustrated by a single snapshot. When the child was engrossed in making the picture, she used the dinosaurs to portray a mating scene, followed by the dinosaur giving birth to its young which may have symbolized her own rebirth.

Figure 29.3

Picture 29.3 is one depicting the negative form of the Great Mother. It was produced by an adult male with severe obsessive/compulsive dynamics, the symptom that precipitated his seeking therapy.

In this picture, the young man illustrated how very castrated he felt. He has used both masculine and feminine symbols; however, almost all of the figures are lying down. The masculine may be represented by the castle (which often symbolizes, for the male, his inner strength), an automobile (often related to positive mechanized energy), a rocket (phallic energy), a cowboy with a gun (also lying down), a lone soldier with its rifle poised is the only erect figure, suggesting there may be some positive masculine aspect available to him. The feminine, or anima images, are also lying down and represented by the little girl on skates, a horse (associated with teen aged girls), a pig (Demeter's animal, She of the Great Mother). A white seashell and a hint of greenery suggest perhaps that this man may be able to connect with some of the more nurturing aspects of the Great Mother. One figure that may hold another key is the black film container in the center that seemingly holds no meaning. Since it is a container, it could suggest a transference object, either to the sand as container of his pain, or the therapist as the photographer (or positive Great Mother) who would record this construction. At this point in therapy he had not yet found the energy to combat the destructive, castrating elements of the Great Mother in his psyche, but he had visually illustrated his struggle.

There is a great deal more that could be said about each of these pictures and about how the therapist used the insights they provided for treatment. It is hoped, however, that this very brief overview has given the reader a glimpse of the world of the Great Mother archetype and a sense of the role that the archetypes can play in Sandplay treatment and healing.

CHAPTER 30

DISMEMBERMENT AND HEALING IN THE WISDOM OF THE SERPENT[170]

PART 1A, BY ILKA LIST

I lingered a little over coffee that morning, daydreaming, unsure of the day's plan. Then it came to me, "I think I'll water the garden." I opened the back door and stepped onto the cedar deck with its flower pots and herbs. Such a beautiful day, warm, not hot, with a slight breeze and a clear blue sky, a perfect day for gardening. A few steps took me to the old cedar gate near the outside faucet where the black garden hose lay coiled on the pavement. The gate creaked and dragged on the deck when I opened it. "I need to tighten up those hinges," I told myself, stepping down to grab the hose. "WHOA!" As I reached down, a black rat snake raised its head high, glared at me and gave a frightening hiss. It lay in black majesty, coiled up just like the hose, blending in perfectly and looking very rubbery. Heart pounding, and insides shaking, I stepped back onto the deck to peer down at it. The snake seemed disinclined to move at first, but then slowly uncoiled its eight-foot length, and slithered away.

I have had other encounters with snakes, copperheads deep in rock crevices on mountain trails, water snakes (looking very like copperheads) lounging on sunny rock, logs, and branches along the borders of a lake or pond, garter snakes treating me to a sudden surprise in the garden, a ring-necked snake under a rock, and even a vicious little baby black rat snake in the house under the porch. But none of these snakes alarmed me as much as the black snake imitating a hose.

---

170 East Coast Journal of Sandplay Therapy, 2011

Snakes are common creatures, after all. No need to be afraid. They are legless, armless, sinuous, dry, cool, and shy basically. They avoid us if they can, preferring flight to fight. But these snakes of gardens, lakes, and forests are not the symbolic serpents of our inner life and imagination, even though they remain the source and image of the symbol.

Remembering the fearless way the black rat snake (rats are its main food) rose to warn me against touching it, I can see that its unpredictable nature is an excellent metaphor for our flowing, changeable inner life, as thoughts, feelings and emotions tangle and confront us with new twists and coils of thought. A mysterious being, the snake is so very unlike us that we feel perplexed about its inner life. Its eyes glint, its tongue waves in and out, it can bite (although relatively few snakes are poisonous, some have a dirty bite because of the food they eat). It is one of the most self-contained of creatures.

Laurens Van der Post[171] describes seeing a cobra in Africa, "making a chain of burnished "s's" in the grass, each "s" strangely reproduced in my stomach, as if the cord of my navel were a serpent unwinding coils of remembered being beneath my heart. "Given our intense feelings on seeing a snake and our natural caution, even repulsion, it is not a wonder that it remains such a ubiquitous symbol. It represents the primordial energy of the Kundalini, the imagery that of a serpent (energy) rising through the chakras. The rising of the Kundalini brings about the union of body, mind and senses, and sponsors a transformation of the personality, described by Jung[172] as the process of individuation.

Henderson and Oakes[173] add that the serpent is "a particularly significant symbol for the life of the unconscious. In its sensuous, unpredictable movement, it frequently illustrates the indirect non-rational approach to the unconscious, most necessary if anything new is to be learned. Jung[174] includes various interpretations of the snake including its role as a transformative object. He posited that because the snake could shed its skin and grow a new one that was one of the numerous

171 Van der Post, L.
172 Jung, C.G., 1967
173 Henderson, J. L. and M. Oakes
174 Jung, C.G., 1967

links to the individuation process. Erich Neumann,[175] one of Jung's followers, linked the uroboros (the snake eating its own tail) as the round "container," i.e. the maternal womb, but the book of Genesis in the Bible gives the snake a voice, and tells it that it is the most subtle of all the beasts. With newly gained arrogance and self assurance, the snake begins to talk with Eve. The snake persuades Eve that the fruit of the Tree of Knowledge is good to eat and not poisonous. Indeed, he says, eating it would make her more like God, with knowledge of good and evil. What an advantage! Now there was nothing to keep Eve from eating the fruit and urging Adam to eat it too. When God asked her, Eve readily admitted they had eaten "of the fruit" and she told God that the snake had beguiled her. God saw that it would not be long before Adam and Eve would eat fruit from the Tree of Life as well. If they did that, they would become immortal. So he immediately expelled them from Eden, along with the snake. God then scolded Adam and Eve. He declared that henceforth snakes would crawl on their bellies and eat dust, and that people and snakes would be enemies. Snakes would bite people on the heel, and people would crush snakes by stepping on their heads. Cherubim were posted at the gates so that they could not sneak back into Paradise (Hebrew Bible). (And obviously snakes could no longer talk to us, except in dreams.)

In Greek mythology,[176] Apollo is the God of Healing and is married to Coronis. Apollo suspected Coronis of being unfaithful to him, so he killed her and removed his baby from her womb by Caesarian section. He named his son Aesclepius, which means to cut open, and gave him to Chiron the centaur, instructing Chiron to care for Aesclepius and teach him everything about healing herbs and remedies. Asclepius grew wise in the ways of healing and became the God of Medicine. He (Asclepius) married and had eight children. Each of his daughters had a role in the healing arts: Hygeia (hygiene), Aceso (healing), Meditrina (the serpent-bearer), Aeglaea (healthy glow) and Panacea (universal remedy). The symbol for Asclepius is a serpent wound around a staff. Asclepius is always shown carrying a rod entwined with a single snake as his symbol. Doctors today continue to use this icon (snake entwined

175 Neumann, E., 1955
176 Kerenyi, K.

about a rod) as a symbol of the healing arts. Asclepius had such success for healing that he brought Hippolytus back from the dead. Hades could not accept this, fearing that the land of the Dead would become depopulated. And so, he persuaded his brother Zeus to kill Asclepius. After that was accomplished, Zeus placed Asclepius in the sky as the constellation Ophiuchus or Serpent Holder. Yet, the work of Asclepius, the god of Medicine, went on, and a healing center called the Asclepion was established in Epidaurus. It is very possible that Hippocrates, the father of modern medicine, may have received his training there. While it is nearly impossible to imagine a doctor's office populated by snakes, they were common in the Asclepion, and were allowed to crawl across the floor of the healing center among the sick and injured. The Hippocratic Oath, sworn by new doctors, says, "I swear by Apollo the Physician, and by Hygeia, and Panacea, and by all the Gods.... "

We turn now to Hygeia. Statues and other depictions often show her carrying a bowl encircled with a snake. Some think that this is a symbol for living in harmony with the earth. Others think of the snake as a patient, who may or may not partake of the medicine, in other words, may or may not take charge of his or her own health. There are many beliefs connecting snakes with wisdom and healing. Such as the belief that snakes have contact with the dead in their travels underground, and bring back the wisdom of the ancestors. The bowl of Hygeia is the symbol for at least four pharmaceutical organizations.

To return to more contemporary thought, Anthony Stevens[177] writes, "While Freudians would doubtless see such dreams (of a snake or snakes) as evidence of phallic symbolism, they can be understood as a phylogenetic hangover, a vestigial warning system from our primate past... Jung's belief that snakes represent brainstem and spinal cord activities may well be nearer the mark..." Hippolytus says, (according to Jung[178]) "The Gnostics identified the serpent with the spinal cord and medulla. These are synonymous with reflex functions." Jung's approach to dreams was essentially biological. "A dream, like every other element in the human structure, is a product of the total psyche. Hence we may expect

177 Stevens, A.
178 Jung, C.G. 1967

to find in dreams everything that has ever been of significance in the life of humanity.[179]"

PART 1B, BY LOIS CAREY

The serpent as a symbol has many meanings and the authors' intention in this article has been to examine those that are relevant to dismemberment and healing. The snake is a particularly significant symbol in the life of the unconscious. Its sensuous, unpredictable movement frequently illustrates the indirect, non-rational approach to the unconscious, most necessary if anything new is to be learned.[180]

Part 1b focuses on the dark side of the image where the story of Medusa comes to mind. Material for this section is taken from *The Eternal Drama, The Inner Meaning of Greek Mythology,*[181] *The Woman's Encyclopedia of Myths and Secrets,*[182] and *Bullfinch's Mythology.*[183]

Medusa was one of the Gorgon sisters who were called "Grey" in Greek because they were all born with grey hair. The other two sisters were immortal (it is unclear why) while Medusa was considered mortal. The Gorgons were monstrous females with huge teeth, claws and snaky hair. However, in another version of the story, it was said that Medusa was a beautiful maiden whose hair was her chief glory. When she dared to vie in beauty with Minerva, the goddess deprived her of her charms and changed her beautiful ringlets into hissing serpents. She became a cruel monster of so frightful an aspect that no living thing could behold her without being turned to stone.

In yet another version of the myth, Medusa was the serpent goddess of the Libyan Amazons, representing "female wisdom," she was the Destroyer aspect of the Triple Goddess. One of her inscriptions referred to her as "mother of all the gods, whom she bore before childbirth existed." She represented the past, the present, and the future. She (Medusa) said "No mortal has yet been able to lift the veil that covers

179 Jung, C.G. 1967
180 Henderson, J. L. and M. Oakes
181 Edinger, E.
182 Walker, B.
183 *Bullfinch's Mythology*

me," because she was Death and to see her face to face was to die – that is, to be "turned to stone" like a funerary statue. She was also veiled because she was the Future, which always wears a veil. Primitive folk linked menstrual blood with Medusa because they often believed that the look of a menstruating woman could turn a man to stone.

Anyone who gazed on Medusa whether human or animal was immediately turned to stone. This caused a great deal of consternation among the townspeople so the King assigned Perseus the task of cutting off her head and bringing it back to the King.

Perseus was the son of Danae and an oracle had told her father (Perseus' grand-father) that his grandson would depose him. He locked his daughter in a dungeon to keep her apart from men. But Zeus came to her in a shower of rain by which she conceived Perseus. (The reader may remember that Zeus was called "the shape shifter" because he could change into whatever form he wanted to be.) Another version of this myth tells us that Danae was seduced by an uncle and was put into the dungeon because of this. This is the sort of ambiguity seen in many myths – a double-parentage theme.

This poses the question about the origin of the hero: is this a divine conception or an illegitimate one? This is familiar ground when one considers the legends surrounding the birth of Christ. The church sources speak of the conception being through the Holy Spirit, something like the shower of rain that came to Danae. However, other legends during biblical times had it that Mary became illegitimately pregnant by a Roman centurion.

Perseus, then, is considered to be the son of Zeus and Danae. After his birth, he and his mother were put in a basket and sent off to sea. They arrived on an island owned and ruled by King Polydectes and that is where Perseus was reared. It was this King who assigned Perseus the task of slaying Medusa.

Medusa, the Gorgon, is seen as a ghastly woman with teeth and tongue protruding and whose hair is made up of writhing snakes. Her image was so fearsome that to gaze upon it, as mentioned previously, was to be turned to stone. She can, of course, be seen as the negative mother archetype in its most terrifying aspect. This is the image that the young person must encounter and deal with if he or she is going to make his/her way forward in life. He/she has to confront the horror of existence itself if his/her life is to proceed and develop, which is what Perseus had to do.

Perseus was assisted in this task by two other Greek deities: Hermes and Athena. Hermes gave him a sickle with which he could cut off the Gorgon's head; Athena gave him a polished shield that acted like a mirror, which enabled him to kill this monstrosity without having to look at her directly.

After Perseus found Medusa and cut off her head, several miraculous things happened. The blood that was shed by Medusa contained a warrior who fathered future monsters and, more significantly, the blood also contained Pegasus, the winged horse that flew out of Medusa's severed head. This is a striking image of released libido – essential to the healing process. The decapitation of the Medusan horror had the effect of transforming the negative energy into positive, creative power. The arts that were derived from Pegasus' libido were directly linked to Medusa, since she was the mother of Pegasus.

Perseus could never have faced Medusa without the reflecting shield of Athena because the shield served as a mirror. That is vitally important in every therapist's work because of the mirroring that helps the client focus. Athena's mirror is showing an image of what must not be looked at directly. In order to grasp what is being dealt with, one has to see it indirectly, which allows for a more objective view.

The mirror shows what we cannot see for ourselves. We do not know what we look like without looking in a mirror. We are too close to ourselves to be able to see ourselves. Similarly, the mirror is a reflecting device and, as therapists, that, too, is what we do – we reflect on what we are seeing and hearing in each and every session. We see this type of projective objectivity in Sandplay Therapy.

In folklore, according to primitive thinking, the reflection in a mirror is actually one's soul. There is also the superstition that breaking a mirror will cause seven years of bad luck. The list goes on and on and these facts are included in order to illustrate just how important the mirror is in this tale of Medusa.

In conclusion, the serpent has many lessons to teach, some positive and some negative. It is hoped that this brief examination of some of its aspects may stimulate the reader to search further for the wisdom inherent in this symbol.

CHAPTER 31

A COMMENTARY SYMBOLS IN ALICE IN WONDERLAND[184]

Story by Lewis Carroll
Commentary by Lois Carey

This story opens with Alice sitting on a river bank with her sister. Her sister is reading and paying no attention to her and Alice is getting bored. It is a hot summer day and, all of a sudden, Alice sees a large White Rabbit run by, saying, "Oh Dear, I shall be too late!!" He takes a watch out of his pocket as he mutters to himself. Alice is intrigued at the sight of a talking rabbit and so runs after him across the field. The Rabbit pops down a rabbit hole with Alice right after him. She falls down, down, down, finally landing with a loud kerplunk. She can't find the Rabbit anywhere, but makes her way into a small room where there is a table with a golden key on it. At the far end of the room is a locked door, but Alice can see through the key hole into a beautiful garden. However, there is no way she can get through the door, as it is locked and she is too tall to get through. She runs back to get the key and finds a bottle on the table that says "Drink Me." Being the obedient child that she is, Alice drinks the bottle and begins to shrink to such a small size that she is terrified. She runs back to the door when she realizes she has left the key on the table. When she goes back to the table, she is so small, there is no way she can possibly reach it. But – as in all good fairy tales, she finds a little cake that says, "Eat Me!!" This has the opposite effect since it makes her grow to over nine feet tall.

Here, let me pause for a moment as I would like to comment on what has been observed so far. First, Alice and her sister are sitting on

---

184 Published with permission – NYAPT *Newsletter* and the Journal of the East Coast Sandplay Association

a riverbank. It appears that her sister is the elder as she is busy reading. Her sister represents an idealized image for Alice, someone to look up to, what she might become when she is older, her future potential. But this idealized figure is not paying attention to Alice, so she (Alice) turns to a meditative or fantasy state and her mind begins to wander. It appears to be like a daydream. The river is also important as it represents the river of life or the waters of the unconscious. The river flows, is never still, is symbolic of the life force, her creative, flowing energy.

The White Rabbit appears. This rabbit symbolically is associated with the feminine, with fleetness, with procreation and, in this case, is White – purity. This, then, is one of Alice's symbols – her pure feminine innocence. But she becomes curious and decides to explore by chasing the Rabbit. She falls down the rabbit hole which symbolizes her descent into her own unconscious process. The White Rabbit is preoccupied with TIME, the sense of time rushing by for child Alice is paramount to the story. She must hurry to catch the Rabbit – very reminiscent of how we all try to cram as much as possible in too little Time. At this point, Alice has lost sight of the Rabbit but has found something else – a glimpse into a locked garden – symbolic of a serene inner space to which she cannot yet be admitted. She must pass numerous tests first.

The garden symbolizes consciousness as opposed to the forest which is much more of an unconscious state. The garden is tamed nature, the Garden of Eden before the Fall. Alice, somewhat frantic, runs back to where she had seen the golden key – another very powerful symbol – as the possibility for entrance to the garden lay with that key.

The key holds entrance to the mystery, and being golden, symbolizes the most precious of inner treasures. However, instead of the key, Alice finds the bottle with the order to "Drink Me." This is where Alice begins to flounder. She impulsively swallows the unknown contents. It (the drink) has transformative powers (to make her smaller,) but her own lack of caution (another feminine attribute) makes her too small, impotent really. She next finds the cake and repeats her first error by eating all of it and growing too much.

So, while she has drunk and has eaten, she has overindulged in both instances so that the extremes are experienced. She is either too tall or too small. Moderation would have been by far the best approach, but she does not learn this until much later in the story.

Now, back to the tale. When Alice finds herself nine feet tall, she begins to cry – and since she is now so huge – she cries huge tears, more and more. She next finds a fan and begins to fan herself. This fan, too, has transformative powers, for as she fans herself she again begins to drown until she finds herself in the middle of a huge lake that contains many strange creatures.

All of a sudden a mouse swims by and she thinks, since everything else here is so strange, that perhaps this mouse can talk. She speaks to it in French, thinking perhaps that is its language since it hasn't answered her in English. Alice asks, unthinkingly of course, "Ou est ma chatte?" (Where is my cat?) This would strike terror into the heart of any mouse. Other birds and animals fall into her lake of tears and all get soaked. Finally, the Dodo suggests that they all have a Caucus race to dry off. This is a rather silly race as they all start wherever they happen to be and end the race when they get tired. Each one is declared a winner. Alice tries to make herself feel better and tells all her new acquaintances about her cat Dinah. She scares everyone away with this as there was a mouse, a bird, etc., all of whom are mortally afraid of cats. Suddenly the Rabbit comes by again and tells Alice to go for his gloves and fan that are in his house. Alice finds her way to the Rabbit's house, goes in and finds another bottle which she drinks. She again grows too large to get out of the house. She is in a trap of her own making. The Rabbit, when she doesn't return, comes to find his gloves and then tries to devise some way to get this creature out of his house.

He puts Bill (a lizard) down the chimney; Alice kicks him out with her foot. Then the Rabbit throws cakes in the window which she eats and then she shrinks again so that she can now run out.

Looking at the symbolism in this section, we find that the fan has transformative powers (wind = spirit); however, she uses it for too long so that she nearly drowns in the lake of her tears – her own unconscious. She meets a mouse which can symbolize something unpleasant in her psyche as the rodent is often symbolic of the devil, something to torment her. However, Alice herself becomes the tormentor of the mouse by the talk about her cat Dinah. The other animals and birds who join in the swim are symbolic of other aspects of Alice's psyche.

Next the Dodo, the simpleton, suggests a ridiculous race – but is it really ridiculous? No one is a loser in this race and it is performed according to each one's particular time frame. It allows for differences in abilities from one species to another.

Then, the White Rabbit appears; however, he doesn't recognize Alice as herself but thinks she is someone else. She decides to do what he asks, thinking, "I better play along with this Rabbit if ever I hope to get back to my home (or myself)." Another transformation occurs when she drinks another bottle of liquid and becomes trapped completely in the Rabbit's house as she is much too large to ever get out. The Rabbit makes an attempt to get this creature out of his house and puts Bill, a lizard, down the chimney. The lizard can be associated with a dragon or snake symbolism as another unconscious aspect in Alice's psyche. The dragon can represent the negative aspect of the feminine and the snake holds large transformative powers. Bill, as lizard, represents multiple aspects. Then the Rabbit, in his own inimitable way, throws some cakes through the window for Alice to eat. These cakes, yet again, are transformative as they cause her to shrink.

From this point on I will try to interweave the story with the symbolism. In the woods (unconscious) Alice meets a caterpillar sitting on a mushroom. The caterpillar is a symbol of another transformative possibility. The caterpillar, as we know, will ultimately be transformed into a butterfly, one of the symbols of the Self – like the inner garden, the golden key and the treasure spot. This caterpillar tells Alice about the Magic Mushroom – eat one side to get taller, the other side to get smaller. This now brings Alice to the position of conscious choice, she no longer has to eat or drink impulsively or entirely, but can choose just how much of what she needs for any given situation. But it is not as simple as that, for Alice doesn't yet know which side was which as the mushroom is perfectly round. Another symbol of the Self is the circle – there is no beginning and no ending. This is also the symbol of death and rebirth, the cyclical nature of time. Alice devises a way, through experimentation, to keep the two halves separate by keeping one part in each hand. In this way, she has achieved the power to make her choices conscious. Finally, when Alice has managed to attain the proper size, she comes upon a four-foot-high house which belongs to the Duchess who is about to go play croquet with the Queen. A Queen, symbolically represents the archetypal woman, magic and supernatural. She is a ruling or governing principle and, when united with the King, can represent the union of the opposites – the masculine and the feminine. The Queen symbolizes the attainment of the individuation process for the woman. The Duchess, in this story, represents a lesser form of the Queen, but with Queen-like qualities nevertheless – Alice's progression towards her own individuation process. But this Duchess, too, is an enigma. She sits nursing a baby which turns out to be a pig. There is a war going on all around them as the cook hurls pots and pans through the air. Alice sets the pig free to be its natural Self – which she is unconsciously trying to do for herself. She next comes across the Cheshire Cat who is grinning from ear to ear, like the cat that ate the canary.

One has the sense that this grin is a mockery as it has the ability to fade and to reappear. The cat, too, has strong feminine components and is the domesticated version of all the animals in the cat family, and is revered as holy in some cultures.

Alice continues on her way and visits the March Hare – certainly another personification of the White Rabbit. The sign for March is Taurus with its many bull-like qualities and is perhaps the negative side of the White Rabbit. The dormouse is also present at this event. They are all having a tea party, but Alice is not invited. She joins them anyway. The Mad Hatter and the March Hare try to explain Time to Alice and they tell her that she can make it (the time) anyway she wants. She can speed it up or make it stop altogether. This typifies how the child perceives Time in the fantasy life as being at one's beck and call. Would that it were so! The March Hare and the Mad Hatter seem stuck in that irrational childlike mode and so Alice goes on her way. She has gotten disgusted with their silliness which suggests her beginning maturity.

Alice eventually finds herself in the beautiful garden – her own symbolic spiritual center – where she meets up with the King and the Queen. This beautiful garden turns out to be the Queen's rose garden where a game of croquet is about to be played. The rose is pure spiritual beauty in appearance, aroma, etc. However, these roses are still in a state of transformation as they are being painted red by the Queen's servants. Red is significant here as it can represent strong emotions and/ or blood (the blood of life). The King and Queen appear – Alice's first full glimpse of her future potential of the masculine and feminine elements for her own individuation process. But this particular Queen has numerous sides, one being quite negative. She continually shouts "off with the head" whenever anything displeases her. However, she never seems to follow the orders through – they are mostly for effect. The rest of the players in this strange game of croquet are Playing Cards that keep flopping over in the wind. This "game" can be viewed as the game of life with all of its many upheavals. The Queen's beheading orders are to be carried out by the executioner, or the Evil, destructive element. The game is played by using flamingoes (more red) as croquet mallets. However, the flamingoes are held upside down and wobble all over the place, possibly indicative of yet another confused state in Alice's search for her true Self. The flamingo, being a bird, can represent a spiritual aspect because the bird flies between Heaven and Earth and is one of the carriers of the Spirit.

Here is where the search for the Self is finally achieved; i.e., in the union of the opposites, the dark and the light, the masculine and the feminine. This process is where the true spiritual center of the psyche becomes balanced in a fully integrated way.

There is a little more to this story as the Mock Turtle discusses Time (mockingly?), the Knave of Hearts (Knave – a trickster figure) steals the Queen's tarts and the trial follows.

This entire story can be viewed as one child's search for her own spiritual truth – through all the unusual and odd elements with which she comes into contact. At the end of the trial, Alice wakes up in her sister's lap and tells her of the strange dream she has just had. Her sister thinks to herself that when Alice grows up, she hopes that she would be able to keep the simple and loving heart of her childhood which would give her pleasure forever.

This tale, then, symbolizes one child's inner struggle as she develops her own unique personality. She has an active fantasy life which allows her to converse with all the animals, to see wickedness and Evil, to experience acceptance and love, to assist the less fortunate and to stand on the side of the compassionate as she confronts the Queen. She goes through many transformations to accomplish this task.

We all have had to come to an acceptance of our own personal symbols (positive and negative) as we have grown and developed. It is a lifelong process, one that has no end. Different psychologists have various terms for this process of finding one's own unique identity – Carl Jung termed it the individuation process. But, no matter what one chooses to call it, the meaning is the same. One has tamed one's inner demons or cantankerous inner forces and has been able to connect with the deepest spiritual center in the psyche. This is what gives our lives meaning. We are thus able to use our abilities in a creative way in whatever our life's work happens to be.

LEWIS CARROLL, pseudonym of Charles Lutwidge Dodgson, an English author and mathematician, born in 1832. He was educated at Oxford and, in 1855, became a lecturer in mathematics there. His fame rests upon a series of fantasies in prose and verse which had their origin in stories told to the dean's young daughters with whom Dodgson had a solid friendship. Dodgson also wrote several mathematical treatises. He died in 1898.

APPENDIX A

ERIKSON'S STAGES

Infancy - Birth to 1, 2 - Trust vs. Mistrust
Early Childhood 1 - 1 -2 to 3-4 - Autonomy vs. Shame-Doubt
Early Childhood 2 - 3 - 4 to 6 - 7 - Initiative vs. Guilt
Middle Childhood - 6 - 7 to 11 - 12 Industry vs. Inferiority
Early Teens - 11 - 12 to 14 - 15 - Identity vs. Identity Confusion
Late Teens - 14 - 15 to 18 - 19 - Intimacy vs. Isolation
Adult - 18 - 19 to 65 - 70 - Generativity vs. Stagnation
Old Age 65 + - Integrity vs. Despair

APPENDIX B

SOME SYMPTOMS SEEN IN LOSS IN THE LIVES OF CHILDREN

- Worrying about seconds and thirds when food is readily available at meals and always in adequate supply in the home.
- Lying about *very* minor issues.
- Confabulating, making up fantastic stories—not infrequently about self and family.
- Treating minor acts as if they were great trespasses.
- Embarrassing family, especially mother, in public.
- Ruining birthdays, anniversaries and holidays. Mothers frequently complain chat they are often treated disrespectfully by their child during the birthday party.
- Occasionally refusal to celebrate and refusal of gifts.
- School underachievement or failure. Academic cheating when native ability would more than allow for average or even superior grades. Many of these children are formally or informally identified as having "learning disabilities."
- Stealing from teachers and peers, often from those who are most liked by the child.
- Going out of the way to get into trouble. Viewing oneself as a "jinx," as having "bad luck."
- Destroying parental, family property. Destroying one's own property or that of others. Often the destruction of the child's own things appears repetitiously "accidental?'
- Sleep disturbances: difficulty falling asleep, nightmares, night terrors. Nighttime insecurity that has no objective cause.
- Failure to learn from experience.

- Indiscriminent attachment in bright, precocious, younger children. Or failure to attach that the parents often think reflects an "inherent" inability to relate in the child.
- Steadfast denial of personal responsibility in the face of incontrovertible evidence.
- Aggression toward peers, insolence toward authority figures—especially in a self-defeating way (Donovan, D.M. and Deborah McIntyre).

It is found that, even when many of the problems and behaviors listed above are not mentioned specifically by adoptive parents during the first contact, a brief review of the list tends to elicit positive findings much more frequently than with children who are not adopted. Many of the adoptive parents that have been worked with have commented that they found questions about specific behaviors to be very reassuring.

APPENDIX C

FOUR PRIMARY CHARACTERISTICS OF CHILDHOOD TRAUMA

ACCORDING TO LENORE TERR[185]

1. STRONGLY VISUALIZED, REPEATEDLY PERCEIVED MEMORIES

To re-see or re-feel a terrible event; stimulated by "triggers." Brain Memory: visual, auditory, physical. Unique to individual – culture, age, background, temperament, etc.

2. REPETITIVE BEHAVIORS

Reenactment, post-traumatic play, psycho-physiologic repetitions; perpetuated over lifetime; repressed and sublimated. Maladaptive behaviors often lead to conduct disorders. Attempts to master the uncontrollable. Need relational model – going through fears using play, writings, art, sand, etc.

3. TRAUMA-SPECIFIC FEARS

Hypersensitivity to fears of loss, abandonment, death, panic, and anxiety, paranoia. Most traumatized children harbor one or two trauma-related fears into adulthood, specific to incident.

4. CHANGED ATTITUDES ABOUT PEOPLE, ASPECTS OF LIFE AND FUTURE

Unable to trust that anyone would care, can't count on anyone, shattered meanings, defensive attempts to create shields of

185 Terr, Lenore, 1983

invincibility. Expect short lives, don't expect marriage, family, fears of intimacy, loss of opinions and choices. Often develop Attachment Disorder.

APPENDIX D

STRATEGIES FOR THERAPISTS

- Keep up professional connections.
- Limit exposure to trauma.
- Enter personal psychotherapy or alternative.
- Maintain rejuvenating relationships and experiences.
- Maintain a personal identity by creating firm boundaries between home and work.
- Get organizational support.
- Find meaningful ways to remain involved with all aspects of humanity.
- Confront and work through intrusive traumatic imagery.
- Recognize the positive feelings associated with this work.

APPENDIX E

COMMON SYMPTOMS EXHIBITED BY THE ATTACHMENT DISORDERED CHILD

1. Acting out - against peers or caretaker.
2. Oppositional behavior.
3. Withdrawal - suicidal concerns.
4. Regressive, clinging behavior - "take care of me."
5. No affect - splitting off the grief which will surely surface later.
6. Psychosomatic problems such as stomach aches, headaches with no physical basis.
7. Sleep problems - inability to fall asleep, nightmares, sleepwalking.
8. Eating problems - food refusal or overeating, hoarding food.
9. Stealing and lying.
10. Enuresis and/or encopresis.

APPENDIX F

PIAGET'S STAGES[186]

The stages of cognitive development according to Piaget:

1. *Sensorimotor stage*: from birth to age two.

   Children experience the world through movement and senses (use five senses to explore the world). During the ensorimotor stage children are extremely egocentric, meaning they cannot perceive the world from others' viewpoints and explore using senses.

The sensorimotor stage is divided into six substages:

(1) Simple reflexes.

(2) First habits and primary circular reactions.

(3) Secondary circular reactions.

(4) Coordination of secondary circular reactions.

(5) Tertiary circular reactions, novelty and curiosity.

(6) Internalization of schemes.

During the last stage children are 18 to 24 months old. During this stage they shift to symbolic thinking.

2. *Preoperational stage*: from ages two to seven (magical thinking predominates, acquisition of motor skills. Egocentricism begins strongly and then weakens. Children cannot conserve or use logical thinking in the early part of this stage; however, by four-and-a-half, they have learned to conserve and think logically but only with practical aids. They are no longer as egocentric.

3. *Concrete operational stage*: from ages seven to eleven (children begin to think logically but are very concrete in their thinking

186 Piaget, J. and B. Inhelder

4. *Formal operational stage*: after age eleven (development of abstract reasoning). Children develop abstract thought and can easily conserve and think logically in their mind.

One of Piaget's most famous studies focused purely on the discriminative abilities of children between the ages of two-and-a-half years old, and four-and-a-half years old. He began the study by taking children of different ages and placing two lines of M & Ms, one with the M & Ms in a line spread further apart, and one with the same number of M & Ms in a line placed more closely together. He found that, "Children between two years, six months old and three years, two months old correctly discriminate the relative number of objects in two rows; between three years, two months and four years, six months they indicate a longer row with fewer objects to have "more"; after four years, six months they again discriminate correctly" (Cognitive Capacity of Very Young Children, p. 141). Initially younger children were not studied, because if at four years old child couldn't conserve quantity, how could a child that is younger do so? The results show however that children that are younger than three years and two months have quantity conservation, but as they get older they lose this quality, and don't recover it until four-and-a- half years old. This attribute may be lost duc to a temporary inability to solve because of an overdependence on perceptual strategies, which correlates more candy with a longer line of candy, or due to the inability of a four year old to reverse situations.

THE DEVELOPMENTAL PROCESS

Piaget provided no concise description of the developmental process as a whole. Broadly speaking it consisted of a cycle:

- The child performs an action which has an effect on or organizes objects, and the child is able to note the characteristics of the action and its effects.
- Through repeated actions, perhaps with variations or in different contexts or on different kinds of objects, the child is able to differentiate and integrate its elements and effects. This is the

process of *reflecting abstraction* (described in detail by Piaget; see Wadsworth, B.)

- At the same time, the child is able to identify the properties of objects by the way different kinds of action affect them. This is the process of *empirical abstraction.*
- By repeating this process across a wide range of objects and actions, the child establishes a new level of knowledge and insight. This is the process of forming a new *cognitive stage.* This dual process allows the child to construct new ways of dealing with objects and new knowledge about objects themselves.

However, once the child has constructed these new kinds of knowledge, he or she starts to use them to create still more complex objects and to carry out still more complex actions.

SELECTED BIBLIOGRAPHY

Adler, A. *The Science of Living,* Minn.: Hazeldon, 1972.

Axline, Virginia. *Play Therapy*, N.Y.: Ballantine Books, 1947.

_____. *Dibs: In search of self,* N.Y.: Ballantine Books, 1971.

Barkley, R. *Attention Deficit Hyperactivity Disorder: A Handbook for Diagnosis and Treatment*, N.Y.: The Guilford Press, 1990.

Bolen, Jean S. *Goddesses in Every Woman: A New Psychology of Women*, N.Y.: Harper and Rowe, 1984.

Bornstein, M., ed. *Sensitive Periods in Development: Interdisciplinary Perspectives,* Hillsdale, N.J.: Lawrence Erlbaum and Assoc., 1987.

Bowlby, John. *Attachment and Loss,* vol. I, N.Y.: Basic Books, 1969.

_____. *Separation: Anxiety and Anger*, vol. II, N.Y.: Basic Books, 1973.

_____. *Loss: Sadness and Depression*, vol. III, N.Y.: Basic Books, 1980.

Bowyer, L. *The Lowenfeld World Technique*, Oxford, U.K.: Pergamon Press, 1970.

Bradway, K., et al. *Sandplay Studies: Origin, Theories, and Practice*, San Francisco: Jung Institute, 1981.

Brody, Viola. *The Dialog of Touch: Developmental Play Therapy,* Northvale, N.J.: Jason Aronson, 1997.

Bullfinch's Mythology, Chapter 15, pp. 74-77, U.S.: Seven Treasurers Publications, 1998.

Carey, Lois. "Sand Play Therapy with a Troubled Child," *The Arts in Psychotherapy,* vol. 17, pp.197-209, Oxford, U.K.: Pergamon Press, 1990.

_____. "Family Sandplay Therapy," *The Arts in Psychotherapy*, vol. 18, pp. 231-39, Oxford, U.K.: Pergamon Press, 1991.

_____. *Sandplay Therapy With Children and Families*, Northvale, N.J.: Jason Aronson, 1999.

_____. *Expressive and Creative Arts Methods for Trauma Survivors*, London: Jessica Kingsley Publishers, 2006.

_____. *A Salty Lake of Tears,* Carmel, CA: il piccolo editions, 2011.

Cicero, T. "Effects of Paternal Alcohol on Offspring Development," *Alcohol Health and Research World*, 18 (1), pp. 37-41, National Institute on Alcohol Abuse and Alcoholism, 1994.

Cirlot, J. *Dictionary of Symbols*, London: Routledge, 1971.

Coles, C., et al. "Effects of Cocaine and Alcohol in Pregnancy on Neonatal Growth and Neuro-behavioral Status," *Neurotoxicology and Teratology*, 14, pp. 23-33, 1992.

Crenshaw, D. in Carey, Lois, ed., *Expressive and Creative Arts Methods for Trauma Survivors*, chap. 1, pp. 21-38, London: Jessica Kingsley Publishers, 2006.

Crenshaw, D. and C. Foreacre, eds. *New York Association for Play Therapy Newsletter,* Rhinebeck, N.Y.: published quarterly.

Davidson, Michele W., RN, Ph.D. *Olds' Maternal-Newborn Nursing and Health Across the Lifespan*, 9th ed., N.J.: Pearson Education, 2012.

Diagnostic and Statistical Manual of Mental Disorders, 4th ed. (DSM-IV), Washington, D.C.: American Psychiatric Assn., 1994.

Donovan, Denis M. and Deborah McIntyre. *Healing the Hurt Child: Developmental-Contextual Approach*, N.Y. and London: W.W. Norton and Co., Inc., 1990.

East Coast Journal of Sandplay Therapy, McCarthy, Dennis and Ilka List, eds., Kingston, N.Y.: published annually.

Edinger, Edward. *The Eternal Drama: The Inner Meaning of Greek Mythology*, Calif.: Shambala Publishers, 1994.

Erickson, M. *My Voice Will Go with You*, N.Y.: Irvington, 1954.

Erikson, Erik. *Childhood and Society,* 2nd ed., N.Y.: W.W. Norton and Co., Inc., 1963.

Feldman, Robert. *Child Development*, 5th ed., N.Y.: The Guilford Press, 2011.

Field, T. "Infants of Depressed Mothers," *Infant Behavior and Development*, vol. 18, pp. 1-13, 1995.

Finnell, N. "Theraplay Innovations with Adoptive Families," in Munns, E., ed., *Theraplay: Innovations in Attachment-Enhancing Play Therapy*, pp. 235-56, Northvale, N.J.: Jason Aronson, 2000.

Fordham, M. *Innovations in Analytical Psychology*, N.Y. and London: Routledge, 1995.

Friedman, H. and R. Mitchell, eds. *Supervision of Sandplay Therapy*, U.S. and Canada: Routledge, 2008.

Freud, A. *The Psychoanalytic Treatment of Children*, N.Y.: Shocken Books, 1946.

Freud, S. *Beyond the Pleasure Principle*, London: Hogarth Press, 1922.

Frey, D. "Puppetry Intervention for Traumatized Clients," in L. Carey, ed., Expressive and Creative Arts Methods for Trauma Survivors, London and Philadelphia: Jessica Kingsley Publishers, 2006.

Green, E. "Jungian Analytical Play Therapy," in O'Connor, K. J. and L. D. Braverman, eds., Play Therapy Theory and Practice: Comparing Theories and Techniques, 2nd ed., pp. 83-121, Hoboken, N. J.: John Wiley and Sons, 2009.

_____. "Jungian Analytical Play Therapy," in O'Connor, K. J. and L. D. Braverman, eds.,

Play Therapy Theory and Practice: Comparing Theories and Techniques, 2nd ed., pp.83-121,

Hoboken, N. J.: John Wiley and Sons, 2009.

Gil, Eliana. *Sexual Abuse: Causes, Consequences and Treatment of Incestuous and Pedophilic Acts,* Holmes Beach, Fla.: Learning Publications, Inc., 1985.

_____. *Play in Family Therapy*, N.Y.: The Guilford Press, 1994.

Grollman, Earl, ed. *Explaining Death to Children,* Boston: Beacon Press, 1967.

Hall, E. *Beyond Culture*, U.S.: Anchor Books, 1976.

Harlow, H. et al. "The Maternal Affectional System in Rhesus Monkeys," in Rheingold, H. L., ed., *Maternal Behavior in Mammals*, N.Y.: John Wiley and Sons, 1963.

Henderson J. L. and M. Oakes. The Wisdom of the Serpent, N.J.: Princeton University Press, 1990.

Horney, K. *Collected Works of Karen Horney*, vols. 1 and 2, N.Y.: W.W. Norton and Co., Inc., 1950.

Irwin, E. and E. Malloy. "Family Puppet Interview," in Schaefer, C. and L. Carey, eds., *Family Play Therapy*, N.J.: Jason Aronson, Inc., 1994.

James, B. *Handbook for Treatment of Attachment-Trauma Problems in Children*, N.Y.: Free Press, 1994.

Jernberg, A. *Theraplay: A New Treatment Using Structured Play for Problem Children and Their Families,* San Francisco: Jossey-Bass, 1989.

_____. "Attachment enhancing for adopted children," in Grabe, P. V., ed., *Adoption Resources for Mental Health Professionals*, pp. 271-79, New Brunswick: Transaction, 1990.

Jolles, I. *A Catalog for the Qualitative Interpretation of the House-Tree-Person (H-T-P),* 8th printing, Los Angeles: Western Psychological Services, 1983.

Jung, C.G. *The Psychology of the Transference*, N.Y.: Bollingen Foundation, 1954.

_____. *Modern Man in Search for a Soul,* 5th ed., N.Y.: Harcourt Brace, 1955.

_____. "The Psychology of the Child Archetype," *CW*, vol. 9, part 1, pp. 151-81, N.J.: Princeton University Press, 1959.

_____. *Memories, Dreams and Reflections*, N.Y.: Vintage Press, 1965.

_____. "Symbols of Transformation," *CW,* vol. 5, 2nd ed., N.Y.: Bollingen Foundation; N.J.: Princeton University Press, 1967.

_____. "The Archetypes and the Collective Unconscious," *CW*, vol. 9, 2nd ed., part 1, N.Y.: Bollingen Foundation; N.J.: Princeton University Press, 1969.

Kalff, Dora M. *Sandplay: A Psychotherapeutic Approach to the Psyche*, Santa Monica, Calif.: Sigo Press, 1980.

_____. Foreword in Bradway, K. et al. *Sandplay Studies: Origins, Theory and Practice,* San Francisco: C. G. Jung Institute, 1981.

Karen, R. *Becoming Attached: Unfolding the Mystery of the Infant/Mother Bond and Its Impact on Later Life,* N.Y.: Warner Books, 1994.

Karr-Morse, R. and M. Wiley. *Ghosts from the Nursery: Tracing the Roots of Violence*, N.Y.: Atlantic Monthly Press, 1997.

Kerenyi, C. *The Gods of the Greeks,* London: Thames and Hudson, 1979.

Kiepenheuer, Kaspar. *Crossing the Bridge: A Jungian Approach to Adolescence*, LaSalle, Ill.: Open Court, 1990.

Klein, M. *The Psychoanalysis of Children*, 3rd ed., London: Hogarth Press, 1959.

Kluft, Richard, ed. *Childhood Antecedents of Multiple Personality*. Washington, D.C.: American Psychiatric Press, Inc., 1985.

Koppelman, Ruby. "Hand Puppetry with a Chronic Psychiatric Population," *The Arts in_Psychotherapy*, vol. 11, pp. 283-88, Oxford, U.K., 1984.

Krementz, Jill. *How It Feels When A Parent Dies*, N.Y.: Alfred A. Knopf, 1991.

Kubler-Ross, Elizabeth. *On Children and Death*, N.Y.: Macmillan, 1983.

Landreth, Garry. *Play Therapy: The Art of the Relationship*, Muncie, Ind.: Acc. Dev. Press, 1991.

Lorenz, Konrad. "Der Kumpan in der Umvelt des Vogels," English trans. in Schiller, C. H., ed., *Instinctive Behavior*, N.Y.: International Universities Press, 1957.

Lowenfeld, Margaret. *The World Technique*, London: George Allen and Unwin, 1979.

Mahdi, Louise, et al., eds. *Betwixt and Between: Patterns of Masculine and Feminine Initiation.*_LaSalle, Ill.: Open Court, 1987.

Mayer, Adele. *Incest: A Treatment Manual for Therapy with Victims, Spouses and Offenders*, Holmes Beach, Fla.: Learning Publications, Inc, 1983.

_____. *Sexual Abuse: Causes, Consequences and Treatment of Incestuous and_Pedophilic Acts*, Holmes Beach, Fla.: Learning Publications, Inc, 1985.

McGoldrick, M. and R. Gerson. *Genograms in Family Assessment*, N.Y.: W. W. Norton and Co., Inc., 1985.

Miller, Alice. *Prisoners of Childhood*, N.Y.: Basic Books, 1981.

_____. *Thou Shalt Not Be Aware: Society's Betrayal of the Child*, N.Y.: New American Library, 1986.

Miller, C., and J. Boe, "Tears into diamonds: Transformation of child psychic trauma through sandplay and storytelling," *The Arts in Psychotherapy*, 17(3), pp. 247-57, Oxford, U.K.: 1990.

Mills, Joyce and R. Crowley. *Therapeutic Metaphors for Children and the Child Within*, N.Y.: Brunner/Mazel, 1986.

Moody, R. and C. Moody. "A family perspective: Helping children acknowledge and express grief following the death of a parent," *Death Studies*, 15(6), pp. 587-602, 1991.

Moustakis, B. *Relationship Play Therapy*, Md.: Rowman and Littlefield, 1997.

Munns, E., ed. *Theraplay: Innovations in Attachment-Enhancing Play Therapy*, Northvale, N.J.: Jason Aronson, 2000.

Nader, K., Pynoos, R.S., Fairbanks, L., and C. Frederick, "Children's PTSD reactions one year after a sniper attack at their school," *American Journal of Psychiatry*, 147, 1526-30, 1990.

Neumann, E. *The Great Mother: An Analysis of the Archetype*, N.J.: Princeton University Press, Bollingen Series, 1955.

_____. *The Child*, N.Y.: Putnam, 1973.

New York Association for Play Therapy Newsletter, D. Crenshaw and C. Foreacre, eds., Rhinebeck, N.Y.: published quarterly.

Noble, E. *Primal Connections: How Our Experiences from Conception to Birth Influence Our Emotions, Behavior, and Health*, N.Y.: Fireside, 1993.

Piaget, J. and B. Inhelder. *The Psychology of the Child*, London: Routledge and Kegan, Ltd., 1955.

Pynoos, R. S. and K. Nader. "Children's Memory and Proximity to Violence," *J. of the American Academy of Child and Adolescent Psychiatry*, 28, pp. 236-41, 1989.

Reitz, M. and K. Watson. *Adoption and the Family System*, N.Y.: The Guilford Press, 1992.

Rogers, C. *Client-Centered Therapy*, Boston: Houghton Mifflin, 1955.

Ross, P. "A Diagnosis Technique for Assessment of Parent-Child and Family Interaction Patterns: The Family Puppet Technique," in

Schaefer, C. and L. Carey, eds., *Family Play Therapy*, N. J.: Jason Aronson, Inc., 1994.

Saint-Exupery, Antoine. *The Little Prince*, N.Y.: Harcourt Brace, 1952.

Sams, J., Carson, D., and A. C. Werneke. Medicine Cards: The Discovery of Power Through the Ways of Animals, N.Y.: St. Martin's Press, 1989.

Satir, V. *Conjoint Family Therapy*, Calif.: Science and Behavior Books, 1964.

Schaefer, C., ed. *The Therapeutic Powers of Play*, N.J.: Jason Aronson, Inc., 1993.

Schaefer, C. and L. Carey. *Family Play Therapy*, N.J.: Jason Aronson, Inc., 1994.

Scharff, J. S., ed., Foundation of Object Relations Family Therapy, Northvale, N. J.: Jason Aronson, 1991.

Segal, R. "Helping children express grief through symbolic communication," *Social Casework*,_65(10), pp. 590-99, 1984.

Sgroi, Suzanne. *Handbook of Clinical Intervention in Child Sexual Abuse*, Lexington, Mass. and Toronto: Lexington Books, 1982.

Shirar, Lynda. *Dissociative Children: Bridging the Inner and Outer Worlds*, N.Y.: W.W. Norton and Co., Inc., 1996.

Siegel, Daniel. *The Developing Mind*, N.Y.: The Guilford Press, 1999.

Sjolund, M. and C. Schaefer. "The Erica Method of Sandplay Diagnosis and Assessment," in O'Connor, K. and C. Schaefer, eds., *Handbook of Play Therapy, Vol. 2: Advances and Innovations*, pp. 231-52, N.Y.: John Wiley and Sons, 1994.

Skinner, B. *Science and Human Behavior*, N.Y.: Macmillan Co., 1953.

Spitz, R. A. "Hospitalism: An Inquiry Into the Genesis of Psychiatric Conditions in Early Childhood," in Eisler, R. S. et al., eds., *The Psychoanalytic Study of the Child*, vol. 1, pp. 53-74, N.Y.: International Universities Press, 1945.

Stevens, Anthony. *Archetypes, A Natural History of the Self*, London: Routledge and Kegan, Ltd., 1982.

Terr, Lenore. "Play Therapy and Psychic Trauma: A Preliminary Report," in Schaefer, C. and K. O'Connor, eds., *Handbook of Play Therapy*, N.Y.: John Wiley and Sons, 1983.

_____. *Too Scared to Cry,* N.Y.: Basic Books, 1990.

Urwin, C. and J. Hood-Williams. *Selected Papers of Margaret Lowenfeld*, London: Free Association Books, 1988.

Van Der Kolk, B. A. "In terror's grip: Healing the ravages of trauma," *Cerebrum 4*, pp. 34-50, N.Y.: The Dana Foundation, 2002.

Van der Post, L. *The Heart of the Hunter: Customs and Myths of the African Bushman*, Fla.: Harcourt Brace, 1961.

Wadsworth, B. *Piaget's Theory of Cognitive and Affective Development: Foundations of Constructivism*, N. Y.: Allyn and Bacon, 2003.

Walsh, Froma and M. McGoldrick. *Living Beyond Loss,* N.Y. and London: W. W. Norton and Co., 1991.

Walker, Barbara. *The Woman's Encyclopedia of Myths and Secrets*, N.Y.: Harper Collins, 1983.

Webb, Nancy Boyd. "The Child and Death," *Helping Bereaved Children: A Handbook for_Practitioners,* pp. 3-18, N.Y. and London: The Guilford Press, 1993.

_____. *Techniques of Play Therapy: A Clinical Demonstration*, N.Y.: A Guilford Press Video Tape and Program Manual, 1994. Winner Bronze Medal, New York Film Festival, DVD, 2007. Korean trans. DVD, 2009.

_____. *Play Therapy with Children in Crisis: Individual, Group, and Family Treatment,* 2nd ed., N.Y.: The Guilford Press, 1999.

_____. *Mass Trauma and Violence,* N.Y: The Guilford Press, 2004.

_____. *Helping Bereaved Children: A Handbook for Practitioners,* 2nd ed., N.Y.: The Guilford Press, 2010.

Webster's New World Dictionary, Second College Edition, N.Y. and Cleveland, Ohio: The World Publishing Co., 1970.

Weinrib, E. *Images of the Self,* Boston: Sigo Press, 1983.

Wells, H. G. *Floor Games,* London, U.K.: Frank Palmer, 1911.

Wickes, F. *The Inner World of Childhood*, N. Y.: Appleton-Century-Crofts, Inc., 1927.

Wilmer, Harry. *Practical Jung,* Wilmette, Ill.: Chiron Press, 1991.

Winnicott, D. *The Piggle: An Account of the Psychoanalytic Treatment of a Little Girl*, London: Penguin Books, 1977.

Wolfelt, A. *Helping Children Cope With Grief,* Muncie, Ind.: Accelerated Development, 1983.

Zametkin, A. "An Overview of Clinical Issues in ADHD," *ADHD Report*, 4(1): pp. 5-18, February 1996.

Zuckerman, B. "Effects of Marijuana and Cocaine Use on Fetal Growth," *New England Journal of Medicine,* 320, pp. 762-68, 1989.

You might also enjoy reading these Jungian publications:

Re-Imagining Mary: A Journey Through Art to the Feminine Self
by Mariann Burke, 1st Ed., Trade Paperback, 180pp, Index, Biblio., 2009 — ISBN 978-0-9810344-1-6

Threshold Experiences: The Archetype of Beginnings
by Michael Conforti, 1st Ed., Trade Paperback, 168pp, Index, Biblio., 2008 — ISBN 978-0-944187-99-9

Marked By Fire: Stories of the Jungian Way
edited by Patricia Damery & Naomi Ruth Lowinsky, 1st Ed., Trade Paperback, 180pp, Index, Biblio., 2012 — ISBN 978-1-926715-68-1

Transforming Body and Soul: Therapeutic Wisdom in the Gospel Healing Stories by Steven Galipeau, Rev. Ed., Trade Paperback, 180pp, Index, Biblio., 2011 — ISBN 978-1-926715-62-9

Lifting the Veil: Revealing the Other Side
by Fred Gustafson & Jane Kamerling, 1st Ed, Paperback, 170pp, Biblio., 2012 — ISBN 978-1-926715-75-9

Resurrecting the Unicorn: Masculinity in the 21st Century
by Bud Harris, Rev. Ed., Trade Paperback, 300pp, Index, Biblio., 2009 — ISBN 978-0-9810344-0-9

The Father Quest: Rediscovering an Elemental Force
by Bud Harris, Reprint, Trade Paperback, 180pp, Index, Biblio., 2009 — ISBN 978-0-9810344-9-2

Like Gold Through Fire: The Transforming Power of Suffering
by Massimilla & Bud Harris, Reprint, Trade Paperback, 150pp, Index, Biblio., 2009 — ISBN 978-0-9810344-5-4

The Art of Love: The Craft of Relationship
by Massimilla and Bud Harris, 1st Ed. Trade Paperback, 150pp, 2010 — ISBN 978-1-926715-02-5

Divine Madness: Archetypes of Romantic Love
by John R. Haule, Rev. Ed., Trade Paperback, 282pp, Index, Biblio., 2010 — ISBN 978-1-926715-04-9

Eros and the Shattering Gaze: Transcending Narcissism
by Ken Kimmel, 1st Ed., Trade Paperback, 310pp, Index, Biblio., 2011 — ISBN 978-1-926715-49-0

The Sister From Below: When the Muse Gets Her Way
by Naomi Ruth Lowinsky, 1st Ed., Trade Paperback, 248pp, Index, Biblio., 2009 — ISBN 978-0-9810344-2-3

The Motherline: Every Woman's Journey to find her Female Roots
by Naomi Ruth Lowinsky, Reprint, Trade Paperback, 252pp, Index, Biblio., 2009 — ISBN 978-0-9810344-6-1

Jung and Ecopsychology: Dairy Farmer's Guide to the Universe (DFGU) Volume 1, by Dennis L. Merritt, 1st Ed., Trade Paperback, 242pp, Index, Biblio., 2011 — ISBN 978-1-926715-42-1

The Cry of Merlin: Jung the Prototypical Ecopsychologist: (DFGU) Volume 2, by Dennis L. Merritt, 1st Ed., Trade Paperback, 204pp, Index, Biblio., 2012 — ISBN 978-1-926715-43-8

Hermes, Ecopsychology, and Complexity Theory: (DFGU) Volume 3
by Dennis L. Merritt, 1st Ed., Trade Paperback, 228pp, Index, Biblio., 2012 — ISBN 978-1-926715-44-5

Land, Weather, Seasons, Insects: An Archetypal View: (DFGU) Volume 4, by Dennis L. Merritt, 1st Ed., Trade Paperback, 134pp, Index, Biblio., 2012 — ISBN 978-1-926715-45-2

Becoming: An Introduction to Jung's Concept of Individuation
by Deldon Anne McNeely, 1st Ed., Trade Paperback, 230pp, Index, Biblio., 2010 — ISBN 978-1-926715-12-4

Animus Aeternus: Exploring the Inner Masculine by Deldon Anne McNeely, Reprint, Trade Paperback, 196pp, Index, Biblio., 2011 — ISBN 978-1-926715-37-7

Mercury Rising: Women, Evil, and the Trickster Gods
by Deldon Anne McNeely, Revised, Trade Paperback, 200pp, Index, Biblio., 2011 — ISBN 978-1-926715-54-4

Four Eternal Women: Toni Wolff Revisited—A Study In Opposites
by Mary Dian Molton & Lucy Anne Sikes, 1st Ed., 320pp, Index, Bib, 2011 — ISBN 978-1-926715-31-5

Gathering the Light: A Jungian View of Meditation
by V. Walter Odajnyk, Revised Ed., Trade Paperback, 264pp, Index, Biblio., 2011 — ISBN 978-1-926715-55-1

The Promiscuity Papers
by Matjaz Regovec, 1st Ed., Trade Paperback, 86pp, Index, Biblio., 2011 — ISBN 978-1-926715-38-4

Enemy, Cripple, Beggar: Shadows in the Hero's Path
by Erel Shalit, 1st Ed., Trade Paperback, 248pp, Index, Biblio., 2008 — ISBN 978-0-9776076-7-9

The Cycle of Life: Themes and Tales of the Journey
by Erel Shalit, 1st Ed., Trade Paperback, 210pp, Index, Biblio., 2011 — ISBN 978-1-926715-50-6

The Hero and His Shadow: Psychopolitical Aspects of Myth and Reality in Israel by Erel Shalit, Revised Ed., Trade Paperback, 208pp, Index, Biblio., 2012 — ISBN 978-1-926715-69-8

Riting Myth, Mythic Writing: Plotting Your Personal Story
by Dennis Patrick Slattery, Trade Paperback, 220 pp. Biblio., 2012 — ISBN 978-1-926715-77-3

The Guilt Cure
by Nancy Carter Pennington & Lawrence H. Staples, 1st Ed., Trade Paperback, 200pp, Index, Biblio., 2011 — ISBN 978-1-926715-53-7

Guilt with a Twist: The Promethean Way
by Lawrence Staples, 1st Ed., Trade Paperback, 256pp, Index, Biblio., 2008 — ISBN 978-0-9776076-4-8

The Creative Soul: Art and the Quest for Wholeness
by Lawrence Staples, 1st Ed., Trade Paperback, 100pp, Index, Biblio., 2009 — ISBN 978-0-9810344-4-7

Deep Blues: Human Soundscapes for the Archetypal Journey
by Mark Winborn, 1st Ed., Trade Paperback, 130pp, Index, Biblio., 2011 — ISBN 978-1-926715-52-0

Phone Orders Welcomed
Credit Cards Accepted
In Canada & the U.S. call 1-800-228-9316
International call +1-831-238-7799
www.fisherkingpress.com

Made in the USA
Coppell, TX
04 November 2026

11289010R00155